RECREATIONAL COLONIALISM AND THE
RHETORICAL LANDSCAPES OF THE OUTDOORS

RECREATIONAL COLONIALISM AND THE RHETORICAL LANDSCAPES OF THE OUTDOORS

Kyle Boggs

THE OHIO STATE UNIVERSITY PRESS
COLUMBUS

Library of Congress Cataloging-in-Publication Data
Names: Boggs, Kyle, author.
Title: Recreational colonialism and the rhetorical landscapes of the outdoors / Kyle Boggs.
Description: Columbus : The Ohio State University Press, [2025] | Includes bibliographical
    references and index. | Summary: "Synthesizes theories of rhetoric, environmental
    studies, and settler colonialism to confront the ways outdoor recreational discourses
    reinforce settler imaginaries and colonial power structures through 'recreational
    colonialism.' Looks especially at the sports of rock climbing, ultrarunning, biking, and
    skiing, primarily in the American West"—Provided by publisher.
Identifiers: LCCN 2025000508 | ISBN 9780814215876 (hardback) | ISBN 0814215874
    (hardback) | ISBN 9780814284148 (ebook) | ISBN 0814284140 (ebook)
Subjects: LCSH: Settler colonialism—Social aspects—West (U.S.) | Indians of North
    America—Recreation—West (U.S.) | Indigenous peoples—Recreation—West (U.S.)
    | Outdoor recreation—West (U.S.) | Cultural property—Protection—West (U.S.) |
    Environmental justice—West (U.S.) | Rhetoric—Social aspects.
Classification: LCC E78.W5 B585 2025 | DDC 978—dc23/eng/20250225
LC record available at https://lccn.loc.gov/2025000508

Other identifiers: ISBN 9780814259450 (paperback) | ISBN 0814259456 (paperback)

Cover design by Susan Zucker
Text composition by Stuart Rodriguez
Type set in Minion Pro

For Klee

CONTENTS

ILLUSTRATIONS

ACKNOWLEDGMENTS

I could not have written this book without the love and support of my partner, Stephanie Capaldo. During the years I spent writing these pages, academia took us from Arizona, to Florida, to Idaho. We endured the personal and political challenges that arose during the prolonged global pandemic, and all the other things, to put it mildly. From my work as a journalist to the years of research, personal reflection, revision, and reimagining that went into this book, she has been there for me. Thank you. She specifically helped me locate and sift through the archival research that appears in chapter 2—and I learned a lot about historical research from her in the process.

I believe that we compose ourselves into the worlds we want to live in, and this includes the worlds we want for those we love. It is with this in mind that I am thinking also about our son. In writing this book through the first six years of River's life, I can't help but acknowledge his fierce sense of justice and curiosity about the world, which certainly inspired me to think prophetically about the kind of book I wanted to write.

I also must be honest and humble when I say this book would not exist without Klee Benally. It was his fierce voice from behind the bullhorn that initially inspired my curiosity as a journalist toward issues of Indigenous resistance to settler colonialism. The interviews I did with him as a journalist and the conversations I had with him as a friend provoked the central questions I return to again and again in this book: What does it mean to be a settler on stolen Indigenous land? How has my proximity to settler colonialism curated my experiences in these lands, my view of myself, and my relationship to Indigenous peoples? What does meaningful alliance and repair actually look like—is it even possible? Engaging with these questions over the last twenty years has literally changed my life and helped shape my sense of justice and responsibility. And that is really what this book is about—outdoor recreation is the vehicle I use to extend those conversations I had with Klee. He wasn't a fan of "activist" as an identity; it hardly does him justice anyway—he was an artist, musician, writer, filmmaker, agitator, and visionary for Indigenous resistance, a truly remarkable and kind human who inspired and taught everyone around him. Rest in Power. And to his family: Princess, Janeda, Clayson, Berta, and Jones—I hold you all in my heart. And thanks to the volunteers at the Táala Hooghan Infoshop, and everyone keeping the memory of Klee alive at Indigenous Action Media and elsewhere.

Thanks as well to Chuck Seiverd and everyone at *The Noise: Arts & News*. In another life, I would have stayed in Flagstaff and written for that little paper forever—it was probably the coolest thing I've ever been a part of. Thank you to Howard Shanker for helping me translate so much legal jargon to the masses. There are many others I'd like to thank—for your time, for your feedback, for your support, and for your encouragement in small and large ways. I'm sticking to first names in case there are some who wouldn't want to be listed: Rudy, Ned, Evan, Dawn, James (×2), Katie, Andy, Ed, Rachel, Rex, Dianna, Uncle Don, Nikki, Bucky, Stacey, Kelvin, Kris, Ilse, Mary, Taylor, Phillis, John, Alex, Bahe, Alicyn, Anne Marie, Christine, and likely many others. Thanks to the scores of Hopi, Diné, and Havasupai people at city council meetings, Forest Service "listening sessions," and elsewhere kind enough to talk to me when you were at your most frustrated and heartbroken; thank you for your patience, but especially thank you to those who were less patient.

Thanks as well to the late, great Katie Lee, who I interviewed over the course of a few days at her house in Jerome—she gave me a lot of great advice as a writer and human, and I never forgot it, nor what it means to be "in step with the stone." And a shout out to Karen Underhill and Sean Evans for helping me out in the archives at Northern Arizona University. Thanks to Goss for nothin' (!). Thanks to Kristen Elias Rowley, Rebecca Bostock, Elizabeth Zaleski, and everyone at The Ohio State University Press for shepherding me through the publication process. Thanks as well to Billie Smith-Haffener for their sharp copyediting. Also, thank you to those who, through the press, reviewed this manuscript, some multiple times. I also want to thank academic colleagues and friends who, at various times and places, helped me think through everything from the structure and purpose of this project to suggested readings and perspectives: Amy Kimme Hea, Adela Licona, Ken McAllister, Laura Gray-Rosendale, Doreen E. Martinez, Jeff Berglund, and Dina Gilio-Whitaker. Thank you to all the Indigenous scholars I cite throughout this book, whose work is absolutely crucial to this project and the critical discussions that I hope extend from it. Thanks to those who gave me permission to reprint their art, specifically Chip Thomas. Thanks to my mom for helping me prepare some images for publication. And of course, thanks to Dez for the long runs.

Another version of chapter 8 appears in *Community Listening: Stories, Hauntings, Possibilities,* edited by Jenn Fishman, Romeo García, and Lauren Rosenberg (University Press of Colorado, 2025). Because I worked on these chapters simultaneously, their feedback in that project improved the final version of the chapter in this book.

The Peaks Are Everywhere

You Are on Indian Land was the name of an art exhibition at the Museum of Northern Arizona in Flagstaff in 2016, which was also my last year living in the region. Banners advertising the exhibit in those words hung all over the city. Within an overwhelmingly white city that lies at the base of a mountain held sacred by at least thirteen regional tribes, the phrase "You Are on Indian Land" clashed provocatively, particularly among all the other ways the land is described through appeals to tourism and outdoor recreation. This clash is even more stark given how these industries—particularly skiing—dominate the culture of the area and are viewed as essential to the economy, despite the local ski resort's tarnished relationship with regional tribes and local Indigenous activists.

For the preceding decade, I had been a community journalist in Flagstaff, covering regional social, cultural, and environmental issues of all kinds. But nothing I covered focused my attention more than the multigenerational controversy over development by the Arizona Snowbowl Ski Resort on the San Francisco Peaks.

The San Francisco Peaks have long been a site of Indigenous resistance to colonialism. In interviews, I learned about how the Peaks are woven into creation stories, serve as a marker of one of the four directions, and are the home of important deities. Based on the stories recounted to me as a journalist and those I read about in archival material as a researcher, Indigenous resistance has taken on many forms, from fighting off early settlers to protecting springs, religious shrines, and medicinal plants and herbs, to maintaining Indigenous rights to conduct ceremonies and practice their religions, resisting mining efforts, and defeating proposals to build gated communities. The Arizona Snowbowl Ski Resort, which operates on 777 acres of land surrounded by now-protected wilderness controlled by the US Forest Service through a long-standing special use permit for commercial activities on federal land, has been a main feature in the modern history of this resistance. Essentially, each change in resort ownership, which has occurred many times since the resort was established in the mid-1930s, has meant new proposed developments. Regional tribes have consistently been against such developments, and each round has been another chapter in the story of Indigenous resistance there. Flagstaff, an old logging community that now relies heavily on tourism to support its economy, has long been a supporter of the ski resort, and the city council has historically bent over backward to make sure the resort gets what it wants even though the resort itself lies outside city limits. While most of these "improvements" have been things like new lifts, ski runs, trails, roads, lodges and other buildings, and parking lots, in 2002 the resort's owners proposed something new to ensure predictable ski seasons.

Among other projects, the 2002 proposal included infrastructure to produce artificial snow from reclaimed municipal wastewater pumped more than thirteen miles from one of two water treatment plants in Flagstaff, out of town, up the mountain, to a reservoir at the resort where it can be tapped for snowmaking. While other resorts make snow from natural sources or supplement those natural sources with reclaimed municipal wastewater, the Arizona Snowbowl was poised to be the first resort in the world to make snow from 100 percent reclaimed wastewater. Concerned citizens voiced their opposition to the absurdity of committing water resources to a ski resort in the dry and drought-prone Southwest, and environmental scientists warned of the risks of introducing contaminated water to a fragile alpine ecosystem. The proposal was also completely unacceptable to the tribes who hold the Peaks sacred. Over a decade of turmoil ensued, once again pitting Indigenous cultural and spiritual survival and ecological integrity against the interests of outdoor recreation and tourism dollars. The proposal was eventually implemented in the winter of 2012–13, but only after several lawsuits and a decade of Indigenous-led resistance in the form of lockdowns, tree sits, road blockades, and a lot more. These demonstrations continue today, as each year the resort opens for the season greeted by a group of people carrying signs that say "No Desecration for Recreation," "Defend the Sacred," "Water Is Life," "No Justice on Stolen Land," "Save the Peaks," and more.

My coverage led me from city council meetings to Forest Service listening sessions, deep into archival research, to courtrooms, and to long interviews and conversations in busy coffee shops to quiet kitchen tables on the Hopi, Navajo, and Havasupai reservations. It forced me to learn how to read and translate court documents and scientific papers on hydrology, biology, and toxicology. My experiences also taught me to read between the lines in municipal resolutions and contracts as well as federal documents like environmental impact statements. This work compelled me to get up in the early hours of the morning to cover Indigenous-led direct actions, road blockades, and demonstrations and risk arrest and harassment to get the truth of their convictions on paper. As a white settler with a press pass dangling from my camera strap, I became intimately aware of how this risk was far more severe for those on the other end of my lens, and how much more they had at stake.

Indigenous resistance to development by a ski resort on the San Francisco Peaks continues to frustrate, instruct, and guide my research, teaching, and ethical commitments in profound ways. The ongoing controversy continues to haunt me, as a writer and scholar who also enjoys other forms of outdoor recreation, in productive ways by which I believe all settlers should be haunted. Such reflection forces us to reckon with the historical truth of our participation in the continued occupation of stolen Indigenous land. The controversy over the Peaks provokes reflection about what it means to be a settler living on stolen Indigenous land, about how colonialism functions through us in ways that may contradict our commitments to solidarity and environmental justice. For me, it continues to expose the myriad ways my identity as a settler, an identity that I didn't choose but nonetheless embody and benefit from, produces particular modes of being in the world that often go unexamined.

Much of my coverage of the controversy over the ski resort on the Peaks focused on telling stories that pushed back against dominant narratives of life in Flagstaff. The city's identity as a "ski town" and the perceived economic benefits from having a ski resort so close have produced a culture in which skiing is not just viewed as important but is often prioritized over what Indigenous activists consistently claim as their cultural and spiritual survival. For those who aren't wealthy, Flagstaff—though beautiful—is a hard city to live in. In 2008 the local NPR station, KNAU, ran a series about Flagstaff called "Poverty with a View," a phrase frequently invoked and resented by people who have struggled with housing affordability there. I remember my years living there as some of the busiest and poorest years of my life. I was not the only one I knew who worked several jobs to string together a rent check, even as Flagstaff is consistently in the top ten for "second home" sales. In fact, more than 23 percent of the residences in Flagstaff are second homes—vacation homes that sit empty most of the year. More than 90 percent of those who ski at Snowbowl are people who drive up from Phoenix. The frustration that comes with knowing the City of Flagstaff, Snowbowl, and the Forest Service seem so eager to accommodate the recreational whims of people who do not actually live there is very real. And, like most anything, it is significantly worse for Indigenous peoples.

Flagstaff is just south of federally recognized boundaries of the Navajo Nation, making it the largest city bordering the largest Indigenous reservation in the country. However, the term "border town," like "public land," obscures the legacy of theft and occupation of Indigenous land. Indigenous peoples are often targeted through racial profiling and harassed in ways that the white population never is, as evidenced by the fact that Indigenous peoples make up just over 11 percent of the population in Flagstaff yet account for the majority of annual arrests.[1] Anti-camping and anti-panhandling ordinances replicated in other cities similarly disproportionately target Indigenous peoples in Flag-staff, and everyone I know has seen police stopping a group of Indigenous folks downtown for drinking in public while college students—visibly intoxi-cated—shuffle right by with hardly a glance in their direction. The data sup-port this observation as well; according to the Flagstaff Police Department's own crime statistics, Indigenous peoples were arrested for public consumption at a rate four to five times higher than white people.[2]

I saw banners for the museum's 2016 exhibition flying on lampposts all over downtown, outside of recreational outfitters, ski shops, bike shops, and all my favorite restaurants and bars in Flagstaff; "You Are on Indian Land" resonated defiantly in these spaces in profound ways. The message within the message is perhaps the most quintessentially, historically, and empirically accurate statement there is for settlers who call Flagstaff home: *You Are on Sto-len Indian Land.* But this is about much more than the Peaks, or a ski resort, or Flagstaff itself.

For those of us racialized as white within a system that institutionalizes white supremacy and normalizes white entitlement to stolen Indigenous land, the truth and recognition of "You Are on Stolen Indian Land" is a confron-tation, one that provokes reflection or defensiveness. Throughout this book, I hope to encourage the former in ways that go beyond acknowledgment. The dominance of settler colonialism, which is a framing of colonialism that emphasizes the ongoing practices, performances, and ways of being that operate structurally in the present, obscures our complicity as settlers in the

---

1. In 2021, 2,432 Indigenous adults and 53 Indigenous youth were arrested, while 1,472 white adults and 70 white youth were arrested. See Flagstaff Police Department, "2021 Flagstaff Police Department Annual Report," 46.

2. See Flagstaff Police Department, 45.

occupation of stolen Indigenous land. And *because* it is uncomfortable, it is worth repeating: *You Are on Stolen Indigenous Land.* It doesn't matter if you are on private property or so-called public land. It doesn't matter if we're talking about a beloved trail or swimming hole, or if the place is now a park or the location of a church or shopping mall. Even land we've defended from developers, worked from behind a plow, land that has big trees that we sat in when the chainsaws came—our years, decades, or even generations of care do not erase the fact that it is all stolen Indigenous land. The Peaks are everywhere.

While this book is grounded in what I hope is a clear theoretical framework that stems from a robust genealogy of scholarship, my audience for this book extends beyond academia. This book should be useful to organizations forging more equitable processes to design, assess, and respond to land-use decisions. It will be useful to those individuals and groups working in solidarity with Indigenous peoples to restore sovereignty on stolen land, and those pushing us all to think about what inclusion and belonging on stolen land looks like. It will be useful to teachers and activists designing place-based curricula that mobilize local material-discursive landscapes in ways that deepen commitments to social and environmental justice. Certainly, there will be interest in these pages for scholars whose teaching and research dip into areas like rhetoric and composition, environmental communication, environmental humanities, leisure studies, and settler colonial studies. Those who have the most to gain from this book, however, are individuals interested in a deeper connection to themselves through the landscapes in which they engage, those seeking a language and a framework from which to respond to the complexity and discomfort of that fundamentally colonial relationship.

While my positioning in this book turns toward settlers, I do not intend to center whiteness, and this book isn't just for white people. It is also my hope that the theoretical frameworks I bring together in this project, animated through a blend of analysis and story, will provoke new forms of engagement for Indigenous activists and other organizers mobilizing resistance to forms of colonialism that operate in ways that might not be immediately recognizable. Settler colonialism, like so many concepts deployed by academics and activists, remains elusive, even unintelligible to the wider public. I do not believe it is the job of every scholar to appeal to the public or that it should be the priority of every activist—especially Indigenous activists—to explain to settlers how they sustain the project of settler colonialism. However, as I reflect on the absolutely crucial conversations that connect settler colonialism to white supremacy, heteropatriarchy, capitalism, environmental justice, and climate change, I also believe there is too much at stake to not do this work. By focusing on the relationship between settler colonialism and outdoor recreation, I aim to bring these important concepts into meaning in ways that I hope are comprehensible and actionable and that provoke much-needed critical engagement within outdoor recreation communities, policy makers, industry leaders, and elsewhere.

The controversy on the Peaks pitted skiers and many business owners against Indigenous and environmental activists, but as significant as the controversy was and still is, the vast majority of people in Flagstaff seemed indifferent. And I imagine when it comes to recognizing and reckoning with settler colonialism, the vast majority of backpackers, hikers, mountain bikers, rock climbers, trail runners, and skiers out there are similarly indifferent. They drive out to the trailhead on Saturday mornings, unload their gear, and prepare for a day of "adventure," "exploration," and "self-discovery" on stolen Indigenous land. Most come in good faith, nonetheless, bringing with them what they believe is a good environmental ethos, adhering to Leave No Trace and Do No Harm principles infused in the language of "stewardship." Many self-described "outdoor enthusiasts," while likely oblivious to whose ancestral land they are on, still side with Indigenous peoples when it comes to clear examples of injustices both historical and contemporary, and I believe the majority want to live in better relation with those communities. They are a growing population that—perhaps more frequently and in bigger numbers than any other group—directly engages with landscapes deeply rooted in a colonial past (federally owned land like national forests, parks, monuments, and other stretches of lands operated by the Bureau of Land Management, and Crown lands in Canada). This is a population that often regards itself as socially and environmentally responsible. For these reasons, I believe this population will be receptive to the arguments and perspectives offered in this book, curious to understand how their legacies and inheritances as settlers on stolen Indigenous land creep into their consciousness in simple and profound ways. For those willing, the processes of recognition may unfold over years of honest self-reflection, processes that are situated and personal.

For me, the controversy over development on the San Francisco Peaks has come to animate so much about settler entitlement to stolen Indigenous land and how rhetorical practices sustain settler colonialism in the everyday, in ways that often escape critique, like in outdoor recreation. But the same settler colonial power dynamics—specifically, white supremacy, capitalism, and heteropatriarchy—play out in other locations across the country and around the world. Consider the controversy over Sand Mountain, which is held sacred to the Fallon Paiute-Shoshone Tribe in western Nevada and is also a destination of recreational ATVs and sandboarders.[3] Considering these dynamics can

---

3. Kniazkov, "Treading on a Shrine."

help us understand the implications of rock climbers at Devil's Tower in Wyoming, who were challenged for decades by the Lakota and five other tribes yet often ignored agreements not to climb during certain times of the year.[4] This type of analysis could also help us understand why, despite a hard-fought legal battle by the Washoe people to protect Cave Rock at Lake Tahoe, some rock climbers choose to climb there anyway.[5] In the Grand Canyon, the Havasupai Tribe's main source of income is tourism to their reservation, where strikingly clear blue waterfalls cascade through Cataract Canyon and campground space is always limited. Yet during their busy season, the tribe has to keep watch as river runners stop along the Colorado River and enter Havasupai land, without paying for and reserving access, to see one of the waterfalls on the outskirts of the tribe's reservation.[6] Today, the discursive formations that make these land disputes possible, the conditions of possibility that produce the response "No desecration for recreation!" on the San Francisco Peaks, are also exported globally. When the Anangu people in Australia worked with the government to make it illegal in 2019 to climb Uluru Rock, after tourists ignored their requests not to climb the rock they hold sacred, climbers "flocked" to the monolith to get in one last ascent before the ban went into effect.[7] On Mount Everest, scores of Nepalese sherpas have died schlepping wealthy mountaineers to the summit. In Peru, there are descendants of the Inca who are trail guides on the Inca Trail; many work so hard serving settler hikers en route that they have never actually seen Machu Picchu themselves.[8] In Quebec, settlers of European ancestry are increasingly self-identifying as "eastern Métis" in order to access Indigenous land to legally hunt out of season.[9] Enduring arduous and complicated lawsuits, Indigenous peoples have been limited in their success in protecting these sites. In all of these cases, settler off-roaders, climbers, hikers, river runners, and others have knowingly dismissed Indigenous cultural survival and disparaged Indigenous peoples so they can have fun. In all of these examples, outdoor recreation functions to accommodate and sustain settler colonialism in the present, and it is the perceived innocence and apoliticalness of outdoor recreation that allow this connection to go unexamined.

---

4. Dussias, "Cultural Conflicts Regarding Land Use."
5. Makley, Cave Rock.
6. Langlois, "Sacred Native American Sites."
7. Williams, "Australia to Ban Climbing on Uluru"; and Rychter, "Climbers Flock to Uluru before a Ban."
8. Shackell, "This Porter Has Hiked."
9. Leroux, Distorted Descent.

Outdoor Recreation

Per the Multiple Use and Sustained Yield Act of 1960, the Forest Service is mandated to balance multiple uses of the forest, including logging, mining, grazing, and also recreation. That the Forest Service is apparently mandated to provide recreational opportunities is one of the central arguments frequently used to defend decisions like the one made in northern Arizona to allow reclaimed wastewater to be used to make snow, despite the clear and consistent oppositions of at least thirteen tribal nations. Examinations between colonialism and resource extraction have been discussed at length in decades of research—from books and articles to documentaries—and while this attention hasn't exactly translated into meaningful policy decisions or reconciliation, connections between colonialism and the ever-expanding outdoor recreation industry have largely escaped this critique.

The Bureau of Economic Analysis quantified the value of outdoor recreation for the first time in 2018, and concluded that this industry, dominated by white people in terms of leadership, ownership, and participation,[10] made up 2 percent of the gross domestic product, in which outdoor recreationalists spent $887 billion.[11] The bureau's 2023 report noted a substantial increase, finding the outdoor recreation industry has soared to $1.1 trillion.[12] It is a massive, growing, and increasingly influential industry that is "redefining the value of public lands."[13] Recent years have seen a groundswell, not just in individuals' participation but also in corporations and small businesses who have oriented toward this rapidly growing market, new national legislation meant to "expand access," the creation of state offices of outdoor recreation, and a dramatic increase in federal, regional, and local nonprofit organizations centered on access, advocacy, and inclusion initiatives. While outdoor recreation can include activities like gardening and birdwatching, this book is primarily concerned with activities and discourses that are more aligned with what most people tend to associate with outdoor recreation, such as trail running, mountain biking, skiing and snowboarding, rock climbing, hiking, camping, and more.

---

10. In the outdoor participation report for 2017, 73 percent of participants identified as white. While statistics continue to show this is the case, and it is more true of some activities, like skiing, than others (see Coleman, "Unbearable Whiteness of Skiing"). People of color are becoming much more visible about their participation, and there are an increasingly large number of organizations that support them such as Diversify Outdoors, Outdoor Afro, Hikers of Color, and the work of academics like Carolyn Finney (Finney, *Black Faces, White Spaces*) and community writers like Glenn Nelson (The Next 100 Coalition and trailposse.com).

11. Outdoor Industry Association, "Outdoor Participation Report, 2017."

12. Outdoor Industry Association, "U.S. Outdoor Recreation Industry."

13. Schimel and Warren, "Recreation Is Redefining."

Outdoor recreation is a massive, growing industry that is codified in law and land-use policies and constitutes a primary relationship between people and the landscapes in which they engage. As a critical scholarly concept, it also has a history that is worth digging into. Leisure, recreation, and tourism are typically regarded as "overlapping concepts," and all three fall under the umbrella of leisure studies.[14] Aristotle positioned leisure as an "intellectual activity," a necessary component to the formation of a meaningfully engaged citizen. He argued that a citizen must be able to "not only work well, but to use leisure well." Therefore, leisure was not simply for pleasure and relaxation; like citizenship itself, leisure was regarded as a privilege, not an entitlement, which helped citizens acquire moral wisdom.[15] The discipline of leisure studies, however, evolved from Marxist critiques of capitalist industrialism that produced a clear separation between work and leisure. In *The Theory of the Leisure Class*, Thorstein Veblen demonized leisure completely, doling out harsh criticism of the industrial society's striking social stratification whereby the "lords of the manor," or the social elite, were able to maintain such status while engaging in "conspicuous consumption" and "conspicuous leisure," which he believed did virtually nothing to better society as a whole.[16] Theodor Adorno and others, however, have criticized Veblen's attitudes toward Marxism as "controversial," even "incompatible," because of his reliance on psychology and "habits of thought" to explain economic facts.[17] Instead, Adorno and Max Horkheimer focused on the cultural production of leisure in relation to work. They posited that leisure is "sought after as an escape from the mechanized work process, and to recruit strength in order to be able to cope with it again."[18] However, considering the limited choices of leisure in relation to determinate social formations, understandings of leisure as simply oppositional to work, or its association with conceptions of freedom and free will, have been further complicated in more recent scholarship.[19]

Since the cultural turn in the humanities and social sciences in the mid-1970s, leisure studies scholars have looked more closely at the cultural production of leisure, not in opposition or relation to work, but in relation to other social formations with regard to race, class, gender, and sexuality, as well as culturally situated local and global conceptualizations of leisure, access to it,

14. Hall and Page, *Geography of Tourism*, 2.
15. Aristotle, Book VIII, in *Politics*, 210.
16. Veblen, *Theory of the Leisure Class*, 28–69.
17. Adorno, "Veblen's Attack on Culture," 77.
18. Adorno, *Minima Moralia*, 98.
19. Spracklen, *Whiteness and Leisure*, 5–10.

its many forms, and what it produces.[20] In his 2013 introduction for the third edition of his important text *The Tourist: A New Theory of the Leisure Class*—originally published in 1976—Dean MacCannell argued that tourism studies has been the "least beholden to postmodernist thinking," which has kept the field from establishing itself outside of professional schools of hospitality management.[21] Those self-imposed limitations prevented scholars from approaching the complex ways in which tourism "spreads itself rhizomatically through every intellectual, economic, cultural, and geopolitical domain."[22] Karl Spracklen has more recently observed leisure as central to "understanding wider debates about identity, postmodernity and globalization . . . a place where late modern identities are defined and defended."[23] MacCannell saw this "place" as ever-expanding and argued that "this world was rapidly remaking itself in the tourists' image of it."[24] Such moves in leisure studies have, henceforth, led scholars to integrate critical conceptions of space into their work, exemplifying a confluence of leisure studies and cultural geography, positioning the everyday life of social space as a way to understand wider social relations.[25] Such efforts have shifted the scope of leisure studies from its roots in Marxism to encompass poststructural and postmodern theories of discourse.[26]

Clearly this history of leisure studies provides a window into the ways that Western intellectual traditions have shaped, and perhaps limited, the way we think about outdoor recreation. Excluded are the many forms of engagement with recreation, sport, and culture that have long been part of Indigenous traditions, from surfing to running,[27] for example, and countless culturally specific games and other forms of competition. However, resistance to co-optation and appropriation of Indigenous sport certainly exist within these and other practices, where they thrive in Indigenous communities. For example, as an Iroquoian invention that functions both as a spiritual practice and a source of collective pride and political agency, lacrosse has been rearticulated as a decolonization practice in the Indigenous communities where it

---

20. Aitchison, "Theorizing Other Discourses"; Spracklen, *Whiteness and Leisure*; Rojek, *Decentring Leisure*; Urry, *Tourist Gaze*; and R. Butler, "Geographical Research."

21. MacCannell, *Tourist*, xvii.

22. MacCannell, xvii.

23. Spracklen, *Whiteness and Leisure*, 1–2.

24. MacCannell, *Tourist*, xvii.

25. Aitchison, MacLeod, and Shaw, *Leisure and Tourism Landscapes*; Urry, *Tourist Gaze*; Lefebvre, *Production of Space*; De Certeau, *Practice of Everyday Life*; Harvey, "Space as a Keyword"; and Bourdieu, "Social Space and Symbolic Space."

26. Rojek, *Decentring Leisure*.

27. For surfing, see Ingersoll, *Waves of Knowing*; and Hough-Snee and Eastman, *Critical Surf Studies Reader*. For running, there are many, but some that link running to Hopi culture specifically include Gilbert, *Hopi Runners*; Nabokov, *Indian Running*; and more broadly among northern Arizona tribes is Brian Truglio's wonderful 2012 documentary, *Racing the Rez*.

thrives.[28] Engaging with the ways in which Indigenous cultures and communities have thought about some of these outdoor recreational activities forces us to reckon with issues of appropriation[29] and with how such activities have been re-created in ways that rely on and sustain settler colonial discourses.

Settler Colonialism

In discussion today, colonialism largely falls into one of two categories: extractive colonialism and settler colonialism. When I was a journalist, I regularly interviewed Indigenous people on the Navajo Nation, Hopi lands, and elsewhere to uncover how environmental justice issues such as mining, water rights, and other forms of resource theft, exploitation, and development continue to impact their physical and cultural survival. I found that readers, especially white liberal readers, more quickly and decisively reacted to stories that boiled down to these forms of extractive colonialism—that is, settler practices, often through industry and government, of extracting physical resources from Indigenous lands to the benefit of their communities at the expense of Indigenous lives and land. These stories fit neatly into the familiar and perhaps comfortable hero/villain, environment/economy, and profit/people frameworks that vilify (quite rightly) big business, the fossil fuel industry, and corrupt politicians. In the United States and Canada, from the legacy of uranium mining and coal extraction to the fight against tar sands and oil pipelines, extractive colonialism is very much a real and present reality in Indigenous communities. The present struggles associated with extractive colonialism also means that "postcolonialism" is neither an appropriate nor accurate framework from which to analyze the position of Indigenous communities and cultures in these contexts. For some scholars, acknowledging the daily, lived experience of colonialism as an ongoing practice—settler colonialism—is a way of positioning oneself within postcolonial theory.[30] Others, however, have taken issue

---

28. Downey, *Creator's Game.*
29. Keene, "Engaging Indigeneity."
30. Postcolonial theory is useful specifically in understanding the legacy of colonialism as a past and present phenomenon that dominates peoples and landscapes, making possible a "critique of the legacy of colonialism that is manifest in many of the structures and practices of contemporary leisure and tourism" (Aitchison, MacLeod, and Shaw, *Leisure and Tourism Landscapes,* 125). Spivak, for example, argues that attention must be paid to the changing identities of colonized peoples in relation to race, gender, ethnicity, and nationality (Spivak, "Can the Subaltern Speak?"). As Bill Ashcroft notes, "We use the term 'post-colonial,' however, to cover all the culture affected by the imperial process from the moment of colonisation to the present day," postcolonial studies encompasses the "'pre,' the 'present,' and an unresolved 'post'" (Ashcroft, Griffiths, and Tiffin, *Empire Writes Back,* 2).

with the prefix "post-" as "prematurely celebratory."[31] Linda Tuhiwai Smith notes, "naming the world as 'post-colonial' is, from indigenous perspectives, to name colonialism as finished business."[32] Settler colonialism is transnational and functions through what Patrick Wolfe describes as a "logic of elimination," a process by which Indigenous populations are replaced by invasive settlers.[33] Settler colonial theory begins from the assertion that this process never ended. "Settler colonialism" is more useful to this project because of its specific applications to circumstances where colonists have never left, where settlement is ongoing. By never leaving, settlement becomes less of an event and more of a structure,[34] and these structures operate directly and indirectly in law and policy but also in everyday decisions, performances, enactments, utterances, assumptions, and beliefs. In short, particularly for readers who are settlers—people of European ancestry who live on stolen Indigenous land and who benefit from colonial structures such as capitalism, white supremacy, and heteropatriarchy—it's a lot easier to point the finger at Peabody Coal Company or ancestors who are long dead than it is look in a mirror.

When European settlers first arrived on this continent, they brought more than just themselves; they brought entire ways of understanding and being in the world. Indigenous scholars like Kim TallBear, Joanne Barker, and Jodi Byrd and settler scholars like Scott Morgensen, Mark Rifkin, E Cram, and others have argued about the ways that European heteronormativity and heteropatriarchy have been at the center of land expansions and the production of the nation.[35] They brought Eurocentric meaning-making systems, philosophies, and religions, codified today through legal, educational, and economic institutions, embedded in everything from land-use policy and property ownership, to notions of family and marriage, to supremacist systems based on their ideas of race. For settlers, the threads of colonialism are woven so finely into the fabric of daily lived experiences that the basic assumptions and worldviews they produce are hardly recognizable, though there are traces everywhere. And it is through this analytic that settler societies constitute belongings, the sites of which compose "how we see the world, what we value, who we are becoming."[36] The constructed self, in settler societies, is forged across shifting sets of relations between peoples and landscapes, histories and

---

31. McClintock, "Angel of Progress," 84.

32. Smith, *Decolonizing Methodologies*, 98.

33. Wolfe, "Settler Colonialism," 387.

34. Here I am recalling Wolfe's observation, key to settler colonial theory, that "the colonizers come to stay[;] invasion is a structure, not an event." Wolfe, "Settler Colonialism," 388.

35. TallBear, *Native American DNA*; J. Barker, *Critically Sovereign*; Byrd, *Transit of Empire*; Rifkin, *Settler Common Sense*; Morgensen, *Spaces between Us*; and Cram, *Violent Inheritance*.

36. Rowe, *Power Lines*, 3.

memories—stories that often rely on disavowal: settler disavowal of the "presence of Indigenous peoples as contemporary agents and of settler colonialism as a persistent shaping force" and ultimately a disavowal of complicity in colonial processes.[37] Settlers move in and out of these sites, often without reflection and in ways that are subtle yet cumulative; settler subjectivities can leave scars and tarnish relationships, unknowingly undermining commitments made to live in better relation.

"Settler," as an identity, signals a specific relationship between land occupation and the uncomfortable realization of complicity in the processes of Indigenous dispossession and violence, which are embedded in economic, legal, and social structures but also "our own day-to-day choices and actions." "Settler" is an identity that people can "claim or deny" but "inevitably live and embody."[38] While I agree with scholars like Scott Morgensen who have used more specific terms like "white settler colonialism" as a "tactic for drawing white people to address white-supremacist settler colonialism multidimensionally,"[39] I prefer the broader deployment of "settler" as an overarching identity/subject position. In other words, an unnecessarily bulky term like "white capitalist heteropatriarchal settler," although quite accurate, is an academic word casserole that isn't helpful to most people, and the additional meanings are already inherent in "settler." There are certainly those who will resist applying to themselves even this simple term, but use of the simpler term does create space for those to enter this important conversation from multiple directions, inviting those who might otherwise feel defensive to recognize the simple and complex ways it may operate in the context of their own lives. By focusing on the discursive and performative aspects of settler colonialism broadly, as normalized and ingrained as they are, I hope to open new space for analysis, reflection, and ultimately responsibility and repair.[40]

"Settler," like "Indigenous," is a political status, not a racial category, and neither should be viewed through binary terms. In their examination of the term "settler," Emma Lowman and Adam Barker discuss the spectrum of affiliations to this term: "There remains a tremendous and changing variety of other people who will pass through these lands and come in contact with Indigenous and Settler communities, and all of them relate to both Indigenous and Settler peoples in multiple and dynamic ways."[41] In *Transit of Empire*,

---

37. This articulation of settler memory in terms of remembering/disavowing comes directly from Kevin Bruyneel, specifically his book, *Settler Memory*, xii.

38. Lowman and Barker, *Settler*, 2.

39. Morgensen, "White Settlers and Indigenous Solidarity."

40. Wolfe, "Settler Colonialism," 388. For more discussion specifically on the relationship between performativity and settler colonialism see Morgensen, "Theorizing Gender."

41. Lowman and Barker, *Settler*, 18.

for example, Jodi Byrd contrasts the term "settler," which is a status imbued with whiteness, with "arrivant." According to Byrd, "arrivants" are racialized non-Indigenous people who inhabit Indigenous lands and participate in colonization but still experience colonial and racial subjugation under white supremacy, heteropatriarchy, and capitalism.[42] I deploy the terms "settler" and "Indigenous" in a deliberate attempt to force readers to reckon with the power dynamics that very much depend on colonial structures. Lived experiences and identities that are situated in different ways, of course, contribute to the complexities of living and being on the land together. I want to acknowledge and account for nuanced Indigenous identities—different tribes and nations but also different family histories and experiences as Indigenous people—while at the same time lingering on the fact that Indigenous people and settler people live in different worlds.

As a settler whose family has occupied every corner of what is now the United States since the mid-seventeenth century, I agree with Onyx Sloan Morgan that it is important to take ownership of my complicit role within the larger and ongoing settler colonial context of these lands.[43] Situating myself as a settler allows for reflection on the contemporary implications of my identity, privileges, and existence as a settler living on stolen land. To identify as a settler is to name the privileged identity through which I write, one imbued with unearned advantages that come from my lineage as an oppressor on this continent, hence today this identity comes with a call to action that can only meaningfully take shape in consultation, coalition, and solidarity with Indigenous communities to dismantle the systems and structures on which settler colonialism depends. I see these not as passive processes but rather as part of a larger commitment to unearth lived and situated histories and reckon with past and ongoing trauma, to learn to recognize the ways "colonial memories function in relation to contemporary contexts."[44] I ultimately see this book and the framework it develops as a way into this work.

---

42. Byrd, *Transit of Empire*, xix (term is also deployed throughout text).

43. Morgan, "Empty Words."

44. O'Riley, "Postcolonial Haunting," 4–5. While this article deploys the useful sociological metaphor of haunting in the same theoretical framework first articulated by scholars like Avery Gordon, academics need to be extremely careful with how they engage with such theories in the context of settler colonialism. This is because of the obvious and complex material and epistemological violence scholars can do to contemporary Indigenous communities by positioning them as "ghosts." O'Riley and others deploy the metaphor in order to critique the myriad ways that settlers are "haunted" not by Indigenous peoples or communities (falsely as part of some notion of the past) but by the ravages of settler colonialism itself in the present. I wish to emphasize this extremely important distinction, as this misinterpretation can easily work against what the theory of haunting is supposed to do.

Analyzing outdoor recreational discourses, or the rhetoric of "the out-doors" as I map out in the first chapter, allows us to recognize the deeply rooted colonial structures that foreground outdoor recreation as a practice dependent on a particular understanding, experience, and treatment of the landscape. I hope to untangle the ways in which settler ontologies have been curated through colonial relationships, which produce and are produced by that which is made certain—certainty about ownership, entitlement, relation, and responsibility. Rifkin observes how these certainties function as "settler common sense" by "normalizing settler presence, privilege, and power." I agree with Rifkin that settler people take as a given "the terms and technolo-gies of settler governance as something like a phenomenological surround that serves as the animating context for non-Indigenous engagement with the social environment."[45] In a lot of ways, this book is about bringing to the fore-ground an identity that draws its strength from operating in the background.

I am drawn to Emma Lowman and Adam Barker's description of "settler" as not just an identity but also a tool, one that is necessary for social transfor-mation. It invites settlers to look inward, opening more space for Indigenous people to be listened to, for their subjectivities to have a greater impact on decision-making processes. "In order to find new ways of living respectfully with one another on this land, Settler people need to take up the responsibility of learning about Indigenous ontologies" and reject the way "Indianness"—a caricature of Indigenous identity forged through settler colonial relations—has been taught. As a tool, "settler" represents "a way of understanding and choosing to act differently."[46] This book is therefore not only a call for set-tlers to reckon with the simple and complex ways they sustain colonial struc-tures in everyday circumstances and experiences; it is also a provocation toward new ways to be accountable to and build solidarity across Indigenous communities.

Recreational Colonialism

Because colonialism functions structurally, it can be understood as permeat-ing all aspects of daily life in a settler state; therefore we should find ways to understand how colonialism works without a set of intentions or conscious commitments to white supremacy or the project of settlement. None of this is meant to dismiss the very real presence of anti-Indigenous racism or, indeed,

---

45. See Epstein, "Mark Rifkin."
46. Lowman and Barker, *Settler*, 20, 2.

vocal commitments to the dynamics of conquest often espoused by white nationalists and others who outwardly embrace white supremacist ideologies. My focus on outdoor recreational discourses reorients us toward the ubiquity, the everydayness, what Rifkin refers to as the "ordinariness," of settler colonialism.

"Recreational colonialism" attends to the ways in which place-based belongings are constituted by settler people through outdoor recreation; it also invites us to confront and challenge white supremacy, heteropatriarchy, and capitalism as they have been narrated through rhetorical practices on so-called public lands. I deploy "recreational colonialism" provocatively to disrupt the idea that outdoor recreation is politically innocent or that good intentions somehow counteract the ongoing legacies of settler colonialism which continue to benefit settlers in direct and indirect ways. By forging new connections between material-discursive theories of rhetoric, environmental studies, and settler colonialism, I examine some of the striking ways that settler imaginaries are accommodated, performed, and sustained in the everyday to reveal outdoor recreation and its spaces to be not just recreational but deeply entangled with the ongoing processes of settler colonialism.

This book examines the often unarticulated ways in which outdoor recreational discourses function as a new language of colonialism. Some of this language is propagated by the outdoor recreation industry, in promotional materials, websites, and events. Some is woven into the writing of individuals as they recount their outdoor recreational experiences and desires; more is produced through public, legal, and policy driven discourses about controversies that involve outdoor recreation on lands held sacred in different ways by a variety of Indigenous tribes and nations. Part of this language is embedded in the landscape itself, where settler belongings are narrated through frontier myths that show up in the names of trails, mountain peaks, historical landmarks, and other land designations. In this way, recreational colonialism, like all manifestations of settler colonialism, regardless of intent, wields outdoor recreation in ways that tokenize or try to erase Indigenous people from the landscape.

Though extractive colonialism and settler colonialism can be described as different frameworks for analysis, they often work in tandem materially and discursively to produce and sustain one another. Recreational colonialism forces us to confront this co-constitutive relationship. While resources like timber may be harvested for profit in the process of building ski runs, trails, and other infrastructure on stolen Indigenous lands, for example, these same resources become sites of extraction that are defined more conceptually through recreational colonialism. Feelings of self-reliance, independence, and freedom cultivated through outdoor recreational practices not only reflect the mythology of the frontier, but are also often emphasized by extractive energy companies, lobbyists, and politicians when they talk about "energy independence," "energy self-sufficiency," and other such terms.[47] Outdoor recreational discourses mobilize Indigenous lands to extract experiences, eliciting performances, myths, and ideologies that sustain settler colonialism. When politicians, government agencies and offices, industry leaders, and municipal officials collaborate to support outdoor recreation projects in defiance of Indigenous opposition, the promise of wealth is extracted from Indigenous lands to settlers and settler communities. As is often the case with resource extraction, Indigenous peoples do not benefit, but they have everything to lose.

In my journalism and academic writing, both woven through this book, I am mindful not to replicate what Eve Tuck refers to as "damaged-centered research," which "operates, even benevolently, from a theory of change that establishes harm or injury in order to achieve reparation." "Without the context of racism and colonization, all we're left with is the damage," writes Tuck.[48] Throughout this book, while I do recount stories of harm, those stories are always rooted in the myriad ways settlers sustain the colonial structures that maintain this damage. As I forge new pathways for settlers to understand themselves in the context of settler colonialism and a new framework from which Indigenous peoples may connect the harm caused by recreational colonialism to broader decolonial movements, ultimately readers may find that I position settlers as the damaged ones: damaged in their inability or unwillingness to implicate themselves, damaged in their compulsion to feign innocence when confronted with harm, limited in their capacity to confront their role in the harm to Indigenous communities and the stolen landscapes in which they engage. It is my hope that by highlighting the pain caused by settler colonialism and expanding our conception of its ongoing effects in ways that are grounded in analysis of its sustaining structures, both settlers and Indigenous peoples might be better positioned to recognize and work against it.

Chapter Breakdown

This book unfolds in two parts, the first of which establishes "recreational colonialism" as an important framing concept, and in which each chapter brings recreational colonialism into sharper focus. In chapter 1, I tell the story

47. For a more thorough analysis of the role of settler colonialism in the production of energy discourses in the American West, see Cram, *Violent Inheritance*.
48. Tuck, "Suspending Damage," 413.

of how I came to this work, the converging exigences that compelled me to think more critically about the relationship between outdoor recreation and settler colonialism. I bridge this personal narrative with the methods that come together in this book, drawing on material-discursive theories of rhetoric, settler colonialism, and environmental humanities, all of which are necessary to broadly describe and apply a rhetorical analysis of "the outdoors" as a constructed space dependent on and sustained by the cultural logics of settler colonialism.

Critical to the framework of recreational colonialism is how settler subjectivity is embedded in the imagined geographies of national landscapes, which foreground the capitalist discourses necessary to promote recreational experiences. Chapter 2 focuses on the relatively recent and growing phenomena of bikepacking, or the practice that combines mountain biking with backpacking, to animate the ways outdoor recreational discourses narrate the landscape as an imaginary dependent on settler colonialism. The imaginary, imbued with whiteness and nationalism, configures the landscape itself as rhetorical, producing a framework through which settlers experience the material world. The imaginary is also crucial toward the marketing of the consumptive experiences of outdoor recreation.

In chapter 3, recreational colonialism is intimately tied to notions of authenticity—an elusive, constructed sense of self that is dependent upon a reading of the material-discursive landscape that places settlers at the center of their story, obscuring Indigenous epistemologies. As the rock climbing narratives in this chapter illustrate, these stories are often dependent upon conquest and discovery and thus reinforce racial and sexual hegemonies. This assertion aligns with Doreen Massey's notion that space is the "product of interrelations" and an assemblage of stories so far.[49] It also aligns with Indigenous gender, sexuality, and feminist scholars who "assume that gender and sexuality are core constitutive elements" in settler societies.[50] Central to my argument in this chapter is that recreational colonialism ultimately mobilizes space in a way that accommodates settler colonial hegemonies and obscures the histories, knowledges, and power relations that foreground settlers' view of the landscape and understanding of Indigenous communities.

How we bring ourselves to the landscapes in which we engage, and what we demand of those spaces, is often curated by outdoor recreational discourses that not only limit our experience but also have profoundly negative effects for Indigenous communities. Chapter 4 analyzes the rhetoric of trail

---

49. Massey, *For Space*, 9.
50. J. Barker, *Critically Sovereign*, 6.

running and ultramarathon running—runs that tend to take place off-road and exceed the 26.2-mile distance of a typical marathon—specifically interrogating the idea of the "destination race." This chapter critically analyzes the legacy of Christopher McDougall's 2009 best-selling book *Born to Run: A Hidden Tribe, Superathletes, and the Greatest Race the World Has Never Seen*, and considers its rhetorical effect on readers and its impact on the Rarámuri, the Indigenous community in northern Chihuahua at the center of his narrative. I contrast McDougall's portrayal of the Rarámuri with Bernardo Ruiz's 2020 documentary *The Infinite Race*. Unlike McDougall, Ruiz centers the Rarámuri people, and their cultural relationship to running and colonialism, from the very beginning of his documentary. The contrast is striking in many ways but ultimately reveals the consequences for Indigenous peoples when they become mythologized in the present. It also animates some of the most salient aspects of recreational colonialism's power to transform Indigenous communities and landscapes into sites of appropriation and extraction. As a trail runner myself, I reflect on my own ruminations on the trail and consider the cultural effects of *Born to Run* on the trail running community during its most influential decade.

Chapter 5 extends from the previous one to analyze historic and contemporary Arizona Snowbowl Ski Resort brochures and maps, illustrating how the resort functions rhetorically to redefine the space of the San Francisco Peaks. In this chapter, I use theories of space that are predicated on the social as well as material production of space to push back against the refrain that the resort makes up "only 1% of the mountain," echoed by a Flagstaff City Council member, the general manager of the resort, and even a former Arizona governor. This chapter digs into how outdoor recreational spaces like a ski resort are much more than the material space they take up; they are also social spaces in which lived practices and interrelationships are embedded, foregrounding perceptions of the whole, not just a piece of it.

The second part of this book returns to and focuses on the controversy over development on the San Francisco Peaks in ways that ultimately led toward various forms of resistance to recreational colonialism. Chapter 6 centers on the common refrain, "no desecration for recreation," a phrase that calls on us to recognize the disproportional effects of land-use policy that Indigenous peoples are forced to contend with in city council meetings, Forest Service listening sessions, and court proceedings. This chapter recounts the extent to which rhetorical exclusion works through colluding legal, political, and corporate entities to limit the way Indigenous voices of opposition may be heard or understood, revealing the structural limitations to Indigenous peoples' advocacy through the legal system. Chapter 7 considers the resistance to development on the San Francisco Peaks as part of a long and ongoing history of resistance to colonialism across a variety of contexts. Separated by 1,300 miles, two pipelines cross stolen Indigenous land—one carrying crude tar sand oil through the Standing Rock Sioux reservation and the other reclaimed municipal wastewater to the Peaks—and the physical sites of their construction mark the location of Indigenous-led resistance. In this chapter, I focus on the inspiring Indigenous-led resistance to snowmaking with reclaimed wastewater that, like at Standing Rock, occurred at the very site of cultural and environmental harm: the pipeline.

Resistance and writing against settler colonialism can look like a lot of different things: a photomural in an alleyway portraying two Indigenous activists head-to-head with the powerful words scrawled on across their faces, "What we do to the mountain, we do to ourselves," or other forms of confrontational public art. Chapter 8 attempts to create more space from which to theorize about the potential of unconventional forms of visual community writing, specifically public art, in ways that reorient our commitments to Indigenous solidarity and writing against settler colonialism. Mobilizing these commitments and intentions requires careful attention to community listening that foregrounds the writing and creating process but, in the case of public art, also shows up in the work itself. In both process and product, community listening is fundamental to building and maintaining trust, establishing structures of accountability; it is necessarily relational and affective, reflecting community connection and collaboration that also "invites us to listen differently, *with* a community rather than *to* a community or *for* a community."[51]

The book ends with a concluding chapter on resisting recreational colonialism that is foregrounded by a practice toward alliance and solidarity I extend from feminist and Indigenous anarchist thinking. "Becoming Complicit" recounts the process(es) by which we enter into meaningful relationships across difference, the process of implicating oneself; this process is situated and unfolds through a commitment to honest self-reflection about positionality and learning to recognize those moments—inflection points— in which a multitude of actions can wield the most leverage toward justice and meaningful and lasting solidarity. My elaboration of becoming complicit builds on challenges to static identity-based proclamations of solidarity, terms like "ally," for example, that lack structures of accountability, individual nuance, or lasting power. I situate the process of becoming complicit within the current state of outdoor recreational management, industry, and education not only to provoke structural changes across these sectors but to infuse dignity and respect at every level of engagement with the so-called outdoors.

---

51. Jackson and DeLaune, "Decolonizing Community Writing," 42.

PART 1

RECREATIONAL COLONIALISM AND THE RHETORIC OF "THE OUTDOORS"

CHAPTER 1

Settler Rhetorics of "the Outdoors"

A Thousand Different Mountains

At a time when I was poring over the archives at Northern Arizona University, writing articles that attempted to historicize the controversy over development on the San Francisco Peaks, I was struck by a quote attributed to former Navajo Nation tribal chairman Peter MacDonald in 1978: "A thousand men can look at a mountain and see a thousand different mountains."[1]

MacDonald's words came at the conclusion of a decade of resistance to "Snowbowl Village," a half-baked proposal by Summit Properties to transform what is now Hart Prairie, a beautiful stretch of aspen groves on the northwest base of the Peaks, into a gated community complete with golf, tennis, and shopping, with a ski lift straight to the resort. That proposal was eventually defeated because the Forest Service failed to obtain the proper permissions from adjacent landowners, but Summit also could not find the water resources to support the project. The proposal nonetheless galvanized regional Indigenous opposition and collaboration with environmental groups and other

---

1. I wrote this quote down in my notes when I found it in the archives in 2008; I used it as part of a headline as a journalist and in many subsequent invited talks. Later when I tried to locate it again in the archives to retrieve the full citation, for the life of me I couldn't find it anywhere! Let this be a lesson to others to write everything down the first time. For my original reference, see Boggs, "Thousand Different Mountains," 12.

concerned citizens—thousands of vocal critics—who basically rode the corporation out on a rail.

In 2009, when I brought MacDonald's observation into the context of my
coverage, I lingered on its meaning, thinking about how differently groups saw
the mountain. There's the City of Flagstaff, the Forest Service, the chamber of
commerce, the Arizona Snowbowl Ski Resort and its shareholders. As far as
I could tell, the mountain they see is a tourist attraction, a management area
broken up into districts, an economic opportunity, a cash machine, a brand.
There's area citizens, skiers, and snowboarders who see the mountain as part
of a sense of place, an outdoor recreational opportunity, and if they believe the
words of Snowbowl's brochures, they see a "year-round playground."

MacDonald's observation that "a thousand men can look at a mountain
and see a thousand different mountains" revealed much about the many ways
the Peaks have been narrated, how the mountains hold different meanings
for different people, reflecting who they are, their cultures, their histories,
and therefore their values. The objectiveness of the observation, however, also
flattens the experience of "seeing," as if any way of understanding is equally
valid and proportionately significant. While the statement attempts to explain
why controversies like this persist, it obscures the unequal power dynamics
at work in colonial contexts. Indigenous peoples have expressed the profound
ways in which the physical landscape—the ecological integrity of that landscape—is directly connected to the cultural survival of Indigenous peoples.
As LeRoy Shingoitewa, then chairman of the Hopi Tribe, reiterated in 2011
when announcing the tribe had filed a separate lawsuit against the City of
Flagstaff, "The health and safety of the Hopi people is indistinguishable from
the health and safety of the environment—protection of the environment on
the San Francisco Peaks is central to the Tribe's existence."[2] I have dozens
of other quotes from tribal leaders and Indigenous activists going back generations that express this same idea in different ways. This way of seeing and
understanding the Peaks is one that has been consistently stated and expanded
upon for generations in countless forums. The question of why the Peaks are
sacred, and how they are sacred, has been answered in as many different ways
as Indigenous people can think of, and the question has become a source of
frustration, as none of their responses seem to be heard in a way that ultimately makes a difference in the outcome.

Even though Snowbowl Village, the gated community proposed in the
1970s, was defeated, the hundreds of Indigenous people who traveled to

---

2. *Navajo-Hopi Observer,* "Hopi Tribe Rallies." This quote is also found in Boggs, "Anti-
Snowbowl Direct Actions."

Flagstaff to voice their opposition to the project were not as influential in that defeat as the laws protecting settler property rights. In the end, despite massive public opposition and sincere testimony from Indigenous leaders attempting to explain why and how the Peaks are sacred and should be protected, the proposal was thrown out because the Forest Service failed to get permission from white landowners, Richard and Jean Wilson, who owned property adjacent to the proposal. While the Wilsons were absolutely allied with regional Indigenous peoples during the process—taking legal action against the Forest Service, and eventually donating the land to The Nature Conservancy so that it would be protected—in the end it was their objections and the recognition of their property, not the testimony of hundreds of Indigenous people and others, that protected Hart Prairie from Snowbowl Village.

Despite constantly being referred to collectively as "the tribes" or "tribal opposition," each of the thirteen regional tribes—Navajo (Diné), Hopi, Havasupai, Yavapai (Apache and Prescott), Hualapai, Tewa, White Mountain Apache, San Carlos Apache, Acoma, San Juan Southern Paiute, Zuni, and Fort McDowell Mojave—have held the Peaks sacred in different ways since time immemorial. These distinct cultures with their own traditions, origin stories, and cosmologies all see a different mountain, distinct from the mountain as it is known by other Indigenous groups in the region as well as from Western understandings. Tribes are not monolithic within themselves, either; belief systems vary within communities, from family to family, generation to generation. Nonetheless, my archival research and interviews reveal nothing but consistency among Indigenous perspectives: the Peaks are sacred and they should be protected from development. With the exception of yet another failed proposal to build a three-hundred-home golf course community in a rare wetland area on the Peaks in the 1990s,[3] in every subsequent public and legal battle since Snowbowl Village—and there have been many—skiing always seems to win out over tribal opposition. The history of the controversy and what continues to unfold in the courts, city council meetings, and Forest Service meetings make one thing abundantly clear: of the thousand different mountains that can be seen, some clearly matter more than others.

Supporters of Snowbowl often dismiss Indigenous opposition outright by recalling that the Peaks are on federally owned land, which should therefore preclude any discussion about Indigenous interventions into these so-called

---

3. In the mid-1990s, James Mehen, one of the principal developers of an exclusive golf course neighborhood in Flagstaff called Forest Highlands, submitted a proposal for Flagstaff Ranch Golf Club, which included plans for three hundred luxury homes surrounding a golf course in the Dry Lakes area of the Peaks. He faced mass and immediate resistance and withdrew his proposal in November 1997.

public land decisions. As if Indigenous peoples need to be reminded of the theft they are still resisting. Such hand-waving dismissals of Indigenous peoples' long-held ties to the land are built on a logic that acknowledges the Peaks only in a post-settlement world, as if the moment that settlers installed toeropes on the Peaks in the mid-1930s was the beginning of time. The mountain range called the San Francisco Peaks became "public land" at the end of the nineteenth century when it was claimed by the federal government after the Arizona Territory decided the land was in the public domain. Indigenous peoples were not consulted, "yet in 1898 and still today, the entire Peaks area was and is traditional unceded sacred territory of thirteen tribes."[4] The Peaks, which have gone by a dozen Indigenous names for thousands of years, were stolen so systematically that this theft is still not fully recognized for what it was. That the Peaks continue to be developed despite consistent Indigenous objection is a continuation of this theft. And skiers who claim Indigenous peoples should not have a say in decisions regarding land they have cared for over millennia express a conscious commitment to sustaining colonialism in the present.

Although Snowbowl Village was defeated at the end of the 1970s, the last fifty years have nonetheless seen it realized in slow motion. Snowbowl Village would have transformed a fragile alpine ecosystem that is holy to thirteen regional tribes into an exclusive community like Aspen or Vail, Colorado. Summit Properties, an out-of-state corporation that made money by developing luxury vacation resorts, made for an easy villain, even among those who aren't against skiing or development in general. A gated community, with restaurants, shopping, golf, tennis . . . it was a lot to demand all at once, and it was difficult for the company to find local support. But since then, the dance has been consistent: Snowbowl proposes new things, the Forest Service approves, Indigenous peoples oppose, and eventually the resort gets what it wants. New lifts, runs, trails, lodges with dining, parking lots, roads, and a thirteen-mile pipeline for snowmaking infrastructure, including pumps, snow guns, and a retention pond, have all been built. The newest proposal—announced in 2019 as part of the resort's Master Development Plan—includes even more lifts, more trails, more facilities, and infrastructure to facilitate night skiing, as well as experiences not currently offered, like mountain biking, a mountain coaster, an alpine slide, ziplines, a climbing wall, and an outdoor concert venue. While Snowbowl continuously highlights that any new developments would take place within the 777-acre boundary permitted by the Forest Service, it is clear that any amount of development will never be

4. Jocks, "Guest Column."

enough. Snowbowl also owns a large parcel of land referred to as Snowbowl Ranch at the bottom of the Forest Service road that leads to the resort.[5] While not all of it has been zoned for residential development, it is adjacent to Snowbowl Ranch Road, which has had several mansions on it since the mid-1990s, with several available lots and new construction in progress. It might not be the exclusive gated community developers wanted in the 1970s, but a form of the village continues to be realized today.

Indigenous peoples have thus far been unsuccessful in their legal and illegal attempts to protect the Peaks from further development, despite consistent and widespread opposition. There have been scores of lawsuits, so many that I imagine Snowbowl just budgets those legal costs into its development plans. Indigenous peoples have voiced opposition when their perspective was invited by the Flagstaff City Council, water commission, and planning and zoning boards, in public comment periods for environmental impact statements, and in Forest Service listening sessions that drew Havasupai grandmothers out of the Grand Canyon thinking their tearful testimonies would make a difference. There have been letters, joint statements, memoranda of understanding, letters to the editor, petitions, and successful appeals to outside parties resulting in more letters reflecting support from environmental groups and human rights organizations. Even the United Nations special rapporteur on the rights of Indigenous peoples wrote in support of Indigenous peoples against the resort's developments. Creative and collaborative Indigenous-led demonstrations ensued: protests, rallies, and vigils, banner drops, then finally lockdowns, road blockades, tree sits, and hunger strikes. As I covered these events as a journalist, I imagined an alternative reality in which skiers had lost in the courts; I tried to imagine them going to such lengths so they could ski, chaining themselves to ski lifts or something. I could not imagine that reality because *it would never happen.*

The stakes for Indigenous peoples are so obviously more severe—illustrated in the conviction of their words and actions spanning generations. Yet the other view of the mountain, what skiers see when they "look at the mountain," continues to take precedence again and again. The recreational whims of settlers who have known skiing on the Peaks in this way for only ninety years somehow trumps the numerous distinct human cultures who have oriented their entire sense of being around the Peaks for more than five thousand years. "No desecration for recreation," reads the protest signs of Indigenous activists

---

5. Snowbowl Road—a nine-mile road that leads from Route 180 to the resort—is still technically a Forest Service road. It was paved for the resort using taxpayer dollars in the early 1980s, which was the subject of a legal battle that ultimately went in favor of the resort.

every year on the resort's opening day as skiers look on totally confused. The disconnect is trivializing, if not absurd.

This book isn't about the Indigenous view of landscapes. It is an interrogation into how settlers have come to understand what they see when they "look at the mountain," or the canyon, the monolith, the river, or the trail. It's about how outdoor recreational discourses are often dependent on a view of the landscape that is fundamentally colonial, and how that view sustains the project of colonialism in the present. It attempts to map out the legacies of settler culture and history that settlers bring to their understanding of themselves and the landscapes in which they engage, and the consequences of those understandings for Indigenous peoples today. But there are also consequences for settlers as well. By coming to recognize the full range of experience inherent to their legacies and inheritances as settlers, rather than the limited vision produced through discourses of outdoor recreation, or the rhetoric of "the outdoors," we open ourselves up to much more vivid, honest, reflective, and therefore more meaningful experiences. This is an ongoing process, one that provokes individual recognition with the goal ultimately of bringing settlers into better relations with the landscapes they love and with Indigenous communities.

Setter Subjectivities and the Rhetoric of "the Outdoors"

When I moved back to Arizona after having lived in Indiana for fifteen years, I reveled in the crisp mountain air and the seemingly endless expanse of ponderosa pine that stretch across the Coconino National Forest. My earliest memories of that time are a mental mosaic: long wandering hikes alone with my dog, the fragrance of the forest, the sound of the wind through the pine needles, the ravens, and me, a small brush free to dance on an enormous canvas.

I saw the forest as full of places to climb, run, and bike, and even though I wasn't a hunter or angler, I knew the forest held those possibilities too. With the right permits, I could potentially feed myself and cut my own firewood. I knew that anywhere, at any time of the day or night, I could find a clearing to temporarily call my own, where I could build a fire and make camp. When I got hot, I could filter water from a seasonal stream, or I could strip down and jump into a cool mountain lake. I fully embraced the promise of so-called public lands, that this land—land that was certainly once taken but is now shared—belongs to all of us. But how did I come to see myself and the land in this way?

These were spaces made familiar to me as a settler through the rhetoric of "the outdoors": the intertwining of physical landscapes with myths of the frontier, the folklore of settlement, and one-sided historiography that positioned my settler ancestors at the center of the story of these lands. Public land-use law and policy, which are historically rooted in Indigenous erasure, carve the land up into different designations and districts under the purview of state and federal land management agencies, and for better *and* worse they also shape our experience. The rhetoric of "the outdoors" produces and is produced by canonized Western environmental writers, artists, poets, and activists. All of this—the historical, cultural, national, philosophical, and the aesthetic—steeped together in my mind to produce a way of being in and experiencing outdoor spaces that is unquestionably colonial and uniquely settler.

I came to recognize my engagement with these processes as both conscious and unconscious, both intentional and unintentional. As I roamed through the forest with my dog, it was so easy to imagine the forest the same way as early settlers—my ancestors—did, full of potential, full of whatever possibilities I wanted to bring. And that is both the allure and the trick of the rhetoric of "the outdoors": it produces an ontology always working to transcend colonial pasts, reinforcing what Tuck and Yang observe as "settler moves to innocence,"[6] but at the same time, it is a way of being that is inherently dependent on the benefits accrued from that very past. By interrogating the rhetoric of "the outdoors," I seek to work against this tension, to make it impossible to disassociate settler orientations, imaginaries, and subjectivities from our experience on stolen Indigenous lands.

During a recent camping trip to Yellowstone National Park with my family, I couldn't help but notice all the ways the mythos of the frontier was present, often relating our experience as visitors to the settler experience. I've seen this play out in many—if not all—of the national parks we've visited, but something that stuck with me this time was the image of tourists in yellow horse-drawn wagons. Yellowstone "Stagecoach Adventures" are advertised all over the park, from visitor centers to signs in campground bathrooms, offering settlers the opportunity to "Energize your Pioneer Spirit on a stagecoach ride." I thought of the people, greeted by two enthusiastic guides in cowboy hats, crowded onto a small wooden wagon, ready to embark on a bumpy ride through the park. As I stared at one of these posters, trying to put into words what exactly the company means by "your Pioneer Spirit" and what practices

---

6. Tuck and Yang, "Decolonization is Not a Metaphor," 3. The phrase "settler moves to innocence" is extended from Janet Malwhinney's usage of "moves to innocence." She observes that "moves to innocence can, and often do, occur anywhere privilege exists" ("'Giving Up the Ghost,'"101).

might "energize" it, I found myself overanalyzing something that was just supposed to be fun, which is what I imagine many might think I am doing throughout the pages of this book. I am suggesting we take seriously that which we are meant not to, that there is much we obscure in the preservation of innocence, and that there is much to be gained when we question how our experiences on stolen Indigenous lands are curated in ways that center settler experiences and histories.

The feelings provoked by the rhetoric of the outdoors through the recreational activities I enjoy are, not surprisingly, the same ones used to describe the hypermasculine virtues embodied in the narratives of early settlers. I wouldn't have admitted it in those early days in Flagstaff because it sounds a bit silly, but it's all there, embodied, animated, and performed, not from horse-drawn wagons but from hiking boots and the view from behind my handlebars: a sense of independence, self-reliance, rugged individualism, and freedom of mobility. While these traits, characteristics, and embodiments are ubiquitous in the histories of western expansion, in settler narratives of the "frontier" and "the West," white US American values like "individualism, self-reliance, risk-taking, and progress" have also been revived in "extreme sports" discourses.[7] However, I gesture here toward new interrogations of rhetorical practices that need not be "extreme" at all but enmeshed in quotidian interactions between settler bodies and rhetorical landscapes. Outdoor recreation, in all its active and sedentary forms, as well as the industries that promote it, functions as a kind of intermediary between the material and the discursive, through which settlers' relationship to colonialism is accessed and activated. The rhetoric of "the outdoors" thus may work to sustain settler colonial dynamics, even if individual participants are not consciously committed to doing so.

The feelings activated through my experience on public lands were surely exacerbated by the fact that I had moved from Indiana, where not even 3 percent of its land is designated as public, back to Arizona, where more than half of it is. Regardless of how many acres, what matters more is the experience of that difference, the imagination it provokes, and the subjectivities it sustains. Even while I was aware of the history of colonialism in Arizona and the continued effect of white supremacy, capitalism, and heteropatriarchy on regional Indigenous peoples who maintain ancestral relations to these lands, I didn't immediately recognize my presence as part of those systems. Instead, the rhetoric of "the outdoors"—the inseparable yet fluid and interdependent relationship between the material and the discursive—was captivating and

7. Kusz, "Extreme America," 209.

comfortable. It was a source of empowerment forged through a deep sense of belonging because of my proximity to white supremacy.

The connection I felt was further rooted in my cultural and personal history of this place. These were the same woods my father had defended as a wildland firefighter in the 1970s, the same place my parents met, a region where I spent time as a kid from Phoenix visiting grandparents in Cottonwood, where my grandfather spent his retirement as a tour guide at Tuzigoot National Monument, an ancient Sinagua pueblo. In my return to the area as a journalist, I would learn a lot about the area's ecology, diverse cultures, controversies, and contested landscapes. I learned to identify plants and animals, and I felt at home in the rhythm of the high desert seasons. I picked and ate mushrooms and pinion nuts, I gathered and steeped Mormon tea, and I befriended ravens and horned toads, or at least I'd like to think so.

Embodying the same settler tropes as so many had before me, from mid-nineteenth-century New England transcendentalists to radical environmentalists like Edward Abbey to others who maintained tragically over-romanticized views of the landscape like Chris McCandless, I, too, found myself constructing some sense of what I believed to be my true authentic self, by being alone in what I believed to be nature, an elsewhere. The more time I spent in that forest, the more I wrote about it, the more I defended it, the more profound I felt the connection to be between those landscapes and my identity. Connection to that land is something I still feel deeply, yet I also understand how the rhetoric of the outdoors has disconnected me from the reality of my legacy as a settler occupying stolen Indigenous land, where occupation and entitlement are reconfigured as forms of identity and belonging.

Mark Rifkin writes about a similar connection he felt when he bought his first house, when the land he suddenly came to own felt like an extension of his own body. "The expansion of self," he describes, lay "somewhere between the realms of the tactile and the imaginary," an interdependent and always changing relationship between the material and the discursive that "encompass[es] the area covered by the official property lines."[8] While Rifkin's sense of ownership, enshrined through Western notions of property, extended to the end of his residentially zoned parcel of land, the connections I felt on federally owned land in northern Arizona extended for hundreds of thousands of acres in all directions. Indeed, I quickly understood all public land in the United States—including land I'd never even been to—in this way. Rifkin explains this connection by observing how "personal identity under

8. Rifkin, *Settler Common Sense*, xv.

liberal modes of political economy often is conceptualized and lived as self-ownership."[9] Like Rifkin, I also extended my "sense of selfhood to the land," but the land is more than just material.

Gregory Clark's repositioning of the material object of "land" as the conceptual "landscape" is a useful distinction here because of how the material can function rhetorically. "Land" becomes "landscape" when it is part of a shared public discursive experience "symbolizing a common home and, thus, a common identity."[10] Samantha Senda-Cook similarly observes that "commitments and investments in places" also contribute to the way groups "bolster their identities."[11] While Rifkin muses on land he legally owned, I'm suggesting that my sense of personhood extended to land I was led to believe was somehow mine because I'm a tax-paying American, and as the popular bumper sticker claims, I'm therefore a "public land owner." Both Rifkin in his backyard and I, running on a trail in a national forest on so-called public land, are both fundamentally occupying stolen Indigenous land, and we have both been conditioned not to recognize how these forms of ownership and other institutionalized frameworks sustain deeply engrained colonial power structures and how they are accessed through a kind of feeling. Indeed, "public land" itself is a euphemism for Indigenous land in the United States: land that was stolen or either recently purchased from Indigenous peoples or Indigenous land that the United States government does not officially recognize as Indigenous land. When mountain biking or trail running or snowshoeing, this is a fact that I can choose to recognize or not, and the very fact of that choice is an exercise in settler privilege. For communities Indigenous to those very same lands, participating in centuries-old cultural practices without consciously acknowledging the federal and state laws and corporate partnerships imposed on those lands could easily result in a wide range of criminal charges.

Like Rifkin, I, too, started to think about how "institutionalized relations of settlement, such as law and policy, help generate forms of affect through which they become imbued with a sensation of everyday certainty."[12] That "feeling" Rifkin describes constitutes my belonging in those spaces in particular ways that are often unrecognizable and therefore difficult to articulate. The cultural histories from which my identity is descended as a settler—the myths of the frontier, the masculinity and heteronormativity wrapped up in the folklore of settlement, the heroic tales of independence and self-reliance—have produced a kind of essence, an aesthetic, a way of being in those spaces.

---

9. Rifkin, xv.

10. Clark, *Rhetorical Landscapes in America*, 9.

11. Senda-Cook, "Long Memories," 421.

12. Rifkin, *Settler Common Sense*, xv.

The resulting narratives that animate our experiences of those spaces demand that we don't think about how we came into possession of this land and cannot be easily untangled without coming to terms with the simple and complex ways white people have been conditioned to relate to the landscape in strictly settler terms through settler ideologies. Outdoor recreational discourses provide useful examples and a frame from which we might come to more fully understand the attitudes, beliefs, and performances that often (but certainly don't have to) accompany these narratives.

"The outdoors," as an idea, is fundamentally colonial. The clarity of this point is rooted in the construction and enforcement of the nature/culture dualism. Among the many ideas European settlers brought to this continent, which are expressed in various ways within the structures of settler colonialism, the categorical separation between nature and culture is primary to the project of settlement and continues to shape settler subjectivities in the present. Environmental historians from Roderick Nash and William Cronon to Patricia Limerick and Dorceta Taylor have established the ways in which this dualistic structure foregrounds the basis of US American conquest and once drove ideas contributing to western expansion, guided by ideologies like Manifest Destiny, a religiously rooted cultural belief among early settlers that it was their divine right to drive Christianity and capitalism westward, across the continent.[13] Under this narrow framing, culture, or civilization, exists in areas that are walled off and fenced in, domesticated, known, controlled. Culture is built, orderly, an organized space constructed under the purview of laws, institutions, and social order. And nature, or wilderness, is that which lies outside of culture; nature is boundless, unknown, uncontrolled space. Nature is contrived as a space of wild animals, and settler cultural beliefs included Indigenous people as part of these untamed landscapes. Nature/culture dualism was central to the articulation of the frontier and the mythic American West, which is less a place and more of a discursive settler formation wrapped in the material reality of the western United States.

As a cultural mythology, the mythic American West tells the story of a self-styled rugged masculinity forged through a sense of independence and self-reliance. In this story, white men are virtuous and Indigenous peoples, if present at all, must be destroyed, and land was justly and heroically acquired. The mythic American West, or the "frontier," is less a geographical reference than an ideological one. The concept of the frontier was popularized by historian Frederick Jackson Turner in 1893, when he used the term as a metaphor

---

13. See Nash, *Wilderness*; Cronon "Trouble with Wilderness"; Limerick, *Legacy of Conquest*; and Dorceta Taylor, *Environment and the People*.

to understand US American identity and politics, often referring to "men of the frontier" or "gentlemen of the west." Turner understood the frontier not only as a male-dominated space but as "the meeting point between savagery and civilization." He also drew a distinction between the US frontier as lying on the "edge of free land" (or stolen Indigenous land) and the frontiers of Europe as being more sharply defined outside of dense populations. While for Turner at the turn of the nineteenth century, the frontier was a useful metaphor, to which "the American intellect owes its striking characteristics,"[14] today historians understand the frontier as a kind of mythology, perhaps best exemplified by the Myth of the American Frontier trilogy by Richard Slotkin. Slotkin defines myth as "a set of narratives that acquire through specifiable historical action a significant ideological charge."[15] The myth of the frontier, over time, has been persistent and pervasive, evolving from ideals of America as the "land of opportunity," where the strongest are valorized through conquest, from exploitation of land through industrialization in the nineteenth century to the present, where it is seemingly cemented as cultural ideology, in popular culture, and in law and politics.

The phrase "the great outdoors" rose in popularity at the turn of the twentieth century, quite suddenly appearing in publications associated with national park tourism and organizations like the Boy Scouts of America. That this cultural shift occurred in the decades following Turner's articulation of "the frontier" is not a coincidence but an extension of the same discursive formations from which settlers have attempted to articulate their complex relationship to land they do not know. The mythology of the frontier coheres to the very notion of an "outdoors" in several ways. "The outdoors," like "the frontier," is a highly mythologized idea of spaces "out there," which lie outside of the comfort of the city, of culture, and that demand exploration. Like Rifkin's characterization of the "wilderness," "the outdoors" is also an "extrapolitical elsewhere."[16] "The outdoors" signals something between nature and culture: spaces that are safer than so-called wilderness but less predictable and familiar than spaces structured by culture and society, and it is this in-betweenness from which it draws its allure. In "the outdoors," a sanitized frontier, one can revel in beauty, can retrieve some lost sense of authenticity, but without the danger evoked in frontier narratives.

---

14. Turner, *Significance of the Frontier,* 60, 64, 10, 11, 80.
15. Slotkin, *Fatal Environment,* 31.
16. Rifkin, *Settler Common Sense,* 108.

The Material-Discursive Outdoors

While "the outdoors" is a concept that cannot be separated from its colonial context, it is also an articulation of language that is at once discursive and material. The outdoors is not a place one lives but a place one visits, a place defined by culturally constructed ideas of nature and wilderness, and practices that are rhetorical in the sense that they are essential to one's identity and linked to the places in which they are imagined to occur. Rhetorical theory is, at its most basic, the study of persuasion in all of its forms. As we teach in freshman composition, rhetoric is that which can be understood as having an author, an audience, and a purpose, and under this framework we analyze "texts," which can be anything from essays, images, films, and song lyrics to speeches and so much more. In this framework for rhetorical analysis, the intention of the author is less important than the effect of rhetoric on an audience. The simple title of Andrea Lunsford's widely used textbook *Everything's an Argument,* now in its ninth edition, makes this point clear for students. If *everything* is, indeed, an argument and can be understood as rhetoric, these same concepts can be applied to analyze the very spaces in which we engage and how the space produces (and has been produced by) various performances and utterances situated within settler colonial contexts. This requires us to consider not just the "texts" themselves but everything that exists in relation to them. Rejecting "the idea that 'everything' is a 'text' to be read" and analyzed in isolation allows us to engage "with text, bodies, materials, ideas, or spaces knowing that these subjects are interconnected."[17] While urban spaces have been observed to "act rhetorically"—which is to say "in ways that shape attitudes, beliefs, and behaviors"—recreational spaces function in this way as well.[18]

Trails, for example, constitute a kind of writing—writing literally etched into the landscape—that is inextricably linked to history, culture, and the social imaginaries that in turn affect the audience, the trail user. When it comes to trail building, a crew makes all kinds of rhetorical decisions about how the trail will traverse the landscape, decisions on the ground that determine the positioning of rocks, turns, drops, which trees stay and which ones will be cut, where the trail will be left rocky and where it will be graded flat. All of these decisions are made in accordance with the purpose of the trail— to be used by the intended user—but also, certainly, assumptions are made

---

17. Riley-Mukavetz, "Towards a Cultural Rhetorics Methodology," 109.
18. Triece, *Urban Renewal and Resistance,* 17.

in the process about those users and their perceptions of nature. These decisions produce forms of accessibility but also "order[ ] the experiences" users expect to have there. Senda-Cook observes how trails (and maps) "function as mediators, lenses through which visitors understand and experience" a place, and elaborates on the lengths trail crews go to "cultivate the perception that nature has not been disturbed by humans . . . to make their efforts invisible." This means that pruning is minimal, debris is disguised, and the cut ends of branches are placed away from the trail so trail users remain unaware anything has been done.[19] These decisions cannot be divorced from the settler colonial context, where settler stories of the landscape surely erase and replace any story that previously existed, and hikers can pretend they are exploring something akin to untouched wilderness. In this context, outdoor recreation may be conceived of as a re-creation; to recreate as a settler is to re-create, to reimagine the landscape in ways that consciously or unconsciously work to sustain settler imaginaries. For those whose research lies at the intersection of rhetoric and culture, oriented methodologically by questions of process and mobilized by decoloniality, "We must recognize that the practices that lead to the creation of these discourses cannot be separated from the systems of power in which they are created."[20] Coming to terms with our participation in recreational colonialism is about recognizing the landscape as affective, written, narrated, and re-created in ways that often reflect fundamentally colonial ideologies, in ways taken for granted as universal when they are not.

Through our relations and identifications, through our cultures, histories, languages, and rhetorical practices like outdoor recreation, we write our landscapes, and in turn, those landscapes write us.[21] Settlers affect and produce spaces of outdoor recreation, and we are then affected and produced by those spaces. The trail is a form of rhetoric, and so are the mountains, valleys, canyons, rivers, and other spaces and places where discourse and physical reality are inextricably intertwined, interdependent, and co-productive. At a ski resort, the carved lines and ski infrastructure alter discourses about the mountain, and that discourse is always rewriting the physical space of the mountain.

Other disciplines have similarly engaged with the relationship between material reality and discourse and have offered several ways to engage with the two, not as separate concepts, but together as a distinct framing lens. Cultural geographers have referred to first space as physical reality, or the "real," and second space as discourse, or "imagined" spaces. Edward Soja, for example,

19. Senda-Cook, "Materializing Tensions," 367, 363.
20. Powell et al., "Our Story Begins Here."
21. I have to give credit to Dobrin, "Writing Takes Place," for helping me think through this affective relationship.

combines them to refer to a "third space," or the "real-and-imagined."[22] More recent work in material feminisms has similarly pointed out that defining the material—such as nature and the body—strictly as products of discourse has "skewed discussions of these topics." Material feminists are concerned with "the interaction of culture, history, discourse, technology, biology, and the 'environment,' without privileging any one of these elements."[23] While some have called for "a new way to understand the relationship between language and reality,"[24] others have answered this need by articulating physical reality and discourse together: "material-semiotic" or the "material-discursive."[25]

Karen Barad's term "material-discursive" is particularly useful in my analysis of the rhetoric of the outdoors because of the relationships under consideration, whereby "imagined" is a potentially condescending term when engaging with powerful identity formations where nature and culture converge in contested ways. Analyzing the rhetoric of the outdoors inherently relies on the relationships between the material and the discursive. Discourse, generally, is not merely a "disembodied collection of statements" but is grouped and "enacted within a social context."[26] For Foucault and, later, Butler,[27] the social context included the materiality of nature and the body. For cultural geographers and spatial rhetoricians, this means that the social context necessarily includes space. Therefore, when engaging the multiplicities of relationships between peoples, cultures, and landscapes, an understanding of the material-discursive in the rhetoric of the outdoors is useful because it privileges neither language nor physical reality but allows scholars to instead focus on the relationship between the two.

While I deploy "material-discursive" throughout this book, I do so hesitantly, knowing that the concept is essentially just an overly complicated articulation for what Indigenous peoples and scholars have always known simply as "the Land"(capital L), as explained by Mohawk scholar Sandra Styres. For Indigenous peoples across what is now the United States and Canada and elsewhere, Styres writes, the Land is an articulation of a duality that is "more than physical geographical space" but simultaneously includes "underlying conceptual principles, philosophies, and ontologies of that space." Space and place together, as "two simultaneously and interconnected conceptualizations," the

---

22. Soja, *Thirdspace.*

23. Alaimo and Hekman, introduction to *Material Feminisms,* 3, 7.

24. Hekman, "Constructing the Ballast," 92.

25. Haraway, *Simians, Cyborgs, and Women*; Harding, *Sciences from Below*; and Barad, "Posthumanist Performativity."

26. Mills, *Discourse,* 10.

27. Foucault, *History of Sexuality*; and J. Butler, *Bodies That Matter.*

Land for Indigenous peoples goes beyond Western ideas of place as "concep-tual, experiential, relational, and embodied."[28] Métis scholar Zoe Todd has criticized movements in new materialisms as repackaging and appropriating long-held Indigenous knowledges and methodologies that articulate discourse as constituted by relationships that include nonliving things.[29] While Todd interrogates Bruno Latour for this kind of appropriation, other scholars have pointed out similar practices across the scholarly landscape.[30] For all of them, the practice of Indigenous appropriation is less about intentional malice; more specifically it points to how often Indigenous scholarship has been ignored in the canons of Western intellectual traditions. Todd asks, "When *will* I hear someone reference Indigenous thinkers in a direct, contemporary and meaningful way . . . without filtering ideas through white intermediaries?"[31] I recognize the utility of "material-discursive" because it appears to linguisti-cally signal the connections I discuss in this book. That these relationships are already apparent in Indigenous articulations of "Land," however, speaks fur-ther to Todd's observations about the settler colonial conditions that structure how meaning is traced in Western academic discourses, which often exclude Indigenous thought.

A material-discursive engagement with a rhetoric of the outdoors is con-cerned with the ways outdoor recreational spaces produce peoples, cultures, and landscapes. By situating spaces of outdoor recreation as a discourse—complete with its own specific set of coding and representation—"tourism landscapes" such as ski resorts may be better understood as "sites and sights of social and cultural inclusion/exclusion and are not fixed but are in a con-stant state of transition."[32] The discourses of outdoor recreation are mapped, codified, and defined in such a way that accommodates and sustains settler subjectivities; outdoor recreational spaces and concepts like the outdoors are therefore ideal to analyze through this framework.

The "material-discursive outdoors" itself is a framing concept that allows for an interdisciplinary analysis of the way recreation shapes social and cultural conceptions of material landscapes.[33] Through the discursive lens of recreation

---

28. Styres, "Literacies of Land," 27.

29. Todd, "Indigenous Feminist's Take."

30. See Rosiek, Snyder, and Pratt, "New Materialisms," for a useful literature review on the rise of new materialisms in political theory and an assessment of the lack of engagement with Indigenous scholars.

31. Todd, "Indigenous Feminist's Take," 7.

32. Aitchison, "Theorizing Other Discourses of Tourism," 19; and Urry, *Tourist Gaze*.

33. Boggs, "Material-Discursive Spaces."

lies a particular construction of nature, the way in which a specific, often narrow understanding and experience of the environment is accommodated and sustained. Yet the validity of this construction underscores the way "power and knowledge gain traction at the sites of affective investment" in some knowledge(s) over others, "between and among those who are constituted through belonging."[34] Therefore, spaces of outdoor recreation exclude non-Western cultures and claims of sacredness but ironically limit the way even Western audiences are meant to relate to other cultures and the natural world.

In southwestern Idaho, where I live now, hikers can traverse sections of the original Oregon Trail; there are signs describing the "epic journey of humanity" where the land is still physically rutted out from the wagon wheels that carried settlers west 150 years ago. Not just the name of the trail but signs, mappings, and conversations one overhears among hikers there indicate the simple and complex ways the trail—as a kind of rhetoric—produces a particular way of being on that trail. In Senda-Cook's work on material rhetoric and memory, she describes the lasting cultural effects of discourse on the material: "If one can read the material space with an eye for the past, then the memories imprinted on the landscape reveal themselves and are telling for the ways that people experience these places."[35] The physical trail remains, as do the discourses concerning its place in US history and the role it continues to play in the narration of the mythic West. So particularly for those settlers who, like me, use the trail, their experience is shaped by both the material and the discursive landscape. When I'm on that trail, and the sun rises to illuminate Barber Valley, I can't help but imagine the landscape the way those early settlers must have seen it. My experience on the trail is produced by the physical characteristics of the trail, the weather, and my body—the material, but also the discursive—how I am implicated by the history of the trail as a settler, and the ways I have come to understand that history through a mesh of fact, myth, and story that quite deliberately centers the experience of my ancestors. This framework allows us to think conceptually about how "we make trails, and how our trails make us."[36] Looking off into the rolling foothills and deep canyons, settlers are meant to recall memories of their own making, a settler subjectivity dependent on the idea of the frontier, the mythic West, and the heroic narratives of conquest.

---

34. Rowe, *Power Lines*, 3.
35. Senda-Cook, "Long Memories," 421.
36. Moor, *On Trails*, 27.

Recognizing Settler Colonial Landscapes

Material objects like monuments, street signs, and building names are key features in the narration of place, and the revising of these material objects indicates a strong belief in the power these objects hold in the everyday lived experiences of those places. During the summer of 2020, a pivotal moment of racial justice movement-building in the wake of the police murder of George Floyd, Confederate monuments were taken down across the United States. Sometimes these were top-down decisions made by city leaders, who were often pressured to do so by constituents; other times, the monuments came down suddenly, by force, by people who couldn't stomach looking at them anymore in light of the worlds they wanted to build together. The monuments represented people who fought to maintain slavery, who were often active proponents and participants in colonial violence, from Confederate leaders like Robert E. Lee to Jefferson Davis but also figures of colonial genocide like Christopher Columbus. The monuments were not compatible with the values of those communities and their commitments to each other. So the statues had to go. Many streets and buildings across the country were also renamed. While the objects were removed and the names changed, they will always be part of the story of that place. The materiality of the object, iron and stone, is bound to the discursive, the cultural and political context, past and present. When a monument is removed or a street name is changed, its previous existence and the fact of its removal become integrated into the narration of that place.

The legacy of white supremacy and colonial violence reflected in monuments and street and building names is not radically different from the ways that settler racism, co-optation, and validation dot and crisscross the landscape. European place-names on Indigenous landscapes, replacing Indigenous names, tell a story of the land that has been described by Indigenous scholars as a "narrative of possession," through which "settler colonialism is (re)lived and (re)inscribed across territory through toponyms."[37] Toponymy "emphasizes the spatial politics of naming and the social production of place,"[38] and political theorists of toponymy like Reuben Rose-Redwood and others have more recently called for great attention to the politics of language in naming practices that contribute to the hegemony of some languages over Indigenous and other minoritized linguistic systems.[39] Cultural geographers working

---

37. Murphyao and Black, "Unsettling Settler Belonging," 317.
38. Rose-Redwood, "Rethinking the Agenda," 34.
39. Rose-Redwood and Alderman, "Critical Interventions," 4.

from a framework of decolonization to challenge the "colonial cartographic frame" have called for Indigenous geographical knowledge to be recentered and for Indigenous communities to be actively involved in mapping practices going forward.[40] The names of trails, peaks, rivers, lakes, canyons, and valleys constitute stories of those places, based as much on discourse—languages, cultures, histories—as on the physical, material details of those places. All over what is now the United States and Canada, Indigenous culture, religious iconography, history, and culture, along with self-styled heroic settler narratives of exploration and white Western-centered frontier fantasies, are woven into the outdoor recreation landscape, where settler entitlement to stolen Indigenous land is as present today as it was three hundred years ago.

Some of these places are in the process of being renamed. Capping off a yearlong process, Deb Haaland, the first Indigenous interior secretary of the United States, identified nearly 650 place-names that bear the offensive word "Squ*w," which are now in the process of being changed.[41] In many cases, Haaland's office has been working directly with Indigenous communities to agree on names that reclaim Indigenous terms or designate new ones, while many names on state and federal land were changed in consultation with local governments. Despite the fact that Indigenous peoples have been demanding these changes for decades, two privately owned ski resorts, the Palisades Tahoe Ski Resort (formerly Squ*w Valley Ski Resort) in California and Big Moose Mountain Ski Resort (formerly Big Squ*w Mountain Ski Resort) in Maine, are being celebrated for "taking the lead" on this issue.[42]

This effort, as important as it is, does not include the thousands of miles of "unofficial" trails that exist throughout the United States and Canada. In a curious case in British Columbia, local mountain bikers illegally built a trail system on Crown land that contains offensive trail names like Squ*w Hollow and The Rapist. As the mountain biking group petitions to legalize the trail system, they fear changing names "right now" would put their bid in jeopardy. In this way, the act of illegal trail building functions as a strategic way to lay claim to unceded Indigenous land; since the trail "already exists," their argument to legalize the trail network appears stronger than it would otherwise. It's easier to ask for forgiveness than for permission, as the saying goes. This strategy and its likely outcome recall the historical practice whereby an invading country would claim land as their own by putting a flag on it—instead of flags, today settlers build trails and acquire land by "expanding access," an

---

40. Rose-Redwood et al., "Introduction: Decolonizing the Map."
41. US Department of the Interior, "Secretary Haaland Takes Action."
42. Rodriguez, "California Ski Resort"; Associated Press, "Name of Ski Mountain"; and Gruver, "U.S. Changes Names."

endeavor universally and uncritically celebrated by the outdoor community and the governmental agencies that manage land-use decisions. Their illegal work promulgates their belonging. "They did invest sweat equity in these trails even though they chose inappropriate names," the president of the group said, adding they will "engage the larger community" to change the names once they are legalized.[43] In short, it would appear that the group's sense of responsibility does not outweigh its perceived entitlement to Indigenous land; in the end, its members get to facilitate the performative community engagement of name-changing without having to fundamentally rethink their relationship to the land.

While name changes are essential, especially the removal of names like this that signal deeply engrained anti-Indigenous misogyny and recall sexualized violence against Indigenous women, changing the name is the easy part. The harder and arguably more meaningful component involves changing the way settlers view the landscape and their place in it, and finding ways to challenge the systems that made these offensive place-names possible in the first place. Klee Benally, a Diné activist, musician, artist, and longtime protector of the San Francisco Peaks against the Arizona Snowbowl Ski Resort, helped me recognize some of the ways gestures like name changes ring hollow when they are not also accompanied by commitments to upend colonial structures that maintain supremacist systems. When the City of Flagstaff moved to recognize Indigenous Peoples' Day, Benally called for "justice, not gestures," and maintained that the city needed to do more to "address historical trauma from settler colonialism," pointing to the city's ongoing support of the Arizona Snowbowl Ski Resort's actions to produce artificial snow from "treated sewage" on the "holy Peaks," as well as continued high levels of homelessness and racial profiling of Indigenous people. He asked, What would recognizing Indigenous Peoples' Day in this context actually do for the Indigenous people who live here? "Our voices matter. Our cultures matter. Our ways of life matter," he said.[44] A name change is simply not enough.

When the effort to remove "squ*w" from the landscape was announced in 2022 by Haaland's office, Benally said it was hard for him to celebrate. "#namechange means little while the state & corporations perpetuate & profit from violence against the land & our bodies," he wrote on Twitter. "Do we really just want a less offensive violent colonial system?"[45] If the Arizona Snowbowl Ski Resort changed its name or petitioned the Department of Agriculture to change the name of the San Francisco Peaks to something that reflected the regional cultural significance of the mountain, this would not

43. CBC News, "Jogger Decries."
44. K. Benally, qtd. in Boggs, "Replacing Columbus Day."
45. K. Benally, "Gesture."

change the fact that the land was stolen from Indigenous peoples, and it would not change the fact that a private, for-profit business operates on a mountain held sacred by at least thirteen regional tribes that have been consistent and unwavering in their resistance to those operations. While name changes are important in different ways, depending on the context, and diminish opportunities for the casual deployment of anti-Indigenous language, they do little to address underlying colonial structures.

For those who recreate on stolen Indigenous lands, hiking, biking, climbing across landscapes made familiar through centuries of narratives that constitute settler belongings, there are perhaps thousands of place-names across the United States that reinforce anti-Indigenous racism and co-optation at the very sites of settler engagement with Indigenous landscapes. Despite the Washington football team owners' reluctantly caving to pressure from years of Indigenous-led organizing against the word "R*dskins," the outdoor recreation community in Colorado continue to use the R*dskin Creek Trail next to R*dskin Mountain. Further to the east is the Tomahawk Trail, and to the west the Kokopelli Trail. Runners enjoy the R*dman Trail in eastern West Virginia, where ATVers connect to the Indian Ridge Trail via the Pocahontas Trail System. Other Indigenous leaders, many of whom infamously led others in resistance against colonization, feature prominently, from the Geronimo Trail in southern Arizona to the Tecumseh Trail in Indiana to the Sitting Bull Mountain Bike Trail in Texas. Despite the fact that teepees are associated with the homes of nomadic tribes in the Great Plains of what is now the United States, mountaineers traverse Teepee Mountain in British Columbia, and hikers access the Teepee Trail near Montpelier, Vermont, and the Teepee Mesa Trail near Crownpoint, New Mexico, and arrive at an actual teepee constructed at the summit of La Canada Teepee Trail outside of Los Angeles, California. In Denali National Park and Preserve, where the traditional Indigenous place-name Denali replaced McKinley, settlers continue to kayak on the nearby S*vage River, where they can access the S*vage River Loop Trail. And in western Maryland, there still exists the Big S*vage Mountain Trail near Little S*vage Creek. Even if our efforts were limited to naming alone, there is still a lot of work to do.

The trivialization and exploitation of Indigenous culture in the context of outdoor recreation also works against efforts toward making better relations. The marketing landscape reflects images of headdresses used to sell outdoor gear;[46] Hopi Kachina and Kokopelli imagery feature on outdoor recreation logos for resorts, outdoor supply companies, trail building organizations, and

---

46. See the website for Warbonnet Outdoors, https://www.warbonnetoutdoors.com/, for an example of a company logo that integrates Indigenous headdresses to sell outdoor gear.

more. What are we to make of the Trail of Tears half-marathon near Jackson, Missouri, which is billed as a "challenging day of dirt, rocks, and tears"? When the Washington Trails Association promotes "8 Trails That Tell a Native American Story," why are Indigenous peoples not actually telling any of those stories?[47] When Indigenous peoples have asserted their ancestral claims to "public lands" and have shared spiritual and cultural knowledge about a place that is held sacred, those insights are celebrated. But if the slightest effort is made to limit settler access to those places, it is often met with profound backlash.

What is today known as the John Muir Trail, for example, was established and used as part of a network of routes for thousands of years before the conservationist arrived. The Paiute, who called it Nüümü Poyo, or "the people's trail," have been working with other regional tribes and a grassroots organization, Indigenous Women Hike, to reclaim these ancestral trading routes.[48] The Sierra Club, whose nonprofit environmental conservation work was founded by Muir in 1892, has recently been honest about his racist attitudes and beliefs about Indigenous peoples.[49] Yet the signs and narrations of the trail in the Sierras that settler hikers get on the ground erase the Indigenous history of belonging, building, and tending of the land, as if John Muir built the trail himself. *Trail Runner Magazine* has brought attention to this in an article, "The Case for Re-Naming Public Lands," in which Zoë Rom reminds readers that John Muir was also an advocate for Indigenous removal and details the extent to which the problem of racist and sexist language for place-names extends across so-called public lands. She writes, "The names of numerous other trails, parks, national forests, wilderness areas and public features bear either racial slurs or are credited to Confederate soldiers, racists and frontier figures responsible for killing or dispossessing Indigenous people."[50] There is much power in naming, and critical inquiry into how places get named, who gets to name them, and what effects those names have on our ability to form meaningful relationships is both revealing and significant. While name changes are an important first step in reorienting settler experiences in ways that decenter whiteness, the difficult work lies ahead: the important process of detangling the everyday attitudes, experiences, and feelings sustained by settler colonialism within outdoor recreational cultures and spaces.

When it comes to outdoor recreation experiences on stolen Indigenous lands, settler colonial narratives that center the pioneer, the prospector, the explorer remain front and center. Settlers still use sections of the Oregon Trail

47. Washington Trails Association, "8 Trails."
48. Chavez, "Nüümü Poyo."
49. Brune, "Pulling Down Our Monuments."
50. Rom, "Case for Re-Naming Public Lands."

where mountain bike races are held, and trail runners participate in the Oregon Trail Ultramarathon Series in Oregon. Thru-hikers trace the route made famous by Lewis and Clark and can even run the Expedition 12K through Lewis and Clark Caverns. Settlers in Sedona, Arizona, mountain bike on the Frontier Trail and the Western Civilization Trail. From the mountains in North Carolina across the west and into British Columbia, old mining routes have been resurrected as popular mountain biking destinations. These trails, where place-names coalesce with local histories and folklore, tell the celebrated tale of grizzled mountain men eking out their fortunes while protecting themselves from "Indian raids"—never ceding the truth that they were the invaders, the raiders, engaged in and benefiting from unfettered extractive colonialism. Making good relations might include removing anti-Indigenous language from the landscape, but this alone does not yet begin to address the centuries of attitudes and beliefs that created the conditions for those names in the first place. There is a lot that needs to be done to unsettle colonized landscapes.

The idea of the trail, particularly the recreation trail, is based on the aesthetics of a romantic social imaginary. Rather than taking a direct route, it meanders and winds through trees and around boulders to arrive in those serene places of wonder and imagination—these moves are part of the trail-building process from the earliest planning to the eventual implementation. The seemingly authentic, solitary experience the user believes they are forging is also heavily curated: "The sublime feeling produced by wilderness is not an innate, universal feeling but a culturally conditioned response."[51] While trail builders actively write the trail, the decisions they make in accordance with the expectations of trail users can also be attributed, at least in part, to the way wilderness spaces have been imagined by painters like Thomas Cole and Albert Bierstadt and photographers like Carlton Watkins. In all of these examples, the land is reimagined as pristine empty space, devoid of the influence of humanity. These images of lush forests that give way to Edenesque river valleys that wind below jagged snow-capped peaks were used quite successfully in conjunction with the Homestead Act to entice settlers to travel west and carve out a little piece of that fantasy for their own. These constructed images that entered the cultural imagination during what Ralph Waldo Emerson deemed the "ocular" age in America—the visual allure of abundant resources and autonomy coupled with the promise of essentially free land and prosperity offered by the Homestead Act—produced a way of perceiving the landscape as a blank slate, waiting to be discovered, explored, settled, written.[52]

---

51. DeLuca and Demo, "Imagining Nature," 555.
52. Emerson qtd. in DeLuca and Demo, 545.

I agree with Gregory Clark, who observes that "the rhetorical symbols we encounter and exchange are not limited to language," that US Americans have always experienced their nation rhetorically as a "scene" not unlike those captured by these nineteenth-century artists. He says it was important, particularly during settlement, for citizens to "seek in their common surroundings some 'objective evidence' of their identity," which grew out of a need to distinguish a uniquely US American identity from the landscapes of Europe.[53] Kevin DeLuca and Anne Demo assert, "Yosemite's mountain cathedrals and majestic redwoods offered cultural legitimacy to a nation seeking a heritage that could compete with Cathedrals and castles of Europe." But of course, these landscapes were not devoid of humanity. They were not uninhabited; they were not waiting to be discovered, explored, or settled. The "scene" observed by US Americans on these landscapes is best described by DeLuca and Demo as a "white wilderness," that is, a space "interlaced by the values of whiteness," where American landscapes are connected to European civilization that is dependent upon civilization/wilderness dichotomies. Within this narrow worldview, diverse Indigenous communities that inhabited those lands were framed as part of that which was understood as wild and untamed. DeLuca and Demo continue: "Within the context of whiteness, those not part of white civilization are, at best, seen as part of nature. At worst they are often expelled from wilderness and forcibly 'civilized.'" There were, and still are, generations of Indigenous peoples whose cultural and spiritual identity are tied to these same landscapes, whose blood has mixed with this soil since time immemorial. Yet "the myth of pristine wilderness is founded on the erasure of the humanity, presence, and history of Native Americans."[54] Through the absence of humanity, the false portrayal of lands as empty, the paintings themselves are based on a lie, one that serves to accommodate a kind of settler gaze.

This same gaze is captured today in the photos mountain bikers often take during trail rides, photos I have taken as well, often without reflection, and post on social media and in other online forums. In the background of the photo, taken when the lighting is perfect, there's the elegant form of the San Francisco Peaks, the red rocks of Sedona, or the deep and colorful expanse seen from the North Rim of the Grand Canyon. The background captures a scene not radically different from those painted by Cole or Bierstadt, or Watson's photographs—dramatic scenes with no human or cultural trace except for what lies in the foreground: propped up beside a boulder or a tree stands alone a dusty, trail-worn mountain bike. When I stage these photos,

53. Clark, *Rhetorical Landscapes in America*, 3.
54. DeLuca and Demo, "Imagining Nature," 544, 550, 554.

they function in the moment to tell my family that I am safe and to say, *look where I am!* Later, when I post the photo on social media, the message is *look where I've been!* and if I'm being honest with myself, the subtext is, *look at who I am.* This scene, which is so ubiquitous within social spaces across the outdoor recreational landscape, also encapsulates DeLuca and Demo's notion of "white wilderness." Here, belongings are constituted through a constructed authenticity, one that is validated through a sense of nostalgia for a time that never actually existed.

CHAPTER 2

Bikepacking

Rhetorical Landscapes and Settler Placemaking

The music begins, an intense and apocalyptic opera reminiscent of Carl Orff's *Carmina Burana* plays. Video and text go back and forth. *To live off the land is a noble human experience.* Black screen. *It's tradition, passion, and birthright.* A pickup truck slows to a stop in the early morning light of some unnamed forest location. *This passion pushes us to look for an edge.* A man pulls a bicycle from the back of the truck and rides off into the woods. *To go deeper, faster.* The man pauses and reads a Forest Service sign. *And leave no trace.* Deeper into the forest the man rides before the screen goes black. *Introducing . . .* At this moment the first full-detailed view of the bicycle comes into focus: A rigid mountain bike with wide knobby tires, a frame painted with dark green camouflage fitted with racks that hold a compound bow and arrows. The remaining images are of different white men hunting and riding, juxtaposed by images of open wilderness. *Hunt, fish, forage . . .* and then the remaining three words flash across the screen, in sync with concluding drumbeats of the music: *Feed. Your. Self.*[1]

---

1. Though Cogburn bicycles have been retired since this book has been published, and some of the advertising is no longer accessible, information about the bikes can be viewed here: https://www.retiredbrandresources.com/cogburn. The ad can still be viewed online. See "The Cogburn CB4 Bike in Realtree Xtra Camouflage," posted August 20, 2013, by Realtree, YouTube, https://www.youtube.com/watch?v=3sRfzdDJVRg.

Critical to the framework of recreational colonialism is how settler subjectivity is embedded in the imagined geographies of national landscapes. This Cogburn bicycle advertisement speaks to a very specific customer, one who seeks to combine mountain biking and hunting through the intersection of frontier masculinity and environmental ethics. The now defunct bicycle manufacturer marketed its products with "hunters and anglers in mind," those who wish to "access more land; taking their gear farther, faster, and quieter with virtually no impact on habitat." Cogburn situated their bicycle within a space that conjures Marc Augé's framework of a "nonplace," a place that is familiar, yet imagined as it doesn't represent any specific location, nor is it situated in relation to any sense of history.[2] It's an idea of a place that exists as an imaginary. This imagination serves as backdrop for a merger between recreation—hunting and riding a bike as "sport"—and self-sufficiency—to "live off the land." Cogburn's goal here was to sell bicycles, but to target their audience, their rhetorical choices evoke a kind of frontier masculinity. The bike is just as capable of commuting in potholed urban conditions, it could be painted any color, and the rack could carry groceries as easily as it could a compound bow. But that's not the narrative Cogburn is conjuring here.

At work in this chapter is how outdoor recreational discourses narrate the landscape as an imaginary dependent on settler colonialism. In terms of identity, the idea of those spaces takes on more meaning than the spaces themselves. The imaginary, imbued with whiteness and nationalism, configures the landscape itself as rhetorical, producing a framework through which settlers experience the material world.[3] The imaginary is also crucial to marketing the consumptive experiences of outdoor recreation.

Imagined Geographies: 1890s Rides from Flagstaff to the Grand Canyon

Bicycling became widely popular in Flagstaff, Arizona, beginning in the late 1800s, and it was immediately tied to tourism to the Grand Canyon.[4] Prior to the 1890s, there was no viable road to the Grand Canyon from Flagstaff, but according to the town's first newspaper, the *Arizona Champion*, there was much potential to bring visitors to Flagstaff if such a road were constructed.

---

2. See Augé, *Non-Places*.

3. See Bonds and Inwood, "Beyond White Privilege."

4. All newspaper articles in this chapter, from the *Arizona Champion* and the *Coconino Sun* (the former became the latter), were accessed through microfilm at Cline Library's Special Collections and Archives at Northern Arizona University.

In 1890 Flagstaff's business elite started making plans. In 1892 the paper ran stories musing about the possibility of Flagstaff as "the gateway to Grand Canyon."[5] With a stagecoach route under way, circling the western slope of the San Francisco Peaks before heading north, hotels were envisioned along the line.[6] By the end of May 1892, the Moqui Stage Coach route[7] opened from Flagstaff, leaving three times a week. During this year, ads for bicycle manufacturers, such as Ben-Hur bicycles, started popping up regularly in the paper, as well as ads for pneumatic bicycle tires.[8] The next year, other ads appeared: Coventry Cross Cycles from Chicago and Buckeye Cycles from Ohio.[9] Stories lamenting the success of the stagecoach route continued to accompany ads for bicycles: Indiana Bicycle Co. and Victor Bicycles.[10]

Bicycling became so popular by the end of 1894 that in the archival index for the newspaper that year, "bicycling" appears as a labeled sport for the first time in either newspaper and has more articles referenced than any other sport, including baseball, hunting, shooting, horse racing, and fishing. The paper documented bicycle races held at local festivals and regional bicycle trips individuals took to Oak Creek Canyon, Prescott, and Sedona; one "Flagstaff bicycle aggregation" used the stagecoach route for the first time to ride to the Grand Canyon.[11] The cultural and technological shift that was taking place in Flagstaff during this time can be drawn from the ads of the Sykes Brothers, local machinists who fell in love with cycling. In 1888 their company ran ads for their specialty in brands for horses and cattle.[12] By 1897 they were advertising their specialization in bicycle repair.[13]

In 1895 they formed the Coconino Cycling Club, which publicized and organized annual supported group rides to the Grand Canyon.[14] During the same year, the *Coconino Sun* did its part to drive tourism to the area, assuring the country that Flagstaff and its surrounding area was safe, no longer the epitome of Wild West lawlessness that so many outside of the area associated

5. *Arizona Champion*, April 28, 1892, p. 3, col. 2.

6. *Arizona Champion*, May 12, 1892, p. 3, col. 2.

7. *Moqui* is a Hopi word that refers to someone or something that is dead. I was told it originated as a term used by the Hopi to name the Ancestral Puebloans, the ancient ones who inhabited Hopi lands.

8. Advertisement for Central Cycle Mfg. Co. Ben-Hur Bicycles and Cleveland Pneumatic tires for bicycles from Halozier and Co., *Arizona Champion*, December 22, 1892, p. 4, cols. 1 and 7.

9. *Arizona Champion*, July 6, 1893, p. 4, cols. 1 and 5.

10. *Coconino Sun*, June 28, 1894, p. 4, col. 6; and December 20, 1894, p. 8, cols. 4–5.

11. *Coconino Sun*, August 23, 1894, p. 7, col. 4.

12. *Arizona Champion*, September 1, 1888.

13. *Coconino Sun*, April 29, 1897.

14. *Coconino Sun*, June 27, 1895, p. 7, col. 3.

with Arizona. The paper said, "For a town that a few years ago was a frontier settlement and as 'wild and woolly' as they make 'em," Flagstaff's crime statistics were at an all-time low.[15] The same article claimed that more visitors had been drawn to Flagstaff that summer than any preceding season in the history of the town and trumped up the town's "superior advantages as a place of recreation." The following year, the Coconino Cycling Club sought to make its annual ride to the Grand Canyon the largest and most successful to date. Realizing the potential of using the ride to help drive tourism, the *Coconino Sun* helped the group publicize the event with a generous amount of column space in which the ride was described in exquisite detail:

> The entire route to the Canyon is a succession of interesting and beautiful sights. The dim, shadowy vistas of the pine forest stretching away on either side, the charming little glades and valleys with which its expanse is broken here and there, the magnificent views of the noble San Francisco triad, the changing hues and shapes of the cliffs and hills along the road, the black carpet of volcanic cinders to the left, Sunset Crater with its sombre slopes and crest of eternal sunshine, all combine to make the first twenty miles of the journey a scenic panorama of indescribable beauty, while the fragrance of the pines and the crisp, fresh mountain air render every breath a delight.[16]

This description recalls Clark's observation that US Americans regard their nation as a "scene," a "symbolic setting where they can enact both individual and collective identity." Clark mobilizes Kenneth Burke's notion of "identification"—his rhetorical theory explaining the connection a speaker makes with an audience when they identify their shared ways—to tourism landscapes and their role in the formation of shared US national identities. In doing so Clark focuses on the "rhetorical power inherent in a particular symbolic experience of their national homeland that Americans tirelessly invite each other to share." The *Coconino Sun*'s description of the landscape exemplifies such an invitation, as the "rhetorical power of a national culture is wielded not only by public discourse, but also by *public experience*," in this case, the way in which the scene unfolds from the view while pedaling a bicycle. The account is colorful and engages multiple senses and scenes, some of which conjure familiarity—like pine forests—while other descriptions such as the "black carpet of volcanic cinders" may sound foreign to people outside the area. At the same time, the description demonstrates Clark's claim that rhetoric functions

---

15. *Coconino Sun*, July 3, 1895, p. 2, col. 2.

16. "A Midsummer Outing: The Bicyclists to Make the Run to the Grand Canyon," *Coconino Sun*, May 28, 1896, p. 1, col. 2.

constitutively. Whether familiar or unfamiliar, the appeal lies in how the vivid description constitute in readers a "sense of shared identity." Clark observes that US American culture teaches Americans to experience their homeland rhetorically, "to encounter for themselves those places as potent symbols of a concept of national community they are to claim as their own."[17] When a material landscape is translated into text, particularly persuasive text like this meant to attract tourists to an unfamiliar space, it is designed to promote a shared experience and a specific way of perceiving the land. It is from this framework that I deploy the phrase "settler subjectivity" in this chapter, to denote a way of seeing and being on the land that has been curated to accommodate and sustain settler belongings.

Clark further observes that rhetoric is "not limited to language," that the "full range of symbols that constitute a person's social and cultural experience have rhetorical functions."[18] Although the *Coconino Sun*'s description of the canyon route is limited to language, it is based upon and draws its rhetorical effectiveness from the material reality that it describes and that the tourist imagines. In short, material-discursive conceptions of spaces of outdoor recreation exemplify "imagined geographies." That is, representations of such spaces become an imaginary, simultaneously appealing to the "desires, fantasies and fears" of a nation and "the grids of power between them and their 'Others.'"[19] "Imaginative geography" was first introduced as a concept in critical theory by Edward Said, who explained it by way of metaphor: "The objective space of a house . . . is far less important than what poetically it is endowed with. . . . Space acquires emotional and even rational sense by a kind of poetic process, whereby the vacant or anonymous reaches of distance are converted into meaning." The space of mountains, trees, and valleys between Flagstaff and the Grand Canyon, like Said's house, is not as significant as its impact on the sociological imagination, which "help the mind to intensify its own sense of itself by dramatizing the distance and difference between what is close to it and what is far away."[20]

The notion of difference also enters the 1896 imaginary, in descriptions not only of landscapes likely unfamiliar to outsiders, such as the "romantic" banks of Oak Creek Canyon, Sedona, but also landscapes linked with cultural differences—however accurate: Montezuma's Well and Castle, and Cataract Canyon "with its magnificent waterfalls, and the picturesque settlement of the

---

17. Clark, *Rhetorical Landscapes in America*, 3, 4, 5.

18. Clark, 3. For more historic scholarship with respect to reading and interpreting the discursive power of landscapes, see Meinig, *Interpretation*.

19. Gregory, *Dictionary of Human Geography*, 371.

20. Said, *Orientalism*, 55.

Yava-Supai Indians which is located in this Canyon."[21] Less important than the imaginary is, perhaps, the fact that there is no such tribe as the "Yava-Supai." One might guess that the writers of the article unintentionally combined the names of the actual tribes Yavapai and Havasupai. However, they were likely referring to the Havasupai, who do indeed live in the village Supai, surrounded by beautiful waterfalls deep within Cataract Canyon, an offshoot of the Grand Canyon.[22] It is perhaps ironic that the article writers, who sought to draw outsiders to bicycle to the Grand Canyon, are ignorant of the diversity of the Pai people who inhabit their destination. Said's point that the imaginary is more significant than the reality is fundamental to my understanding of rhetorical landscapes: they are based on something tangible and real but rely on discourses—powerful stories and mythologies—that bring those landscapes into meaning. The story that is told in outdoor recreational discourses sustains modes of being that center the settler experience of those lands.

A week before the group's 1896 bicycle ride from Flagstaff to the Grand Canyon, the paper ran another article that captured the group's enthusiasm. "It is expected that one hundred wheelmen" would show up for the ride; the ride further involved several local businesses and would include "handsome ribbons" for participants and a parade to see them off.[23] The day after the group left, however, the paper published a few short paragraphs about the start of the ride. Ride organizers expressed disappointment that of the sixty cyclists from outside Flagstaff who had committed to join them, only seven showed up for the event.[24] The fact that so many people from all over the country read the initial article, with its vivid description of the landscape and difference, and signed up for the event, yet so few actually participated further illustrates the powerful allure of imagined geographies. Months before the ride, it existed as an exciting fantasy; one can only guess that the reality of logistics and physical capability weighed more heavily on would-be participants as the date approached. Though the club conducted small annual group rides to the canyon into the twentieth century, the stagecoach itself was closed after 1900, in part because a rail line was constructed from Williams, Arizona, to the canyon, and later, a paved road was built from Flagstaff.

Even though the Moqui Stage Coach line was short-lived, it represented early efforts to draw outdoor recreational tourism to the area. Furthermore, the way in which the bike rides were promoted outside the area through

21. *Coconino Sun,* May 28, 1896, p. 1, col. 2.
22. Hirst, *I Am the Grand Canyon;* and Jacoby, *Crimes against Nature,* specifically chapter 7, "The Havasupai Problem," 149–70.
23. *Coconino Sun,* August 13, 1896.
24. *Coconino Sun,* August 20, 1896, p. 7, col. 4.

colorful descriptive language that emphasized connections between recreation and settler subjectivity exploited a kind of imagined geography that continues to pervade outdoor recreational discourses today.

Frontier Fantasies and the Settler Aesthetics of Bikepacking

Adventure mountain biking, or "bikepacking"—the practice of traditional backpacking done by bicycle—has, in practice, occurred for as long as people have ridden bicycles. The power of the imagined geography described in the 1896 newspaper excerpt is made more intense because of its associations with concepts like wilderness, rugged individualism, and self-reliance—all of which complement the hegemonic archetype of white US American masculinity today. It is through these associations that the rhetoric of bikepacking, and the identity of riders, is implicated today. As the Flagstaff riders of the 1890s can attest, the first bicycle owners were driven by the impulse to see what they could do with them, how far they could go, how capable these new-fangled, self-powered machines were, and how those machines would stand up against existing technologies such as the stagecoach. They learned, even though they could not carry as much, they could travel more swiftly and efficiently than the stagecoach. No doubt, there was something refreshingly satisfying about what that technology allowed them to do and the confidence it inspired. The description of the 1896 ride noted that, although tents would be provided at the canyon, bedding would also be supplied for those who wanted to sleep under the stars. "This will be found preferable to the tents" because "sleep in the open air is most refreshing and invigorating."[25] The article also lauded the "sense of freedom" riders will feel from "widespread views" in the prairie, "extending many miles on every hand." When it turned out that the 1896 group got caught in a heavy rainstorm on the way to the canyon, the weather did not dampen their spirits but tested their "power of endurance."[26] Within these spaces, not only is there a particular way of *being* in the wilderness but also a specific settler subjectivity that characterizes who belongs there and how they belong. In this way, settler subjectivity, imagined geographies, and whiteness merge to form a logic in which wilderness experiences are narrated. The curated experience of this narration recalls and romanticizes the experiences of early settlers: the freedom of mobility, feeling of self-reliance and individualism, the seeming emptiness of the land,

25. *Coconino Sun,* May 28, 1896, p. 1, col. 2.
26. *Coconino Sun,* Aug 27, 1896, p. 7, col. 4.

the low-stakes risk that provokes a touch of danger and discomfort from a position of relative privilege. It's an imaginary that relies on the histories and cultures of the settler experience that is bound to the landscapes of settlement, mythologies of the frontier, and ideas of wilderness.

Informed by Roderick Nash's *Wilderness and the American Mind* and Max Oelschlaeger's comprehensive *Idea of Wilderness,* among others, Cronon argues that there is nothing natural about the concept of "wilderness," which he claims is "quite profoundly a human creation"—indeed, the creation of very particular human cultures at very particular moments in human history.[27] DeLuca is careful to point out that this postmodern view does not imply that the idea of wilderness should be dismissed in favor of privileging humans. Rather, by deconstructing "modernism's foundational concepts and Truths," postmodernism "represents an even more sustained questioning of the human than of wilderness."[28] Carolyn Finney aptly applies DeLuca's concept of "white wilderness" to describe the way the natural world is "socially constructed and grounded in race, class, gender, and cultural ideologies." Finney argues, "whiteness as a way of knowing, becomes *the* way of understanding our environment, and through representation and rhetoric becomes" entrenched in our national psyche.[29]

This imaginary, a kind of settler landscape, is steeped in cultural myths that sustain white supremacy—the settler and the frontiersman blur through recreational colonialism to become the outdoorsman, the mountaineer, the angler, the mountain biker. The mythic American West tells the story of a self-styled rugged masculinity forged through a sense of independence and self-reliance—where white men are centered, virtuous and heroic, a narrative frame that works against the humanity of Indigenous peoples. The mythic west ultimately tells one story, however, obscuring Indigenous genocide and displacement that precipitated white settlement, as well as the resilience of Indigenous communities who resist colonization through the present, and maintain claims to their ancestral lands. Historian of the American West Malcolm Rohrbough helped Patricia Limerick draw this point out in her important book *Legacy of Conquest: The Unbroken Past of the American West*: "The settlers of the West took the view that the land was there to be taken, and that the rules and regulations of the government did not change their natural rights as citizens."[30] In this story, the land was justly and heroically acquired, and white men replaced Indigenous peoples as the true keepers, stewards, and guardians of the land.

---

27. Cronon, "Trouble with Wilderness," 7.
28. DeLuca, "Wilderness Environmentalism Manifesto," 38.
29. Finney, *Black Faces, White Spaces,* 3.
30. Malcolm Rohrbough qtd. in Limerick, *Legacy of Conquest,* 61.

Furthermore, the concept of a "white wilderness" signals class privilege as well. It is not a coincidence that members of the Coconino Cycling Club included what would appear to be some of Flagstaff's wealthier citizenry: a local physician, the owner of Riordan Mercantile Company, the treasurer for Arizona Lumber and Timber Company, and other businessmen. They did not find themselves in the wilderness, traversing the landscape on their own exertions, out of necessity, but—like those who engage in bikepacking today—by choice. It was fun; it was—and still is—recreation.

It follows, therefore, that the ethos of the "white wilderness" drives the way these bicycles are sold and consumed—an affective relationship driven by capitalism's exploitation of identity. The interplay between production, consumption, and the culture created is affective, in the sense that bicycle frame builders respond to the desires of those who seek to ride deeper into more remote areas for longer periods of time by producing bicycles capable of doing that, and when the technology begins to fulfill that perceived need—first for a fringe group of riders—the marketing of that technology on a larger scale produces that desire in other riders. The desire produces the technology, and the technology produces the desire. Those without previous inclinations to pedal over a frozen creek bed in the canyons of southern Utah may begin to ponder the possibility when they see a bike capable of this in a bike shop or in a photo online. Slowly a culture coalesces around this consumptive process.

The last half of this chapter interrogates some of the ways settler colonial discourses have informed the practice and culture of bikepacking, beginning with the cultural moment in the early 2010s when the industry responded to this phenomenon. More and more manufacturers today have embraced the "adventure bike" as a new and separate genre of bicycle that, in many ways, combines the utility and nimbleness of traditional touring bicycles with the off-road capability of mountain bikes. From gravel bikes to fat bikes, these bikes share a lower center of gravity that makes heavy loads more manageable, and clearance for larger tires, as well as many features on the frame designed to allow for multiple racks, fenders, and water bottle cages.

There is a relationship between the technology and aesthetics of the adventure bike and identities among those who ride them. One blogger took issue with the way these new bicycles were being marketed, drawing sharp contrasts between the rhetoric of professional mountain biking and the lifestyle of adventure biking. He claimed that by depicting pro mountain bikers performing feats most riders of fat bikes couldn't possibly do, such as flips or carving lines down steep sandy terrain without showing them walking the bikes back up, marketers were being dishonest and failing to pitch the design platform. But more importantly, it was clear these videos did not portray the kind of relationships he sought between this technology and settler authenticities and aesthetics he crafted for himself. "Utility sells itself," he wrote before asking, "Where are the edits about fat bikes being ridden on snowy back roads, with campfires and bourbon and beards and cooking your whole breakfast in a cast iron pan full of bacon grease?"[31] His question appears to be more about his identity than the bicycle itself, and clearly, a fat biker is necessarily masculine, white, and legitimized through a cliché performance of the frontiersman. At the same time, his identity is intimately tied to that technology, which in turn affects and is affected by his nostalgic identifications. In this description, a trail-worn horse could easily stand in for the bike, and that is very much the point.

Manufacturers of these bikes have answered this call. Surly Bikes and Salsa Cycles, for example, understand that selling a bicycle today means would-be buyers must be persuaded by the technology but also by messages that speak to their identity as bikepackers. For example, the Salsa Fargo was initially described in a manner reminiscent of the imagined geography described in the newspaper excerpt that promoted the 1896 bicycle rides to the Grand Canyon from Flagstaff:

> A unique creature with a special set of skills, it is always willing to fulfill the most imaginative endeavor. It has developed a cult status as an off-road touring and bikepacking machine, and fuels our passion for long days in the saddle in distant lands. Fargo is designed to take you wherever it is you wish to go, be it the Camino de Santiago route between France and Spain or a trip down the Tour Divide route.[32]

Notice the emphasis on other, exotic, or in their words, "distant lands" in various countries as well as rugged North American landscapes that follow the Tour Divide route, which traverse the Continental Divide in the United States from Canada to New Mexico. The difference is that Salsa mediates the imagined geography with the marketing of their emergent bicycle technology. While both the 1896 excerpt and the Salsa bicycle ad are selling an experience, the Salsa ad takes it a step further, using the allure of the imaginary to sell a product.

Surly Bikes, however, takes a more direct rhetorical approach in linking their technologies with the rider's identity, specifically with their description of the ECR when it was first introduced in 2013: "ECR has multiple mounts

---

31. Roggeman, "Bike Companies."

32. Salsa Cycles has since removed this language from the description of the Fargo on their website (http://www.salsacycles.com).

on the frame and fork for water bottle cages and larger gear cages, so you can bring lots of water, stove fuel, milk, a sleeping pad, small mammals or what have you. . . . It's a pack mule, a pedal-powered escape pod. Wherever you want to explore, this is the bike that can get you there."[33] While the ECR has been discontinued, descriptions for all of Surly's bikes take on this tongue-in-cheek, no-nonsense rhetoric. As the owner of two Surly bikes myself, I have long admired their commitment to innovation, reinvention, and versatile design. Even though I am a fan, I have to be real with the fact that descriptions like this also flag settler belongings, inviting riders like me to imagine myself performing and embodying all the ways of being that come with it.

Alongside the technology, these companies speak to a lifestyle, an identity, and a foundation for the way in which environmental ethics are framed, positioning the wilderness as a place to explore, to "escape." Both bicycle ads further describe the technology itself as something that belongs in nature: a "creature," a "pack mule." Another Surly bike, Krampus, is described alongside a quote from one of the company's lead engineers: "Lean back, hang on, and ride that wild horse."[34] Likening the bicycle to a pack mule or a wild horse further allows the rider to align their recreational activities with nostalgic, simpler, more authentically perceived forms of transportation when "long days in the saddle" meant traveling by horse or burro.

But more than utility, manufacturers have further capitalized on what they perceive to be the aesthetics of a bikepacker, which—like settler subjectivity—is very much dependent upon frontier fantasies of exploration, settler-centered narratives, and myths about Indigenous peoples. These interrelationships are forged through textual descriptions as well as visual rhetoric. Regarding the Surly Pugsley, for example, the bike manufacturer proclaims, "Many moons ago we began producing the Pugsley because we wanted to ride a bike that could be ridden where other bikes simply faltered."[35] Surly likens the passage of time with the appearance of the moon, a practice associated in the stereotypical portrayals of Indigenous cosmology. The phrase, a remnant from the traditionally defined American colonial period, has surfaced again and again in Hollywood portrayals of Indigenous peoples.

Visual aesthetics further capture the interrelationships. For example, Kokopelli, a Hopi deity that has been appropriated widely across the Southwest in art and in souvenir shops, has also entered mountain biking discourses.

---

33. Surly Bikes has since removed this language from the description of the ECR on their website (http://www.salsacycles.com).

34. Surly Bikes, http://www.salsacycles.com.

35. Surly Bikes has since removed this language from the description of the Pugsley on their website.

Representations of Kokopelli are integrated into the logo for the Colorado Plateau Mountain Bike Trail Association, where the dancing fluteplayer's curved form functions as the "C" in the group's acronym, COPMOBA. Similarly, Kokopelli Bike and Board, a business in Cortez, Colorado, features Kokopelli riding a bicycle in its logo. In this example and in others, settlers engage in what refers to as "narrative transfer," which renders Indigenous peoples' claim to the land no greater than settlers'—but not just claims to land.[36] Narrative transfer can apply as well to Indigenous cultural aesthetics. For example, Kokopelli has been co-opted and rearticulated by settlers so many times that, at least under this framework, Indigenous peoples are not connected to the proliferation of its meaning.[37] Such integrations of Indigenous iconography within mountain biking discourses are important to the production of recreational colonialism, removed from its original context and trivialized as an aesthetic.

Other examples make further connections between settler subjectivity and the imagined geographies that elicit nostalgia for the frontier, for a white wilderness. In many cases, these aesthetics are integrated into the physical bicycle frame itself. In 2016 Specialized Bicycles partnered with Poler, a bicycle touring-bag company, to make an adventure bike, AWOL. Beyond the utility of the bicycle itself, the frame was covered in decals: pine cones, animal tracks, and various foliage from evergreen trees. Where text illustrating imagined geographies falls short, the visual aesthetics of the decals take over. "With AWOL," the description reads, "the only thing holding you back is your imagination."[38] Yet it appears that much of the imagination has already been developed for riders, mediating the material and the discursive, the physical environment and discourses that narrate the environment. This was also exemplified on the mountain graphics featured on the Specialized Fatboy, or the hunting camouflage print on Cogburn's fat bike frames. The natural imagery juxtaposed with the technology of the machine suggests a desire that can never be fully realized, which is to say that by literally wrapping the bicycle in images of nature manufacturers can bring the object no closer to being "natural."

The 2016 Salsa Deadwood used this same aesthetic marketing tactic for its frame, but Salsa went to greater lengths to overemphasize the interrelationships between frontier fantasies that necessarily include the idea of Indigenous peoples, or what Philip Deloria refers to as "Indianness."[39] Etched into the

---

36. Veracini, *Settler Colonialism,* 42–43.

37. See also Rogers, "Deciphering Kokopelli."

38. Specialized, https://www.specialized.com/us/en/awol-x-poler/p/101430?color=190281-101430. While the link is to the bicycle I discuss here, Specialized has since removed this language from its description.

39. P. Deloria, *Playing Indian.*

frame is a jumble of pseudo–Indigenous American imagery reminiscent of hieroglyphics such as the outline of a hawk, a buffalo, and an arrow through the Deadwood logo. These appear alongside a pair of axes and a deer skull, among others. Inclusion, with respect to "Indianness," or the image of Indigenous iconography through a settler lens, forces us to ask, "included how?" Here, the "Indian," the wilderness, the lumberjack, the outdoorsman, and the explorer are all mixed together to appeal to one uniquely settler subject. Other bicycles, such as the Tumbleweed bicycle company's Prospector, rely on frontier rhetorics that constellate within the same settler colonial relationships at work here. With all these examples, the visual portrayal of these relationships is put on as an aesthetic for settlers.

Recreational Colonialism as Settler Placemaking

Recreational colonialism encourages performances of colonialism through outdoor recreational practices. Today, the original Moqui Stage Coach route exists within a complex web of Forest Service roads that crisscross and intersect the historic seventy-mile-route to the Grand Canyon. Though people do hike sections of it and even run it as an ultramarathon, mountain bikers have made great efforts to mimic the efforts of those cyclists in the 1890s. The annual Flag2GC, "a Charity Fat-Tire Bike Ride," draws riders from all over the Southwest to "pedal through Arizona history"[40] from Flagstaff to the Grand Canyon. The website claims that the idea for the ride was kindled in 1994, when a small group of mountain bikers heard of the old stagecoach route: "Armed only with trail snacks, water, a local map, credit card and a thirst for adventure, they were off to follow the original Moqui Stage Coach route to the Grand Canyon."

To "pedal through Arizona history" speaks to the way in which contemporary riders (re)constitute space as settler place. Michel de Certeau links places to narrative, noting that every place has its own story, or an accumulation of stories: "Every spatial practice constitutes a form of re-narrating or re-writing a place, over and against the . . . 'geographical' space."[41] The ability to "re-narrate" and "re-write" is evidence of a kind of privilege that comes to define spatial practices in particular contexts as they are "dependent on the stories that already occupy it."[42] In this way, the bicyclists that trace the Moqui Stage

---

40. Quotes and descriptions of the Flag2GC annual ride come from their website, https://flag2gc.com/.

41. De Certeau's framework of space qtd. in Blanco and Peeren, "Possessions," 396.

42. Blanco and Peeren, 397.

FIGURE 2.1. Mural in Denver, Colorado, 2016. Photograph by the author.

Coach route are re-narrating place in ways that are based on and therefore limited by the stories of the original stagecoach rides. This re-narration also produces another layer, a step further removed from the truth of Indigenous dispossession of those lands by settlers.

Consider the visual rhetoric of a mural (figure 2.1) photographed in Denver, Colorado, in 2016. Bicyclists ride in the foreground, and in the background ghostly Indigenous people ride on horses. Again, how are Indigenous peoples narrated into the story this artist is telling? Depictions of Indigenous peoples—narrated as tribeless, timeless, existing in the past, literally in the background—are superseded by modern bicyclists in the foreground. Given their positioning, the artist seems to draw a relationship between the two, but what is that relationship? Perhaps the artist sees the cyclists as somehow inspired by Indigenous cultural traditions, carrying on their ways of knowing and being on this land on bicycles instead of horses. This view, however, would position settlers, who benefit from the structures of settler colonialism that aim to erase and replace Indigenous peoples, as also carrying on Indigenous legacies in their perceived absence. Building on the descriptions of adventure bikes quoted earlier, this view animates the fantasy that the bicycle is like a horse, but it also sustains the idea that settlers are the rightful inheritors of this land. This is how outdoor recreational discourses unknowingly or unwittingly produce bad relations. This analysis assumes of course that the cyclists are settlers to begin with, an assumption that is safe, I think, given the mural's location and the statistics that support the fact that cyclists in the

FIGURE 2.2. Idaho State Parks and Recreation logo for the Trail of the Coeur d'Alenes, a seventy-three-mile rail trail in northern Idaho.

United States are still overwhelmingly white. I don't know what the artist's intentions were, but it's also safe to say that this mural is for settlers, not for Indigenous peoples. The artist's intentions, however, don't matter as much as the effect the story narrated through these depictions has on its intended audience. Yes, the work is the result of a process that obviously did not include the Cheyenne, Arapaho, and Utes who historically inhabited the area, who could have helped define the terms of their representation. But for the settlers who are meant to see themselves as one of the cyclists in the foreground, their belongings are constituted in ways that depend on Indigenous erasure and co-optation.

Such imagery can also be state sanctioned, and similarly promote outdoor recreation while relying on the myth that Indigenous peoples no longer exist. Take, for example, the official Idaho State Parks and Recreation logo for the Trail of the Coeur d'Alenes (figure 2.2), a seventy-three-mile trail that traverses the panhandle of northern Idaho. While the rail trail, and presumably the logo, was apparently created in partnership with the State of Idaho, the Coeur d'Alene tribe, and the Union Pacific Rail Road, the similarities with the Denver mural are striking. Even the colors are similar, with the mural and the logo reminiscent of a setting sun with fading oranges and yellows. Not radically different from the Denver mural, ghostly in the background is the figure of an Indigenous person on a horse, and in the foreground, a cyclist. Because of the fact that the trail was an old railroad route, a steam engine also

FIGURE 2.3. Cogburn Bicycles' display at Frostbike 2014, an industry trade show in Minneapolis, Minnesota. Photograph by the author.

appears in the faded background. The difference, of course, is that the steam engine is long gone, but the Coeur d'Alene people have not gone anywhere. This is not an image for the contemporary Coeur d'Alene people. Clearly, the steam engine as a symbol of western expansion alongside a one-dimensional portrayal of "Indianness" work together to produce a particular experience on this trail, an experience meant to accommodate settler riders view of a mythic West, as themselves engaged in their own frontier narrative. In both of these examples, settlers do not just recreate but re-create, re-narrate, and reimagine the stories that occupy the landscape in ways that center their experiences, sustain their belonging, and preserve their innocence.

Cogburn's bicycles are designed to accommodate a rather niche group that seeks to combine mountain biking with hunting. Their bicycle frames often come in one of two versions of camouflage print, the typical green and brown or the gray and white of winter camouflage. These bicycles are designed to carry things like rifles and compound bows. When I saw their display booth at Frostbike (figure 2.3), an annual convention for all things winter cycling, I was struck by the level of thought that went into narrating the bicycle within a constructed environment that is at once cultural—signified by a masculine mannequin dressed up as a hunter posed with a compound bow attached to the bicycle—and material—exemplified by positioning of actual wooden logs, mulch, rocks, and trees. While the company sought to maximize their allotted convention space to allow potential customers to imagine the context in which it is designed to be used, the material-discursive rhetorical choices also activate settler belongings: masculinity, frontierism, rugged individualism, fetishization of an unknown and empty landscape. Although this piece is an advertisement, the settler colonial ideologies are assembled in ways that go beyond "buy this bike" and toward historical and cultural persuasions that reinforce particular ways of knowing and being on the landscapes in which we engage.

Fredric Jameson wrote that under postmodern capitalism, history and culture are uncoupled from a sense of the past; where once we might have lived through history, we now go somewhere—to the store, or cinema, or online—and purchase a simulacrum of it.[43] In 2014, when I attended Interbike, an annual mountain bike convention held in Las Vegas, Nevada, I saw countless examples of this simulacrum literally on display. Mission Workshop and Acre Supply—two companies that produce bags, panniers, and other necessities for bikepacking—transformed their indoor convention space to resemble a campsite. They rolled out real grass, set up lawn chairs, and parked a weathered Volkswagen Bus. The year before, Chumba displayed its bikes atop real logs and a scenic wilderness display in the background. In 2015 Ryders Eyewear, which specializes in sunglasses and eye protection for cyclists, built its display as if it were an 1800s saloon, complete with swinging doors and a fake horse tied to a post in front. Another display from a company that makes heavy-duty bicycle racks included a faux campfire next to a stuffed dog.

As marketers are tasked with making artificial settler space, they are engaged in the ongoing process of settler placemaking elsewhere. While de Certeau links places to narrative, Homi Bhabha suggests the nation itself, as an evolving idea, is narrative, that we "write the nation" as a "form of social and textual affiliation."[44] In settler colonial contexts Rachel Busbridge observes that "nations always necessitate a certain 'writing over' by the dominant settler party if it is to fashion a space to match the world it wishes to create."[45] The scenes in the displays are familiar, yet they have no history and could represent any number of environments near or far from those enticed by this imaginary. In the absence of a history, settlers make their own, and real landscapes are rewritten through rhetorical practices like bikepacking. As stolen Indigenous land is rewritten, it becomes "domesticated," becoming familiar and complementary.[46] Such "writing over" contributes to settler entitlement to Indigenous land and erasure of Indigenous peoples, the implications of which extend far beyond the commercial spaces of convention halls and to virtual spaces as well, as exemplified by the Cogburn commercial recounted at the start of this chapter.

43. Jameson, *Postmodernism*, 244.
44. Bhabha, "DissemiNation," 292.
45. Busbridge, "On Haunted Geography," 473.
46. A. Wilson, *View from the Road*, 200.

One of the most powerful ways these hegemonies are reproduced digitally among mountain biking and bikepacking circles, however, is via photography on social media by everyday people. As N. Katherine Hayles reminds us, the virtual is always inseparable from the material infrastructure that it supposedly erases, and "this illusion of erasure should be the subject of inquiry, not a presupposition that inquiry takes for granted."[47] These images are of majestic landscapes—a mountain, valley, canyon, river, or forest lies in the background, and in the foreground, propped against a tree, is the photographer's bicycle, dusty and sometimes loaded with camping equipment. Digital rhetoric, unlike traditional rhetorical theory, is less interested in persuasion and more invested in how it can promote "self-expression" and "creative collaboration for the purpose of building communities of shared interest" in digital, virtual, and online spaces.[48] Because the emphasis is on building communities, digital rhetoric is necessarily participatory; therefore, the way in which rhetoric is delivered takes on new meaning in digital environments. Text can be shared in the traditional way—in speech or on paper—but it can also make use of other forms of sharing through media that interact with each other.[49] Digital spaces like social media therefore become spaces—like any "environment" in which identities produce and are produced by collaborations and interactions. They are also capable of reproducing and sustaining settler subjectivities that displace Indigenous peoples and affect real landscapes.

---

47. Hayles, *How We Became Posthuman*, 28.
48. Zappen, "Digital Rhetoric," 321.
49. Zappen, 321.

CHAPTER 3

Rock Climbing

Frontier Authenticity, Whiteness, and "Desert Pioneers"

In his guidebook, celebrated rock climber Eric Bjørnstad articulates the allure of tracing the climbing routes first made and used thousands of years ago by Indigenous peoples in Utah. He writes that climbers like him "relish the idea of following the paths of the ancients and, perhaps like them, have the same gut-wrenching fear when the route is run out and the steps becoming thinner and more tenuous." He continues:

> Envision an Indian on Comb Ridge, a hundred-mile-long escarpment immediately east of Cedar Mesa, working his way up a vertical 200-foot wall. Either barefoot or wearing deerskin moccasins, our athlete chips a small platform into the sandstone, just big enough for toes and the ball of a foot. Balancing, he now pecks a handhold, then another foothold. On and on he goes. Each hold takes up to an hour to fashion, and no rope holds him when his forearms pump out. Days pass and his compatriots watch him working the route, downclimbing at night, upclimbing early in the morning to start the work again. Finally he reaches the top. This route still exists and is plainly visible from the Comb Wash road.[1]

---

1. Bjørnstad, *Rock Climbing*, xxvii.

Bjørnstad's fictional portrayal promotes a particular way in which rock climbers "relish" the past during present-day excursions. The stone is not simply material, but the climber brings himself to the rock—his race, class, gender, sexuality, ability, and his culture and history, all of which produce his experience and his expectations. The rock climber *envisions himself as* the "Indian," so it is not a coincidence that the Indian-as-main-character embodies the physical prowess, strength, and determination to which Bjørnstad aspires. Richard Slotkin observed that narratives involving Indigenous characters always ultimately reinforce the heroism of whites, yet conversely "the Indian is portrayed as inferior to whites, his presence remains necessary to the revelation of the heroic stature of the Anglo-American hero."[2] Clearly Bjørnstad writes about this encounter with much reverence, but the liberties he takes in the story are worth examining. How does he know this "Indian on Comb Ridge" is a man? How does he know the route was the work of one person? How does he know there wasn't some kind of safety mechanism in place? Why the focus on the forearms "pumping out" instead of the dexterity required of fingers or toes? This isn't a story about the "Indian on Comb Ridge" at all. It's a story about Bjørnstad and the rock climbing community to which he writes, both of whom no doubt relish in imagining themselves as the main character in this story. Recreational colonialism positions the settler as the subject, free to leave, grow, and return, while the idea of the "Indian" is forever trapped in time, a static character. Rather than make up this story, after all, he could have probably just asked the Ute people, who know more about it than he ever would, whose land Comb Ridge is on. But his story isn't about the Utes either. Stories like this, told by settlers about Indigenous peoples in the past tense, are always actually about those telling the story. And those stories contribute to the erasure of contemporary Indigenous peoples.

In this chapter, recreational colonialism is intimately tied to constructions of authenticity. As the rock climbing narratives in this chapter illustrate, these stories often depend on conquest and discovery, and thus reinforce heteronormativity and heteropatriarchy. This assertion aligns with Doreen Massey's notion that space is the "product of interrelations" and an assemblage of stories so far.[3] It also aligns with Indigenous gender, sexuality, and feminist scholars who "assume that gender and sexuality are core constitutive elements of imperialist-colonialist state formations"; the heteronormativity and heteropatriarchy that predicate the settler state are revealed in ways that often go

---

2. Slotkin, *Regeneration through Violence,* 189.
3. Massey, *For Space,* 9.

unexamined.[4] As discussed in the previous chapter, settler identities are also dependent upon the material reality of the monoliths they climb and the landscapes in which they engage. Recreational colonialism ultimately mobilizes space in a way that accommodates settler colonial hegemonies: heteropatriarchy and white supremacy. Recreational colonialism's racialization of space obscures the histories, knowledges, assumptions, and power relations that rock climbers bring to their view of the landscape and the people who live there.

Because of the sacred status of many desirable climbing locations, it is illegal to climb anywhere on the Navajo Nation, but with such alluring rock formations like Shiprock, Totem Pole, Spider Rock, and Castleton Tower, among others, many settler climbers have chosen to disregard the ban and re-enact the original climbing routes "discovered" by other climbers in the early 1970s. Recent climbers have gone as far as to locate an enrolled tribal member to bring along with them as "proof" of legitimacy, belonging, and authenticity. Climber resistance to the ban on the reservation also invites a critique of the idea of ownership. The chapter also interrogates the term "dirtbag," a celebratory self-identifier deployed in rock climbing communities that masks climbers' privilege and participation in recreational colonialism.

The Pioneer and the Indian

In "Natural Indians and Identities of Modernity," the fourth chapter of *Playing Indian,* Indigenous historian Philip J. Deloria examines the founding philosophies of the Boy Scouts to highlight turn-of-the-century anxieties about how best to reclaim an authentic US American identity. According to Deloria, the perception was that with the rise of modernity came fears that something innate, something authentic about what it means to be an American was being lost, forgotten, and needed to be clearly defined and taught to boys—specifically white boys.

Robert Baden-Powell, the founder of the Boy Scouts in England, quintessentially epitomized masculine anxieties when, at the turn of the twentieth century, he wrote, "We badly need some training for our lads if we are to keep up manliness in our race instead of lapsing into a nation of soft, sloppy, cigarette suckers."[5] Deloria highlights the same "problem" in the United States in a growing concern regarding how best to foster "modern American character in children (especially boys)" who were perceived at the turn of the century "to

---

4. J. Barker, *Critically Sovereign,* 6.
5. Marsiglio, *Men on a Mission,* 33.

be imperiled by an effeminate, postfrontier urbanism."[6] In the United States, there seemed to be two central archetypes that young boys were meant to emulate: the "Indian" and the "Pioneer."

William Marsiglio's text detailing the history of boys' "youth work" notes the way this problem was addressed by Ernest Thompson Seton, the founder of the Boy Scouts of America, who sought to accentuate "aspects of the frontier spirit while honoring Native American Indian culture and lore."[7] Philip Deloria's research confirmed Seton's admiration for "Indianness," quoting the founder: "The Red Man is the apostle of the outdoor life." The first rendition of the Boy Scouts was Seton's Woodcraft Indians, a "group of local vandals" seemingly in most need of social rehabilitation. Philip Deloria recalls this history in *Playing Indian*: "After regaling the boys with Indian tales, he organized them into a make believe tribe, the Sinaways, led them through nature study games, and put them to work making Indian costumes."[8] Seton's make-believe tribe never involved any actual Indigenous peoples but instead relied on what Deloria called "Indianness" to reclaim an authentic US American masculinity.

Seton, however, was later challenged by other aspiring youth development leaders at the time who disagreed that "Indians" should be portrayed as "'manly heroes' to boys" and argued for a more patriotic approach.[9] P. Deloria contrasted Seton with Daniel Carter Beard, who emphasized that "Americanness" was better learned by "recreating the lives of the pioneer scouts who had tamed the wild American Frontier"; thus Beard formed the Sons of Daniel Boone, which contrary to Seton's Woodcraft Indians focused on the "pioneer experience," pitting his boys against the "Indian characters" that Seton's group used. While Beard's vision toward progressivism embraced innovation and technological advancement, Seton "feared the alienating effects of the machine and the system" and therefore turned toward a vision of a primitive past. Although it would seem these two visions were irreconcilable, as Deloria points out, "Primitivism and progress defined the dialectic of the modern."[10] The way in which both the Indian and the Pioneer were performed through dressing up and storytelling highlights a relationship whereby one narrative necessarily involves the other, and the two together highlight the performative aspects of a settler colonial identity, the legacy of which is *played* out today in a multitude of ways, including outdoor recreation. Both the Pioneer and the Indian were once based on real peoples, but no longer. Instead, through

---

6. P. Deloria, *Playing Indian*, 96.
7. Marsiglio, *Men on a Mission*, 33.
8. P. Deloria, *Playing Indian*, 96.
9. Marsiglio, *Men on a Mission*, 33–34.
10. P. Deloria, *Playing Indian*, 97, 100.

the lens of white supremacy, these caricatures are meshed together as a single fictional archetype curated to accommodate settler belonging on stolen Indigenous land.

The Heteronormativity of "Desert Pioneers"

Settlers confront the rock with much more than just their presence. They bring their histories, experiences, assumptions, and values; they bring their ideas about what it means to be a man, to be an American. What is seen in the rock is as much a reflection of these discourses as it is the sandstone.

In 2014 the American Alpine Club published a colorful online history of rock climbing on the Colorado Plateau, centered on locations within the Navajo Nation. *Desert Pioneers* covers the climbing adventures of white people in the area from the 1800s to the present and describes the "never-seen-before mountain ranges" as "too forbidding, too alien." Shiprock, in northwestern New Mexico, is described as "dark, ghostly, and disturbing."[11] The roles that "pioneers" take on in this "alien landscape" have been that of explorers, adventurers, and mythic frontier heroes, an ethos the American Alpine Club fuses with rock climbing. In order for this mythical role to be played out successfully, some assumptions—however incorrect—must follow. The argument relies on the notion that these settlers were the first to see the landscape and that it was previously devoid of other people. It also characterizes the landscape from the position of settlers, marking that space as "alien," as radically different from that which is familiar. Climbing icons from the sixties, seventies, and eighties like Eric Bjørnstad, Fred Beckey, and Huntley Ingalls are often memorialized as "pioneers" of climbing, having "pioneered the earliest ascents" in the area.[12] The introductory slide to *Desert Pioneers* features the following quote from Huntley Ingalls: "These untouched, fiercely protected sandstone towers—known only to birds—seemed more fantasy than reality. . . . There were not only unclimbed towers but untouched areas. Part of the wonderful experience of pioneering these climbs was the feeling of exploration. We were fantastically privileged to be the first."[13]

In order for the pioneer narrative to work, the towers must be described as "unclimbed," "untouched," and "known only to birds." These statements are of course based on unfounded assumptions but are necessary to infuse settler belongings onto stolen landscapes—the implication is, *we were the first to*

11. American Alpine Club, *Desert Pioneers*.
12. Bartlett, "Huntley Ingalls."
13. American Alpine Club, *Desert Pioneers*.

know it, therefore they belong to us. Recreational colonialism, and the "feeling of exploration" it provokes, necessarily erases the multitude of ways that Indigenous peoples have come to know those towers, diverse cultural affinities formed over thousands of years suddenly replaced by a few settler climbers who had a "wonderful experience."

This characterization is obviously a celebratory one, given the language and its presumed intended audience of rock climbers. This framework, however, reveals much about the performance of the mythic frontier embedded in the identities of rock climbers and how the materiality of the rock has produced various discourses about it. Frontier masculinity comes to life through narratives marking these early climbers as self-reliant, independent, and traversing unfamiliar landscapes presuming to be the first to enter such places, to see such places, to touch such places. Another slide was dedicated to the climber John Otto, who embodied the "spirit of western self-reliance" and used the "techniques he had learned as a hard rock miner" to summit a sandstone tower near Grand Junction, Colorado. Because he summited the tower a "couple days into July," Otto named the rock Independence Monument, choosing to cement his achievement alongside his national identity.[14] Otto's Route, marked by the holes he drilled into the rock, continues to reveal the way to the top for climbers today. Contemporary climbers are no doubt delighted to retrace his steps, and in doing so, his story, which is steeped in rugged masculinity and nationalism.

In another slide detailing the first attempts to summit Shiprock, which is also on the Navajo Nation, the American Alpine Club briefly recounts a story about Robert Ormes, who in the 1930s nearly fell to his death in his last of several attempts. He recounted his efforts in great detail in an article for the *Saturday Evening Post* called "A Bent Piece of Iron." The article is significant, as it was one of the first detailed accounts of rock climbing distributed to such a wide audience. In the article, Ormes similarly positioned himself as an explorer who learned how to rock climb based on the routes of "pioneers" before him.[15]

Ormes's account serves as a stark reminder that a key characteristic attached to the pioneer narrative necessarily includes heteronormative masculinity. When it came to the allure of climbing Shiprock, he noted a "sudden fear" that "some other party would be the first to conquer its summit," which he detailed as his primary motivation for climbing it himself. Throughout Ormes's narrative, he employs words like "frontal attack" and "assault"

---

14. American Alpine Club.
15. Ormes, "Piece of Bent Iron," 13.

to describe his climbing.[16] His word choices indicate an association between the recreational activities of rock climbing as an expression of dominance, even violence. The use of war metaphors and similar language choices that position men as the aggressors in a fictional narrative enacted through sports are, however, not exclusive to rock climbing. As Michael Kimmel and others have pointed out, it is quite common in team sports such as football.[17] Within the context of rock climbing on the Navajo Nation, words denoting settler "conquest" directed at the monoliths on the reservation take on a different meaning, serving as a productive example of how settler colonial identities are accentuated through rock climbing as an activity but also as part of a larger discourse that recalls colonialism through recreational discourses.

Today, however, the "heroic" characteristics of the pioneer narrative are not expressed through words like "conquest" and instead have taken on a strong sense of environmental ethic. Jackie Kiewa's sociological analysis observes how modern climbers have "rewritten the heroic script" in a way that still depends upon the pioneer identity, exemplified through the prolific use of terms like "independence" and "self-reliance," as well as how the expression of the hero has evolved to accommodate rock climbing. For example, while self-reliance is crucial to what it means to enact the hero, because rock climbing requires some level of interdependence and the forming of relationships for safety, the concept of the hero—and similarly, the concept of authenticity—proves to be malleable yet contextual. While the authentic rock climber no longer holds on to the traditional need for "conflict and conquest" as part of the heroic persona, those elements have merely taken on different forms. As Kiewa notes, there are increasingly more women rock climbers, but the men climbers, in particular, "tended to be more aggressive [than women] in this respect in that they denigrated those (inexperienced) climbers who abused the natural environment." One climber even compared the act of bolting a cliff— drilling bolts into the rock to aid in difficult climbs—to the rape of a woman. This marks men rock climbers' affinity toward the environment as inherently contradictory; even as they seem to distance themselves from the idea of conquest or control over the environment, they assert it in different ways. Kiewa concludes, "climbing relationships frequently mimic the gendered stereotypes prevalent in society."[18] While the concept of "individualism" in climbing may seem like a relic from the past, Kiewa's observations gesture toward a kind of difficulty, if not impossibility, involved in settlers' wishes to move away from settler colonial structures. Even among the most well-intentioned climbers,

16. Ormes, 13.

17. Kimmel, *Guyland*, specifically his chapter "Sports Crazy," 123–43.

18. Kiewa, "Rewriting the Heroic Script," 37, 34, 38.

the embeddedness of settler colonialism is difficult to recognize, let alone escape, and in profound ways continues to shape settler experiences with each other and the landscape.

Like spelunkers do when they believe they discover a new cave system, rock climbers traditionally award themselves the right to name the monoliths they summit; "first ascents" are then named by those who "discover" them. Even previously summited cliffs may contain several different climbers' routes, which are also named after them (e.g., Otto's Route). *Rock and Ice* magazine featured an article online listing "Climbing's Greatest Route Names" with locations all over the world. For example, located in Joes Valley, Utah, is a climb named Trent's Mom, and according to the article, climbers jokingly refer to how they "did Trent's Mom," or "Every time I go to Joes, I work on Trent's Mom."[19] There are a lot more, too many to recount here, many of which have been more recently exposed and challenged by climbers of color. Third Reich, A Woman's Place, Clean Shaven Girls, Welfare Crack—the list goes on and on.

Much is revealed about those who bring their discursive legacies to their interactions with material landscapes, obscuring Indigenous identifications in the process, often with disproportionate harm to Indigenous women. Each one of these names by itself may seem like an aberration, dismissed as a one-off, but together they begin to tell a story about the kind of subjectivities settlers write onto the landscape that also produce various forms of exclusions. According to a survey conducted by *SNEWS*, an outdoor industry magazine, in partnership with 57hours, an app that connects users to mountain guides, 91 percent of *SNEWS* readers and 65 percent of 57hours mountain guides have encountered route names "they considered racist, sexist, discriminatory or otherwise offensive."[20] While Secretary of the Interior Deb Haaland has made it a priority to rename places and trails that use the derogatory term "squ*w," there are thousands of official and unofficial climbing route names, and it often takes individuals in the climbing community to make changes. Melissa Utomo, an Asian American climber who has been engaged in this work alongside a growing number of Black, Indigenous, and other people of color, commented in 2020, "We've normalized worshiping the first ascenders. . . . If you're a new climber, it takes a lot of courage to speak up."[21] Outdoor recreational discourses narrate the landscape through the lens of settler heteronormativity and patriarchy, together as heteropatriarchy. For example, the name Squ*w Crack[22] not only takes rhetorical possession of Indigenous

---

19. Parker, "Climbing's Greatest Route Names."
20. Loudin, "Climbing Routes."
21. Loudin.
22. Bjørnstad, *Rock Climbing*, 9.

land the way these other settler names do but trivializes the pervasiveness of sexual violence against Indigenous women. The very real and ongoing reality of sexual violence, including murder and disappearance,[23] is not just a contemporary tragedy articulated through symbolic orange shirts and a hashtag (#MMIW, referring to missing and murdered Indigenous women) but rather a historical and political legacy tied directly to settler colonial violence.[24] Resisting recreational colonialism, however, involves much more than campaigning to change names, as this book will continue to reveal, challenging the ways settlers have been conditioned to imagine themselves as the rightful inheritors of stolen Indigenous lands.

Many scholars have noted the relationship between conquest of nature and sexual conquest of women's bodies,[25] and more recently, Indigenous scholars have taken on the work of connecting settler colonialism to the sexualization of Indigenous women.[26] Many are engaged in revitalization efforts based on traditional practices to heal from the intergenerational trauma associated with sexual violence.[27] There is a long history of settlers referring to a "virgin" landscape, a sentiment that is certainly echoed in the accounts of rock climbers, who used phrases like "untouched," recounting how privileged they were to "be the first" as captured in *Desert Pioneers.* Carolyn Merchant points out the implications of using the term "virgin" to refer to land (and women) that have not yet been and therefore must be "conquered and controlled."[28] While individual men climbers today may not use the term "conquest" to describe their feats, the "pioneers" they celebrate through embodied action certainly did, and that knowledge is transmitted to climbers through a discursive legacy inscribed both as an imaginary and literally on the settler-named monoliths they climb. As an episteme, rock climbing as a performance demonstrates the way climbers "learn and transmit knowledge through embodied action."[29] Diana Taylor notes that "performances function as vital acts of transfer, transmitting social knowledge, memory, and a sense of identity."[30] Rock climbing on the Colorado Plateau, especially on the Navajo Nation, on monoliths held sacred in different ways to different tribes, highlights the colonial relationship between settlers and the materiality of the rock. The performance of the

23. Anderson, Campbell, and Belcourt, *Keetsahnak.*

24. Deer, *Beginning and End of Rape.* For more discussion on the trivialization of violence against Indigenous women, see Bird, "Savage Desires."

25. Merchant, *Ecological Revolutions*; and Griffin, *Women and Nature.*

26. J. Barker, *Critically Sovereign,* specifically the introduction.

27. Baldy, *We Are Dancing for You.*

28. Merchant, *Ecological Revolutions,* 231.

29. Diana Taylor, *Archive and the Repertoire,* xvi.

30. Diana Taylor, 2–3.

Pioneer in this context highlights a broader notion of conquest as it relates to settler colonial conquest of land and people, even when it is not outwardly acknowledged. Settlers take part in a performance that reveals their investments in heteropatriarchy and white supremacy through conquest not just of nature but of gender and race; the act of rock climbing becomes a way in which the conquest of Indigenous peoples, Indigenous women's bodies, and nature can be performed, shared, and replicated. While understanding climbing as a performance exposes its dependent interrelationships, rock climbing as mere recreation evades the notion that the authentic self is discursive.

Just "You and the Rock": Settler Authenticities

A visit to the south rim of the Grand Canyon during peak season will yield a familiar phenomenon: hundreds of people in line to take their turns to snap that one picture of themselves on a ledge, with the vast labyrinth of purple and vermilion canyons stretching out behind them. The picture posted later on social media shows one alone on a precipice: *adventure!* The reality is that they're one of a thousand in line that day trying to take that same picture. At the end of 2023, *Merriam-Webster* announced its word of the year—the word most searched for in the dictionary that year—"authentic." The reasons for this word's popularity have been explained by the rise of artificial intelligence in the context of a world already plagued by deepfakes, post-truth, and a general sense of distrust across the political and media landscape.[31] It's curious, however, that this term also coincided with dramatic growth in the outdoor recreation economy[32] and overall increases in outdoor recreation participation, both characterized by the mainstreaming of #vanlife during the pandemic,[33] bicycle sales, record-breaking visitations to national parks, the (un)availability of campsites, and other trends. Authenticity is something we construct, and it is undoubtedly important to the formation of identity in outdoor recreation discourses.

For centuries, philosophers like Hobbs, Locke, Rousseau, and Kant produced a litany of theories attempting to uncover the idea of a "true self," an autonomous, authentic human self that exists internally, as opposed to an

---

31. Associated Press, "What's Merriam-Webster's Word."

32. I'm referring specifically to the 2023 report from the Outdoor Recreation Industry that notes this once $887 billion a year industry was in 2023 a $1.1 trillion industry.

33. Here I am referring to the surge in camper van sales during the height of the COVID-19 pandemic. See Pietsch, "How Veterans of #Vanlife Feel."

external "fake self."[34] Artists focused on self-portraits, and writers turned to autobiographies. Transcendentalists occupied freshly stolen land to sit in nature and espouse the virtues of the self as something separate and away from the degradations of civilization. The assumption is that by looking inward, without any distractive influences from the periphery, only truth and goodness will be uncovered. Poststructural theorists like Foucault and Deleuze waged sharp criticism against the notion of an authentic self, arguing instead that identity is in perpetual flux, a constant state of becoming. In the concluding section of *The Order of Things*, Foucault argued that there is no individual that exists outside of the discourses that produce and are produced by determinant historical and social formations.[35] In *Archaeology of Knowledge*, he posits, "Do not ask me who I am, and do not ask me to remain the same," making an argument against the idea of authenticity and claiming that one's identity—their values, ethics, morals, and how they shape thoughts and actions, their understanding of the past and present and sense of responsibility to the future—changes moment to moment.

Surface-level constructions of authenticity look like a lot of different things in outdoor recreation—from specific clothing, gear, or brand choices to more embodied details like beards and Chaco sandal tan lines. These kinds of details and embodiments are always changing. At a deeper level, participants construct expectations for authentic experiences through rhetorical practices that contribute to how we understand ourselves in certain contexts and are also thus always changing. In her essay "Rugged Practices: Embodying Authenticity in Outdoor Recreation," Samantha Senda-Cook uses ethnographic evidence and surveys to detail the often-unspoken norms of trail etiquette, where authenticity is tied to an understanding of social and situational knowledge. When that knowledge is performed, it can generate forms of affect that can "become indicators of authenticity in that they demarcate one's knowledge and membership in a community."[36] Is a hiker authentic when they stay on the trail to protect the environment and maintain safety? Or is the person who leaves the trail to see more and rely on their own means of navigation more authentic? The answer is situated and personal, but also cultural. The question of whether to leave the trail or stay on it, whether to climb that rock that Indigenous communities hold sacred, depends on the kind of ethics that foreground identity and the cultures that coalesce around those constructions. All of this is to say that the idea of an authentic self is not only a construction, but belief in it sustains existing relations of power. For the delicate bio-crust

---

34. Straub, *Paradoxes of Authenticity*, 14.
35. Foucault, *Order of Things*.
36. Senda-Cook, "Rugged Practices," 137.

landscapes of the US Southwest and for Indigenous communities working to protect sacred sites, it is fortunate that identity is a process that is continuously unfolding because that means people can and do change. Nonetheless, outdated Eurocentric notions of an individualistic, morally good true self that can only be discovered in what we believe to be nature persist in outdoor recreational discourses and communities.

The tension between an internal "core" self and that which is affected by external expectations speaks to an inside/outside dichotomy that shows up in rock climbing narratives in many different ways in conceptions of nature, gender, and sexuality. The idea of wilderness continues to hold much allure in the US American imagination as it relates to claims toward authenticity.[37] Massey refers to "wilderness" as a "dubious category," a contrast to the city, meaning that wilderness serves a rhetorical function with which we use to "situate ourselves."[38] Another familiar inside/outside dichotomy, nature/culture, is embedded in the idea of wilderness as that which is wild, uncontrolled, unknown, a concept dependent upon its perceived opposite, the domesticated, the fenced-in, the familiar.[39] As opposed to culture, following Massey, nature is perceived as unchanging, as "timeless," which might explain why we use it to "ground ourselves" and to "convince ourselves that there is indeed a grounding."[40] The concept of a "true self" located in nature, always in relation to culture, expressed itself in US transcendentalist writers such as Emerson, Whitman, and Thoreau, who believed that true knowledge and wisdom exists within all people, that by looking inward, self-destructive social conformity could be transcended. Emerson and Thoreau believed this was best achieved by seeking solitude in nature, according to Emerson, to find "an original relation to the universe."[41] But the self is constantly changing; the "core" self as transcendentalists and others before them sought does not exist. The physical reality with which the "timelessness" of nature is constructed is also in a perpetual state of becoming: "This 'natural' place to which we appeal for timelessness has of course been (and still is) constantly changing."[42] These investments in identity that are dependent on solitude in whatever we believe to be nature profoundly limit the way settlers imagine themselves and relate to Indigenous peoples and landscapes.

37. Nash, *Wilderness and the American Mind*.
38. Massey, *For Space*, 131.
39. Nash, *Wilderness and the American Mind*, 1–7.
40. Massey, *For Space*, 131.
41. Emerson, *Ralph Waldo Emerson*, 3.
42. Massey, *For Space*, 133.

Rock climbing is often described as something exclusive of everything but the climber and the materiality of the rock, a constructed relationship that relies upon a strong sense of self-reliance and individualism. "It's an extreme activity with only you and the rock and the will power to get that extra inch behind you," wrote one climber in the Northern Arizona University student-run newspaper.[43] In a different exposé on climbing in the same paper, another student remarked that he liked rock climbing because "you basically have to rely on and support yourself. . . . It's just you and the rocks. It's energizing."[44] Even within critical academic discussions about rock climbing and identity,[45] the larger social and cultural processes that shape the way in which climbing takes places is evaded. For example, while Ian Heywood demonstrates how "imagination and a social dimension remain important to climbing," he asserts, "the core experience of climbing is to do with a real relationship with the material world and gravity, not an imaginary or symbolic one with other human beings." To Heywood's credit, his claim is within the context of spectator sports, but commentators and large audiences are typically absent from the participant sport of rock climbing. He also makes clear that he does not intend to theorize climbing from a sociological or cultural theoretical position "external" to "the everyday life of climbing."[46] But doing so obscures the settler colonial context in which rock climbing occurs. A dynamic relationship between discourse and physical reality that is neither fully internal nor entirely external is precisely what produces the "everyday life of climbing."

The "it's just you and the rock" trope that is so common in rock climbing discourses mirrors Emerson's guiding philosophy that somewhere *out there* alone, in nature, one's true self can be reclaimed. In terms of masculinity in the United States, the notion that a more authentic masculine identity lies outside of culture and can only be found in nature has a long history, one that seems to resurface again and again. From Thoreau's *Walden* to Ed Abbey's *Desert Solitaire,* men have sought solitude in the wilderness out of a distrust of emerging technology, urbanization, and changing cultural norms whenever the traditional roles and status of men have been disrupted.

Men's flight into nature has also signified what is known across academic disciplines as a "crisis in masculinity." Rooted in a perceived "ideological weakening and collapse of patriarchy," the crisis is expressed as men reevaluate what "masculinity is imagined to comprise."[47] Lynn Segal powerfully captured

---

43. Karakey and Leach, "Bouldering," 11.
44. Escudero, "Students Climb to New Heights," 9.
45. Robinson, *Everyday Masculinities and Extreme Sport.*
46. Heywood, "Climbing Monsters," 457, 458.
47. MacInnes, "Crisis of Masculinity," 322.

the crisis of masculinity: "The 'crisis of masculinity' springs from a situation where those men who benefit most from the continuing social and ideological position of their sex are not likely to be the same people as those who suffer from the disadvantages of shifts and insecurities in men's lives."[48] The notion itself is predicated upon the idea that there is an innate, authentic masculinity waiting to be found, based on assumptions that there are "certain psychological or social traits that inherently come with being biologically male." Specifically in the context of the United States, Robert Jensen summarizes hegemonic masculinity as "marked by the struggle for control, conquest, and domination. A man looks at the world, sees what he wants and takes it."[49] Sociologists like Jackson Katz have characterized hegemonic masculinity as a "John Wayne ethos"[50] displayed through outward displays of toughness, ruggedness, invulnerability, aggression, violence, heterosexuality, and whiteness, among other perceived traits. This is also a useful description because of the emphasis on the fiction, the character, the performance. It's an archetype, but as R. W. Connell and James Messerschmidt are careful to point out, it is "normative" and found in "things done," or "the pattern of practice," that allow men's dominance over women and other men to continue.[51]

The concept of masculinity within this framework is also predicated upon a heteronormative conception of gender that "essentializes male/female difference and ignores difference and exclusion within the gender categories." Masculinity, according to Connell and Messerschmidt, "represents not a certain type of man but, rather, a way that men position themselves through discursive practices."[52] The belief that an authentic masculinity can be reclaimed through rhetorical practices—those associated with outdoor recreation, for example—underscores the elusiveness of authenticity as fraught with paradox. Jonathan Culler describes this paradox in the context of the perception of authenticity as experiential: "The paradox, the dilemma of authenticity, is that to be experienced as authentic it must be marked as authentic, but when it is marked as authentic it is mediated, a sign of itself, and hence lacks the authenticity of what is truly unspoiled, untouched by mediating cultural codes."[53] Julia Straub directs readers of her edited volume *The Paradox of Authenticity* to Virginia Richter, who playfully captured the paradox in the title of her essay, "Authenticity: Why We Still Need It although It Doesn't Exist." She

48. Segal, "Being a Man," 18.
49. Jensen, *High Cost of Manliness*, 1.
50. Katz, *Tough Guise*.
51. Connell and Messerschmidt, "Hegemonic Masculinity," 832–33.
52. Connell and Messerschmidt, 836, 841.
53. Culler, *Framing the Sign*, 164.

writes, our "collective investment in it is so high that even after decades of deconstructivism and anti-essentialism it is impossible to get rid of it."[54] Not only is authenticity important to the construction of the self (rock climbing as more than what one *does* but fused to identity: *I am* a rock climber), but it is also essential to the construction of place.

That authenticity is sought within the idea of a "true self" assumes an Other, inauthentic external world that must be escaped or evaded; that authenticity is claimed in nature assumes an Other, inauthentic urbanization. Those climbers who seek to locate their authentic selves by choosing sites that are perceived to be untouched, that are foreign to them—physically, but also culturally—necessarily mark these landscapes and the cultures within them as Other. Following Philip Deloria, the never-ending paradoxical search for authenticity is a simultaneous quest for the Other, which is coded in many different forms: "This Other can be coded in terms of time (nostalgia or archaism), place (the small town), or culture (Indianness). The quest for such an authentic Other is a characteristically modern phenomenon, one that has often been played out in the contradictions surrounding Americans' long and ambivalent engagement with Indianness."[55]

"Far from a static thing," the coded and ever-changing status of the Other—other cultures, other landscapes, other ways of being—is why Edward Said refers to "Othering" as a "process." The process of Othering, like Said's concept of "Orientalism," is tied to language, both in possibility and in limitation. Said quotes Nietzsche, who suggests language is essentially "the sum of human relations, which have been enhanced, transposed, and embellished poetically and rhetorically."[56] A material-discursive conception of language would suggest that physical reality—red sandstone spires, cliffs, crags, monoliths and the very spaces they inhabit—function discursively as "rhetorical symbols" and are therefore inexplicably linked with discourse as a component of human relations. In his book *Rhetorical Landscapes*, Clark notes that the "rhetorical symbols we encounter and exchange are not limited to language," so when a climber interacts with physical reality, it is a "relational encounter" that "constitute[s] a person's social and cultural experience."[57] Recalling Sherene Razack's observation that the "national mythologies of white settler societies are deeply spatialized stories," I suggest that for rock climbers, the settler colonial situation is always already embedded in these encounters with the

---

54. Richter quoted in Straub, *Paradoxes of Authenticity*, 11.
55. P. Deloria, *Playing Indian*, 101.
56. Said, *Orientalism*, 332, 203.
57. Clark, *Rhetorical Landscapes in America*, 2–3, 3.

landscape.[58] Even when alone, climbing hand-over-hand in a remote area, the encounter is relational: the climber brings their ways of knowing and being to that encounter, weaving them into the palpable realness of the experience—the sensation of the wind and sandstone and sweat. The discursive powerfully collaborates with the material on this canyon wall, substantiating the feeling of authenticity—so powerfully the climber may scarcely recognize their implication in this constructive and co-constitutive process.

"Daring to Go": The Appropriation of Indigenous Landscapes

One of the most well-known controversies with respect to rock climbing on the Colorado Plateau is the climbing ban on the Navajo Nation. Although a reservation-wide ban has been in place since 1971, several individual formations were banned from climbing as early as the 1960s. According to an open "letter to rock climbers," written by Charles S. Damon, then director of the Navajo Parks and Recreation Department, the 1971 ban was instituted for two main reasons.[59] First, due to the fragile "nature of the rocks themselves," climbing was prohibited in order to protect the rock. And second, rock climbing was prohibited because "the monoliths of the Navajo reservation are considered sacred places. To climb them is to profane them." The letter clearly asserts that the Navajo Nation would make "no exceptions" and accept "no argument" posed by any "would-be climbers." Nevertheless, as the years went by, the climbing ban has been and continues to be violated.

A widely circulated and iconic photo featuring renowned rock climbers Fred Beckey and Bjørnstad (figure 3.1) was taken to celebrate their first ascent in Monument Valley in the 1960s. Together they hold up a sign reading, "Absolutely No Rock Climbing" with the monolith they had presumably just summited in the background. As the pair memorializes their accomplishment, the rhetoric of the image looms large as marking their legacy as climbers. This is best captured in a profile of Beckey's lifetime accomplishments as a climber: "The iconic image encompasses everything that Fred stands for: rebellion, freedom, and a penchant for daring to go where few others would imagine."[60] The image was also prominently displayed in the 2014 obituary for Bjørnstad featured on climbing.com under the title "Desert Pioneer Eric Bjørnstad Has

---

58. Razack, *Race, Space, and the Law*, 3.
59. American Alpine Club, *Desert Pioneers*. The letter is dated May 12, 1971.
60. Restivo, "Fred Beckey."

FIGURE 3.1. Fred Beckey and Eric Bjørnstad pose in an iconic photo taken at Monument Valley in northern Arizona in the 1960s. Photo used with permission from Mara Bjørnstad and the American Alpine Club.

Died."[61] In my research, speaking also with people who knew him, I came to know Bjørnstad as kind and humble, having climbed with a great reverence and cultivated knowledge of the plants and animals in the areas he climbed. Yet what it means to be a "pioneer," to be "a rebel," and to be "daring" meshes seamlessly in the rhetoric of the photograph. Climbers who have been inspired by this legacy should not shy away from contending with the fact that the photo also communicates egregious dismissals of tribal requests not to climb. The fact that the image is celebrated as part of the legacy of climbing history is at the heart of recreational colonialism: while Indigenous cultural differences

61. MacDonald, "Desert Pioneer Eric Has Died."

are met with disdain, the climbers simultaneously rely on those differences to mark themselves in opposition, drawing pride from positioning outdoor recreation above the cultural sensibilities of those marked as Other. From the Doctrine of Discovery in the mid-1400s to the Homestead Act in 1862, the assumption that Indigenous land was not being used as productively as settlers would use it, and therefore that Indigenous peoples should have no claim to it, has been a prominent theme in the ongoing story of settler entitlement to Indigenous land. The image further depicts a "new" Manifest Destiny via outdoor recreation, whereby the appropriation of Indigenous landscapes is not only inevitable and necessary but essential to sustaining settler authenticities. While the posturing is meant to signal rebellion—and certainly it is read that way by other climbers—Bjørnstad and Beckey ironically embody quite the opposite. They may be breaking a rule, but on these lands, we can conversely think of them as settlers following a long-established norm.

Several articles in rock climbing publications have contributed to more recent confusion around the fact of the ban, which has remained unchanged since 1971. In his 1995 article for *American Alpine Journal,* "Shiprock's East Face," Cameron Burns detailed an experience he had on the Navajo Nation while out photographing Shiprock. A "young Navajo" at a nearby convenience store told him he could climb Shiprock if he wanted to and noted that many people do it regularly despite the ban. He didn't climb it, but the experience kindled interest.[62] Years later, in 1992, Burns was with a friend standing outside their parked car admiring Venus Needle, a rock formation near Window Rock, Arizona, when they were again approached by a young man who asked if they wanted to climb it. As it turns out, the man's family held the grazing permit. The man explained "that climbing was OK if climbers got the local landowner's permission."[63] As rock climbing forums over the next decade indicate, this article fostered much confusion about the fact of the ban. This finally resulted in another letter written May 30, 2006, to rock climbers from the Navajo Parks and Recreation office, making it clear that the ban was still in effect. "Please abide by the humble religious requests of the Navajo people and do not climb the monuments," said the press release.[64]

The February 2014 issue of *Rock and Ice* magazine featured a cover story enticing would-be climbers with a color photo of two people climbing Cleopatra's Needle next to text that read, "Illegal Not Necessarily: Navajolands Climbing Re-Examined" (figure 3.2). Upon first glance it would appear that the climbing ban had been lifted, or at the very least that the Navajo Nation

---

62. Burns, "Shiprock's East Face," 66.
63. Burns, 66.
64. Martine, "Monument Valley Tribal Park."

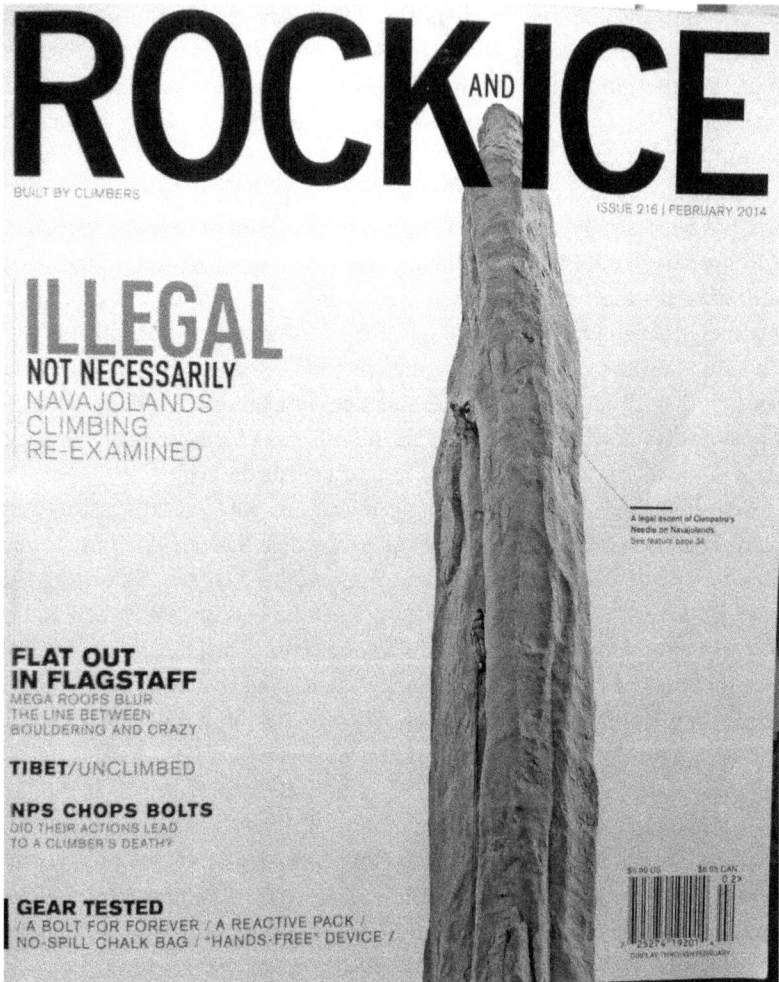

FIGURE 3.2. Cover of *Rock and Ice* magazine from February 2014. Pictured are climbers scaling Cleopatra's Needle on the Navajo Nation. The image in combination with the language "Illegal Not Necessarily" brings ambiguity to the fact that a climbing ban on the reservation remains in effect.

created a process for allowing climbing on the reservation. The actual title of the article was even more ambiguous: "Sacred or Profane: A Future for Navajolands Climbing?" Would this article answer this question with news, or was it simply asking it again? The article celebrated previous illegal climbs and climbers, describing them as "stealthy," "banditos," and "clandestine," before explaining how the writer had completed his own climbs on the reservation. He located a Diné climber whom he met on the Internet and used him to manufacture permission and justify his presence.[65] Obviously, Diné people are not a monolith, and if one searches for an individual willing to break long established tribal laws and defy traditional beliefs, they can be found. But advocating for this in a national publication as a valid process is not only extremely problematic but also replicates historical colonial strategies of land theft tied to constructions of authenticity.

Both articles give the impression that climbing is legal through two forms of authenticity. The *American Alpine Journal* article defers to a level of authenticity that is in line with the pioneer—respect for the individual, the person who owns the land—as a reflection of his own values. The *Rock and Ice* article relies on locating an authentic "Indian" who holds the same values as the climber, who can pretend to speak for everyone else on the reservation. The Indigenous rock climber is valued because of his "Indianness," the way in which his perceived authenticity enables the climber to illegally summit monoliths on the Navajo Nation. In this way, the Indigenous climber functions as an accessory to the construction of authenticity in the climber. This tokenization is not radically different from the played-out cliché of white people who parade their "one Black friend" as a way to substantiate their commitments or shield themselves from criticism. Searching the rez for an Indigenous climber who will sign off on actions the vast majority have rejected is not a productive path toward better relations.

There is a lot of emphasis in climbing communities on first ascents, first free ascents, first descents. But "not everything needs to be climbed," Diné climber and guide Aaron Mike wrote on *Common Climber*. According to Mike, the expectations that everything needs to be climbed represents a "western 'take' culture," which is often not compatible with Diné culture. "Recreation must take a back seat to respecting Indigenous practices that have existed for millennia," he writes, advocating that climbers push one another and local climbing organizations "to provide information on how to recreate with respect on or near sacred lands and to develop relationships with local Tribes," and build a world that "honors our sport, our land, and the Indigenous communities associated with that land."[66]

---

65. Haas, "Sacred or Profane," 38. *Rock and Ice* magazine is now owned by *Outside* and is titled *Climbing*.

66. Mike, "Navajo Rising."

The Whiteness of "Dirtbaggers"

The term "dirtbag" is deployed in rock climbing communities to signify a climber who has obtained a coveted status. The term is used widely in rock climbing magazine articles, blog posts, and online forums at near constant frequency: "Becoming a Modern Dirtbag," "10 'Dirtbag' Climbers Convert Vans into Mobile Homes," "Considering Pursuing the Dirtbag Lifestyle," "How to Be a Dirtbag Climber," "The Rules for Dating a Dirtbag," and "You Might Be a Dirtbag If." Rock climbers aspire to be dirtbags; they denigrate "wannabe dirtbags"; "dirtbag" can be a noun; "dirtbagging" can be a verb. In the introduction to his book *The Great American Dirtbags,* Luke Mehall avoids a direct definition of a "dirtbag," claiming that each person will have their own idea of what it means: "At its essence, a dirtbag lives in the dirt, out of a bag. She or he spends their days in the outdoors, engaged with some recreational activity, and works just enough to pay for the basic necessities of a dirtbag existence."[67] A blog post titled "Dirtbag Explained" lists ten characteristics under the question, "How do I know if I'm a dirtbag?"[68] Answers include your willingness to give up necessities because of your love of the outdoors and passion for climbing all day every day; you cannot remember the last time you bathed; you live out of your pickup truck; you know when and where to acquire free food from dumpsters, leftover food at restaurants, and expired food from the grocery; you can talk about climbing with anyone at any time; you drink lots of beer; all your clothes come from a thrift shop; you live nomadically as the seasons change; and "you love your life and love the freedom it has given you to explore the world." The list concludes with the idea that "dirtbag" is a term of "admiration" and "endearment."[69]

The highly romanticized term is also steeped in race and class privilege. Evidenced by photographs that accompany each article on the "dirtbag," another characteristic that is overwhelmingly present, but left unsaid, is that a dirtbag is almost always white. While dirtbags are often poor, their poverty is "self-inflicted" and worn like a badge of honor.[70] One climber traced his romanticizing of "dirtbagging" to US literature: "There was something that resonated from classic pieces of literature like *The Adventures of Huckleberry Finn, On the Road, Dharma Bums, The Electric Kool-Aid Acid Test, Fear and Loathing in Las Vegas, Rock Jocks, Wall Rats and Hang Dogs,* and

---

67. Mehall, *Great American Dirtbags,* 8.
68. Climbing House, "Dirtbag Explained."
69. Climbing House.
70. Samet, *Death Grip,* 76.

Desert Solitaire that unfolded before my eyes in those dirtbag days."[71] In all of these examples, the main characters, the heroes these narratives are centered around, are also white. The context of the climbers' whiteness within the outdoor recreational space of rock climbing, and the fact that poverty has been chosen "in the name of screwing off to climb full-time," allows the term "dirtbag" to take on a different aspiring quality than it would outside those contexts. "The term [dirtbag]," as recounted in Matt Semet's celebrated memoir, *Death Grip*, "has its romantic connotations, evoking images of self-sufficient outlanders with no need for society or its trappings, but instead only the company of 'the tribe' and the rocks."[72] Semet's book intertwines his struggle and recovery from addiction with his love of climbing, conveying powerful ideas of strength and resilience. Yet descriptions like this further identify "dirtbag" with ideas of authenticity that hinge on romanticized forms of Indigeneity.

This context recalls Doreen Massey's observation that bodies occupy particular positions in space and Razack's argument that the geographical turn in critical theory has the potential to map out the ways white supremacy is implicated in everyday life.[73] The authenticity of the climber is, therefore, intimately tied to whiteness and class privilege, to being able to move in and out of poverty, but equally important is the way this authenticity is also bound by space, by material reality. Outside whiteness, outside class privilege, and outside spaces of outdoor recreation, "dirtbag" would not be a compliment. That the term is only deployed within certain spaces and applied to certain bodies illuminates the way the very spaces of outdoor recreation are racialized and coded in a manner that accommodates the subjectivities of those rock climbers who readily embrace the term.

Performing Pioneer

It is curious that many of the rock climbing narratives on the Navajo Nation, even Ormes's article detailing his near-fall in the 1930s, provide detailed explanations of Diné culture and spirituality. In the 2014 *Rock and Ice* article about defying the climbing ban on the Navajo Nation, Haas also recounts his experience with Diné people, their creation story, and how they define the sacred. These narratives feature no sources, quotes, or any evidence that a Diné person or community were involved at all in the way those stories were recounted. Beyond this, why is Indigenous cosmology relevant at all to an article on rock

71. Mehall, *Great American Dirtbags*, 8.
72. Samet, *Death Grip*, 76.
73. Massey, *For Space*, 6.

climbing? Why do these authors insist it is their place to discuss this alongside rock climbing? The answer: it is necessary for their construction of authenticity. The rock climbing communities reading these publications defer to the authority of the author, and part of that ethos depends on the perception that he is accepted in those communities in order to manufacture his own sense of authenticity. Settlers recount Indigenous culture and spirituality to foreground their own self-imposed states of peril and triumph in places where settlers have systematically displaced Indigenous peoples.

In his 1984 article for *American Alpine Journal* "The Unclimbable Summits," David Kozak wrote about why climbing is illegal on the Navajo Nation, dedicating roughly half of the article to explaining Diné culture to the journal's largely white audience. He began by noting a particular passage from another piece featured in *Climbing* magazine that "distressed" him: "The Four Corners desert area sees very little climbing traffic, and those with a taste for the bizarre, virgin rock and no crowds might find the area attractive. However, it is still illegal to climb anywhere on the Navajo Reservation, *so discretion is encouraged.*"[74] The article goes on to remind people that climbing on the reservation, indeed, remains illegal, despite the author's promotion of it. Following Foucault, to articulate knowledge is to impose a kind of dominance, or ownership of it.[75] Even as rock climbers need the "Indian" as an Other, there remains a compulsion to also speak for Indigenous peoples. There is an allure to climbing on the Navajo Nation, perhaps because it is illegal, perhaps because of the challenging climbs, perhaps both. Articulating rock climbing through both pioneer and "Indian" legacies, however, weaves a kind of nostalgia into settlers' sense of entitlement to Indigenous lands, regardless of legality or respect. There are few places today where the idea of Manifest Destiny can unfold the way it once did,[76] but outdoor recreational discourses remind settlers that it can be performed again and again, and that these enactments of frontier exploration are central to accessing the notion of an authentic self.

---

74. Kozak, "Unclimbable Summits?," 122, emphasis mine.

75. Foucault, *Archaeology of Knowledge.*

76. It is important, however, to underscore resource colonialism, perpetrated by governments and multinational corporations, as a continuation of a mindset that is certainly an evolution of Manifest Destiny. For more on these connections see Endres, "Rhetoric of Nuclear Colonialism"; and Gedicks, *Resource Rebels.*

CHAPTER 4

Ultrarunning

Settler Imaginaries and the Born to Run *Effect*

Much of this book thus far has attempted to provoke discussion about settler colonialism and its performances, embodiments, and enactments in outdoor recreation. I have tried to establish some of the ways settler colonialism has produced modes of thinking and being that show up in outdoor recreational discourses. This chapter returns to some of those points of inquiry as I reflect on my experiences as a trail runner, particularly in light of my research on recreational colonialism during a time when the sport of trail and ultrarunning has grown exponentially.

In this chapter, I mobilize these experiences and observations to animate some of the inherent problems that arise when tourism, ultrarunning, and Indigenous communities and lands intersect in destination races. I use this context to articulate some of the challenges faced by well-meaning and well-intentioned race directors, homing in on two individuals who are no longer with us, whose legacies offer valuable insights into the deeper challenges of settlers working to resist settler colonialism in outdoor recreational spaces. Matt Gunn, for example, organized ultramarathons in the four corners area of the American Southwest, and his race organizing involved working directly with tribal communities to rebuild structures in need of repair and helped build water infrastructure. And Micha True, a.k.a. Caballo Blanco, founder of the Ultra Maratòn Caballo Blanco in the Indigenous Rarámuri community in the Copper Canyons region of northern Chihuahua, Mexico—the same community mythologized in Christopher McDougall's book *Born to Run*—True mobilized funds from participants to help secure food vouchers for the Rarámuri people, who he lived among for decades and understood as facing profound threats to their cultural survival. Gunn and True were both known as humble, often soft-spoken individuals who fused their love of ultrarunning with a profound respect for Indigenous communities. Yet intentions and commitments like theirs are too easily obscured by the larger settler colonial context in which their running events occur, deeply entrenched in the imaginaries that participant runners bring to a destination race.

The destination race—both a material-discursive concept and a practice whereby runners travel to participate in a running event somewhere else, sometimes far away but not necessarily—holds the conditions of possibility from which recreational colonialism thrives in all the ways previously discussed in this book. This chapter, however, digs deeper by highlighting some of the effects of recreational colonialism on Indigenous communities and attempts to map out pathways from which settlers may confront their historical role as settlers on Indigenous lands in ways that are situated and personal yet generative. The destination race allures and entices as an elsewhere, illustrated through race reports, magazine covers, podcasts, and anything else that plants a seed in the minds of runners' imaginations. Runners ruminate on these landscapes for months, sometimes years, as they train for the event and learn all they can about the course. Often this knowledge is limited to the physical experience of the terrain: elevation gains, varying trail conditions, the number of river crossings, the climate, and the number and locations of aid stations that will support them. By focusing only on the physical, material conditions without also engaging the discursive, settlers confront those landscapes bringing their own imaginations, assumptions, and claims to innocence. When settlers describe running in these ways without acknowledging their political identity as settlers—their legacies and inheritances—they animate what Tuck and Yang describe as "settler moves to innocence."[1] These moves refer to a variety of rhetorical strategies that "attempt to relieve the settler of feelings of guilt or responsibility without giving up land or power or privilege."[2] Much is obscured in the preservation of "innocence." These moves may not be malicious or even made consciously; settler colonialism has created the conditions that prevent settlers from recognizing themselves as participants in the colonial present.

---

1. Tuck and Yang, "Decolonization Is Not a Metaphor," 1.
2. Tuck and Yang, "Decolonization Is Not a Metaphor," 10.

Other forms of destination races, those facilitated by organizations with names like Ultra Expeditions and Vacation Races, generate opportunities from which settlers can re-create colonial narratives of exploration by tracing the paths of their frontier ancestors who traveled by horse and wagon, or by engaging landscapes that would otherwise be too remote, if not restricted. Native American reservations, for example, contain many locations outsiders are not allowed to access alone, without a permit or guide, such as Antelope Canyon on the Navajo Nation. But Vacation Races obtains annual permission from the tribe to give a limited number of runners special access via the Antelope Canyon Ultramarathon series. In these cases, quite literally, participation in outdoor recreational events like ultramarathons becomes the primary way in which settlers engage with Indigenous communities and experience these landscapes. By going somewhere else, an elsewhere that is real but has also been produced by trail running discourses, settler trail runners perform a process that is inescapably colonial. This is how outdoor enthusiasts may problematically import recreational colonialism to other lands, and how settler colonialism is built into the very structures of these events, despite the well-meaning efforts of race directors and organizers. Ultra Adventures, the event organization run by Matt Gunn, used to host several ultramarathons on the Navajo Nation, including one in Monument Valley, but when he sold his organization to Vacation Races, the Monument Valley race didn't follow, and it's now run by NavajoYes. Some of these movements suggest a larger pattern among tribal communities who rightly want control over how settlers and other outsiders come to view their lands, cultures, and communities.

Ultramarathons can be transformative experiences that test the limits of one's mind and body, and therein lies immense potential toward radical self-reflection about the land itself, a palimpsest of culture, identity, competing histories, and contested belongings. Yet runners often arrive at an event given little information about the lands they run on, the lived experiences of local communities—their struggles and their joys—or how the race is situated in that community. Destination runners arrive a few days or weeks before a race as tourists in a land that is not their own. And they bring with them a tourist gaze not radically different from any vacation-goer engaged in the consumptive experience of landscape, the expectation of safety and an infrastructure of accommodation. Race directors and organizations play a crucial role in how an event is framed long before runners arrive—by providing resources, outlining their intentions, working with local communities to ensure dignity and respect in terms the community defines, and more. Yet even the most celebrated, self-reflective, and well-intentioned settlers who direct races and trail events in Indigenous communities have had limited success in challenging the deeply entrenched colonial mindsets participants bring to those events. This only reinforces the broader need to engage settlers more directly in ways this book attempts to do, by provoking deeper understandings that, like the act of running itself, force us to "confront who we are, at the deepest level," a phrase I borrow from a running coach. Ultimately, resisting recreational colonialism is a lifelong process full of difficult questions, through which we are constantly humbled; when we do the work required to recognize and resist recreational colonialism in ways that are situated and personal, the process brings us closer to ourselves, makes us more present and more responsive, and connects us more meaningfully to the landscapes in which we engage and activities we love.

"Discovering" the Rarámuri

As this book has taken shape over the last decade, participation in ultramarathons—marathons usually on mixed terrain that exceed the typical marathon distance, from fifty kilometers to one hundred miles and beyond—has increased by 345 percent, and these events continue to grow.[3] Due to restrictions on the number of people the Forest Service allows in wilderness areas at one time, the most popular ultramarathons have had to institute lotteries to gain entrance. In 2023 Western States, which has been described as the "Super Bowl of ultramarathons," drew more than 7,000 hopeful participants for only 369 spots.[4] Epic races across the country and around the world come to life for would-be participants in race reports, podcasts, and beautiful magazine cover photos featuring muscular elite athletes in vast mountainous landscapes. New data has busted a lot of myths about age and gender with respect to athleticism, revealing that people well into their forties, fifties, and sixties can thrive as long-distance runners, and women outperform men as distance increases beyond 195 miles.[5]

A popular trail running podcast, *Trail Runner Nation,* reflected on this massive growth in participation in its final episode of 2022 and discussed some of the inflection points that resulted in the mainstreaming of this

---

3. "State of Ultra Running."
4. Western States Endurance Run, "Lottery."
5. See Ronto, "State of Ultra Running 2020." According to a study analyzing running data over twenty-three years, conducted by RunRepeat in collaboration with the International Association of Ultrarunners, "in 5Ks men run 17.9% faster than women, at marathon distance the difference is just 11.1%, 100-mile races see the difference shrink to just .25%, and above 195 miles, women are actually 0.6% faster than men." Two words: Courtney Dauwalter.

once-fringe sport. While a few different factors were discussed, all three of the hosts agreed that one of—if not the biggest—influence was the 2009 best seller by Christopher McDougall, *Born to Run: A Hidden Tribe, Superathletes, and the Greatest Race the World Has Never Seen.* The first-person narrative follows McDougall deep into the Copper Canyons region of northern Chihuahua, Mexico, to find a US American expatriate—Micha True—who had been living and running alongside the Rarámuri for some years, and to learn the tribe's "secret" to their longevity as distance runners who run in homemade huarache-style sandals or barefoot, apparently injury free. What ensues is a tale from McDougall's first-person perspective that culminates in a race pitting a handful of invited elite US American trail runners against the Rarámuri, who McDougall referred to as their "prehistoric counterparts."[6]

According to one review for the *Washington Post,* the book is written in a style "straining to be gonzo," "engaging and buddy-buddy, as if he's an enthusiastic friend tripping over himself to tell a great story."[7] As a trail runner myself, especially one also engaged in this kind of research, I've had a *lot* of people recommend this book to me. By now, every trail runner has likely learned about the legendary feats of the Rarámuri people, which McDougall describes as a "near-mythical tribe of Stone Age superathletes."[8] The book not only brought a lot of people to the sport; it also generated a lot of interest in the running practices of Indigenous peoples, specifically the Rarámuri community in the Copper Canyons, inspiring many trail and ultrarunners to seek out ways to be like them. One of the hosts of the *Trail Runner Nation* podcast commented that when he read *Born to Run,* he was so inspired to run like the Rarámuri that he cut the soles down on his running shoes to mimic the minimalist footwear of the Indigenous community and started eating traditional pinole on the trail (on air, he actually misremembered it as "polenta"), detailed in the book as a powerful and essential Rarámuri running fuel. When *Born to Run* hit the shelves, the story and the Indigenous peoples McDougall mythologized immediately became the stuff of Western trail running lore. It's hard to overstate the impact of this book, which has sold over three million copies and continues to be especially popular in trail and ultrarunning communities.

Not only is *Born to Run* credited with bringing people to the sport, but it has also inspired dynamic changes to the running industry by introducing the Western running world to barefoot running and kickstarting the minimalist running shoe trend of the mid-2010s. LUNA sandals, Vibram FiveFinger toe shoes, and others made their mark during this time as bigger shoe companies

---

6. McDougall, "Born to Run."
7. Zak, "Book Review."
8. McDougall, *Born to Run,* 4.

produced minimalist shoe models due to consumer demand, which led to injuries and a class-action lawsuit.[9] McDougall's primary concern centered on uncovering what the Rarámuri people could teach him, and the Western world, about running pain-free. In the book and in interviews promoting it, he recounts the story of how he had been trying to be a runner but kept getting injured—common injuries like plantar fasciitis and Achilles tendonitis plagued him, sending him from doctor to doctor for advice. And those doctors would often administer cortisone shots, prescribe expensive custom orthotics, and tell him that running was bad for him. He wanted to know what the Rarámuri people knew about running that he did not. McDougall's description of the book during interviews and TED Talks always went something like this: "I discovered the Tarahumara Indians of Mexico's Copper Canyons. And the Tarahumara can somehow run hundreds of miles at a time in thin homemade sandals without ever getting hurt and running into old age. So I went down into the Copper Canyons to find out what it is the Tarahumara were doing that we're not, and once I figured it out that was it, that was my last running injury."[10]

Because running injuries are so common, he spoke to an audience who hung on his words with bated breath. McDougall concluded that running shoes cause running injuries; that because the Rarámuri people grew up not only running prolifically, but in homemade huarache-style sandals, they run in a way that is more "natural," in ways that rely on the body's evolved biomechanics perfected over millennia; that we are all "born to run" if only we throw out our fancy running shoes. "The shoes are the root of the problem," he told Jon Stewart on the *Daily Show*. "Without the shoes you can run painlessly forever."[11] In terms of the success of the book, McDougall speculated that it resonated with multiple kinds of readers. "It is whatever you want it to be," he said. "If you want it to be about the sport of ultrarunning, it is. If you want it to be an anthropological exploration of this reclusive tribe, it is. If you want it to be a rant against the destruction caused by running shoes, it is."[12] Yet McDougall himself is a journalist. When he wrote the book, he wasn't an ultrarunner, and he is neither an anthropologist nor a podiatrist. As a journalist, McDougall is an effective storyteller with a good grasp of how to capture the imagination of his audience—this chapter digs into that imagination. I am less interested in debating the validity of the claims McDougall makes with respect to running shoes, minimalism, and running form, and more interested

9. Doyle, "Switch to Minimalist Running Shoes."

10. *New York Times*, interview with "Roving Runner" blogger, YouTube, October 5, 2009, https://www.youtube.com/watch?v=iIT7t2jtdP0.

11. Stewart, "Christopher McDougall."

12. Yang, "Christopher McDougall."

in the rhetorical effect of his book on the trail running community, specifically his portrayal of the Rarámuri people and the landscape of the Copper Canyons.

While McDougall's book and its stances on the issue of running shoes and minimalist running practices continue to be a topic of debate, there has been very little attention brought to how his book, his perspective, and his language choices are so deeply entrenched in settler colonial logics. "Near-mythical tribe of Stone Age superathletes" is quite a phrase. While "superathletes" and "near-mythical" might at first sound complimentary, these are two ways of communicating forms of otherness that have profound consequences. This description further conjures near parallel constructions to the historical term "noble savage," which denotes an impossible standard: an idealized human whose innate goodness can only be cultivated outside of the corruptions of civilized life but is also characterized by brutal savagery. Likewise, "Stone Age" distances the Rarámuri from their cultural identity, binding them to a prehistoric past. When McDougall refers to the Rarámuri as "Stone Age guys in sandals"[13] as he does in the book, or as "a Smithsonian exhibit come to life," as he does in an invited talk for Google,[14] he prevents the Rarámuri from being understood as contemporary people resisting settler colonialism in the present. Throughout the book, McDougall describes the Rarámuri as having "superhuman toughness," having a "superhuman tolerance for pain," and able to "run all day without rest,"[15] characterizations that may at first appear to be praise but that come at the expense of the actual Rarámuri people, who like so many other Indigenous peoples have had to fight essentialism, romanticization, misrepresentation, and dehumanization.

While language like this is common throughout McDougall's book, I want to be clear that I do not think McDougall, nor the majority of his readers, maintain a conscious commitment to colonialism. This is precisely why this language is important to dig into. The casually embedded everydayness of settler colonialism permeates yet often goes unrecognized by those who use reverence to mask the limited ways they actually engage with Indigenous peoples. There is hardly a moment in Born to Run when any Rarámuri speak for themselves—what readers get are short snippets of quotes here and there, but it is mostly McDougall writing about the Rarámuri, based on his impressions and what others have told him. Whether intentional or not, McDougall's narrative is representative of a longer story of settlers speaking for Indigenous peoples and Indigenous peoples struggling to be understood on their own terms. When he told Jon Stewart on the Daily Show that he "discovered the

---

13. McDougall, Born to Run, 79.
14. McDougall, "Born to Run."
15. McDougall, Born to Run, 4, 15.

Tarahumara," he was likely referring to when he personally became aware of the Rarámuri, not that he had actually "discovered them," whatever that would mean. All intention aside, as a settler on television using the word "discovered" in reference to how he came to understand an Indigenous community, McDougall unwittingly attached himself to language that has a deep colonial history. When he describes the Rarámuri as "near-mythical" and "superathletes" McDougall is appealing to readers' sense of wonder and imagination, but at what cost to the Rarámuri? All too often, settlers get the benefit of the doubt, which is another way of articulating the preservation of innocence that Tuck and Yang describe. Whether as writers or runners, or both, we should not shy away from structures of accountability that allow us to better recognize ourselves and our roles as situated in a historical and cultural context. Further, these phrasings recall Gilio-Whitaker's observation about the way that the popularity of surfing "carried with it the story of Hawai'i and her people,"[16] yet those stories are often divorced from the conditions of imperialism and settler colonialism from which the Rarámuri have fought to resist, structures in which McDougall himself is enmeshed.

The last half of this chapter spotlights three ultrarunning events I encountered in 2015 in various ways, which is also when sales of *Born to Run* and the minimalist running trend were at their peak—the Paatuwaqatsi ("Water Is Life") 50K on the Hopi Reservation, which I ran that year, the Monument Valley 50-mile Ultramarathon on the Navajo Nation, and the Caballo Blanco Marathon in the Copper Canyons. I pivot from each of these contexts to animate Tuck and Yang's articulation of innocence as a framework from which settler appropriation and co-optation in Indigenous communities may occur, regardless of race organizers' intentions, reflecting the profound challenges of resisting settler colonialism in outdoor recreational spaces. But first, it is necessary to further discuss *Born to Run* and its effects. It is worth examining how *Born to Run* speaks directly to settlers in ways that mythologize Indigenous peoples and accommodate settler imaginaries, as evidenced in the 2020 documentary *The Infinite Race* by Bernardo Ruiz.

The *Born to Run* "Journey"

In 2015, at the height of *Born to Run*'s best-selling success and influence on the trail running community, I was doing little else beyond writing my dissertation and running the trails near the house we were renting in Mountainaire, a small neighborhood nestled in the forest about nine miles south of

---

16. Gilio-Whitaker, "Appropriating Surfing," 227.

Flagstaff. I wanted to use this time to train for my first ultramarathon; there was something empowering about the everyday accomplishments of training alongside writing that was incredibly challenging and using my time on the trail to recharge as I outlined chapters in my head. As I researched what race I wanted to run, I read a ton of race reports from individuals with blogs or other forms of social media who recounted their experiences running events across northern Arizona. This was also a time when this subculture was seemingly obsessed with *Born to Run*. Traces of the book's influence were everywhere as runners discussed the book, experimented with huarache-style running sandals and Indigenous foods, and expressed in various ways how they sought to infuse what they learned about the Rarámuri, translated as "The Running People" and otherwise known by their Spanish name, the Tarahumara, into their running practices.

In his 2020 documentary for ESPN, *The Infinite Race,* filmmaker Bernardo Ruiz centers the Rarámuri people as he documents this time period and highlights the consequences for Indigenous peoples when they are mythologized and written into outdoor recreational discourses. *The Infinite Race* contrasts the deep cultural tradition of running among the Rarámuri in the context of historic and ongoing resistance to colonialism with a complicated case study showcasing the effects of the relatively sudden attention they received through Western narratives, specifically McDougall's *Born to Run.* The film examines a cultural heritage race that was transformed into a globally recognized ultramarathon; as a consequence of the continued success of *Born to Run* in the years after the death of the ultramarathon's founder, Micha True, the race tripled in size by the 2015 event documented in the film, attracting runners from all over the world and the attention of local municipal tourism officials. Because of the massive success of McDougall's book, Ruiz's film necessarily contends with his depictions of the Rarámuri people and their cultural running practices, how the increased attention has affected them, and what the book misses. There are many moments in the film that brought attention to the settler imaginaries provoked by the book.

Luis Escobar, a photographer and runner who participated in the first Caballo Blanco marathon, documented in *Born to Run,* was interviewed in Ruiz's film, and commented on the influence of the book: "Our story has become a legend in the running circles and beyond." He continued, "That journey that we were on, and the way that Christopher documented it, it just resonates with people; people are looking for something big, outside of their office, outside of their home, and that is exactly what this story is about."[17] I would argue that the rhetoric of the "legend" and the "journey," as Escobar

---

17. Ruiz, *Infinite Race.*

evokes in opposition to the everyday spaces, experiences, and capitalist logics of work and leisure, reflects the way the book activates an imaginary that is quintessentially colonial. As I have shown throughout this book, settler colonial logics—those taken-for-granted ways of knowing, being, and orienting oneself in the world discussed throughout this book—foreground the pursuit of authenticity. Runners who come to the Copper Canyons because they were inspired by the book attempt to bring what was once imagined, mythologized, and romanticized into knowing, mimicking the colonial process from which settlers come to possess land that does not belong to them.

This settler drive to possess land might not always translate to literally taking physical land. Outdoor recreation nonetheless creates opportunities from which settlers bring themselves *as settlers* to lands that are not their own, where they redefine those lands through rhetorical practices inspired by narratives that accommodate their belonging. *Born to Run* is an example of such a narrative. Referring to his experience captured by McDougall and the sudden attention the Copper Canyons and Rarámuri received because of it, Escobar commented in Ruiz's documentary that "people wanted to re-create that experience that we had." In doing so, the hundreds of runners who showed up for the 2015 race also chased a feeling that only existed as an imaginary produced by McDougall. One of these hundreds of settler runners who had been drawn to the Copper Canyons for the 2015 race because of McDougall's book was Ryan Van Duzer, who confirmed and expanded on the imaginary he brought with him:

> That book in particular really just grabbed my heart and my soul. It's dangerous and it also has the beauty of the people, this long lost tribe. And North American runners coming down to see who was best. It had all the elements of a good Hollywood movie. All the runners that were there from all over the world were there because they read the book *Born to Run*. It was almost like they had all read the Bible and they were following their pilgrimage to this sacred place.[18]

There is a lot going on in Van Duzer's statement in which he reflects on the emotional effect *Born to Run* had on him, a statement made in good faith with which many likely would identify. But let's be clear: the Rarámuri have never been "lost"; they have been purposely hidden to maintain their own physical and cultural survival in the face of colonial violence. According to

---

18. Ruiz.

the Rarámuri featured in *The Infinite Race,* the tribe fled to this area to escape the colonial violence of the Spanish in the 1500s[19]—they live in this remote and dangerous area because they didn't want to be found. While the tribe might have recently become known to some, the Rarámuri have always known where they are. As Van Duzer details his observations in terms of the influence of the book, it's also worth examining his comparison to the Bible, characterizing *Born to Run* as a spiritual text that narrates the Copper Canyons as a "sacred place" for settler runners. Bringing these once unfamiliar landscapes into meaning in this way is not radically different from articulations of Manifest Destiny that sustained European settlers' belief that expanding westward was not just their right but a divinely inspired mandate. Lorenzo Veracini observes the circular logic produced by settler colonialism that forges belongings in places that settlers have never been to—"special locales," as he writes, are "intimately linked" to a "particular lifestyle."[20] Runners moved by *Born to Run* in this way do not come to the Copper Canyons to settle the land the way that European settlers did, but that doesn't mean they don't come to possess it in other ways. Possession occurs through the re-narration of place, a process that largely excludes the Rarámuri, where settlers become the primary storytellers of Indigenous cultures and landscapes, curating experiences, assumptions, and belongings. Van Duzer also said he didn't know much about the Copper Canyons outside of what he read in the book.[21] If the vast majority of runners present for the 2015 race were drawn there because they had read *Born to Run,* it's also worth lingering on how McDougall's descriptions of the Copper Canyons drove so many settler runners there.

So to be clear, hundreds of people from all over the world flew great distances to run great distances in a remote canyon in northern Mexico, with little else framing their expectations and experiences beyond the descriptions contained in this one book. This indicates a degree of rhetorical effect that is undeniably powerful. In previous chapters, I have traced some of the ways that narrations of material-discursive landscapes in outdoor recreational contexts often reflect and sustain settler belongings. The Copper Canyons, according to McDougall, are "treacherous," "mysterious," and "seem haunted," they are the "Bermuda Triangle of the borderlands," with "man-eating jaguars, deadly snakes, and blistering heat."[22] These descriptions may not sound very inviting,

---

19. This history is told in nearly every book about the Rarámuri. I also consulted Fontana, *Tarahumara;* and Irigoyen-Rascón and Paredes, *Tarahumara Medicine.*

20. Veracini, *Settler Colonialism,* 55–56.

21. Ruiz, *Infinite Race.*

22. McDougall, *Born to Run,* 34, 33, 5.

but consider the audience—a subculture of athletes that relish in the physical and mental challenges involved in running incredible distances on mixed terrain, fifty, one hundred, two hundred miles on courses with thousands of feet of elevation gain in every kind of weather imaginable. Or certainly an audience that daydreams about such things, and one specifically looking for such an "adventure" outside the daily structures and spaces in which they live. This recalls Rifkin's observation about the idea of the frontier as a "movable space of exception," translating Indigenous lands into a space of settler possibility.[23] Young's critique of Deleuze and Guattari's articulation of "the Rhizomatic West" animates this process, as he positions settler tales of exploration as historical and mythic narratives of western expansion that "constitute a coercive expression of sovereign power rather than an escape from it."[24] So there is an appeal based on the challenges inherent to the physical landscape, but McDougall also appeals to his audience's sense of a discursive landscape, a vague mixture of myth, historical fact, and romanticized danger in which settlers envision themselves triumphant.

McDougall curates a colorful list of dangers present throughout the history of this landscape: "Over the past hundred years, the canyons have played host to just about every stripe of North American misfit: bandits, mystics, murderers, man-eating jaguars."[25] Yes, he mentions the jaguars twice in the book—jaguars that most certainly would prefer not to eat people, but that's not the point. As enthusiastic participants in a fringe but growing subculture of athletes who are often asked *why*, ultrarunners may easily identify as a kind of misfit themselves, drawn to the challenge of navigating such dangers real or imagined. The list continues: "Comanche warriors, Apache marauders, paranoid prospectors, and Pancho Villa's rebels have all shaken pursuit by slipping into the Barrancas."[26] This is a list of associations that connect the canyons to myths of the frontier and Indianness—the ideas of Indigeneity produced by settlers—associations that have nothing to do with the Rarámuri and everything to do with establishing imaginaries that provoke settler subjectivities. At least in part, it is these imaginaries and provocations that brought runners to the Copper Canyons. Trail and ultrarunning communities should be aware of how these framings continue to bring settler people to the sport and what this phenomenon reveals about how they understand themselves in those spaces.

23. Rifkin, "Frontier."
24. Young, "Settler Sovereignty," 123.
25. McDougall, *Born to Run*, 33.
26. McDougall, 33.

Reckoning with Settler Imaginaries

Unlike McDougall's *Born to Run*, Ruiz's film *The Infinite Race* centers the voices and experiences of Rarámuri people. The result is an intimate and complex portrayal of Rarámuri people's actual lives, the unique challenges produced by their proximity to colonialism, such as poverty, anti-Indigenous racism, drought and other impacts related to climate change, and the effects of the drug trade. Two powerful voices in the film were Silvino Cubesare, who opened the film saying, "We Tarahumara are born with a gift, but we all run for our own reasons," and Irma Chávez, who said, "*Born to Run* is a nice story. But I don't consider the ultramarathons to be part of our culture," making a distinction between the cultural running traditions of the Rarámuri, which she said are "fundamental to our community," and the organized events like Micha True's Caballo Blanco Ultramarathon. While McDougall definitely touches on the fact that the Rarámuri are terrorized by drug cartels, who use the shaded, remote canyons as grow sites, his descriptions do not give readers a sense of what this is actually like for the Rarámuri. By glossing over these dangers as one of many present in the canyon, like the man-eating jaguars, the daily lived reality of cartel violence is abstract and might also be understood as exaggerated. Ruiz's documentary, however, painted a more detailed picture by giving space for Rarámuri people to talk about their experiences. Chávez described a time when she spoke up against the cartels and was threatened with violence and was forced to leave or face a similar fate as the many who have been killed for doing the same. The documentary gives an overview of the unique threats the cartels pose to the Rarámuri, who exploit their reputation as talented runners capable of swiftly covering distances others cannot to run drugs across the border. The consequences of not doing this work have resulted in forms of violence that range from murder to sexual assault.[27] These are the circumstances that left Cubesare locked away in prison for six months, which took him from his family and his ability to provide for them.

Yet, in *Born to Run*, the full weight of these realities is obscured by the near-utopic sense of being that accompanies McDougall's time in the canyons. McDougall writes,

> In Tarahumara Land, there was no crime, war, or theft. There was no corruption, obesity, drug addiction, greed, wife-beating, child abuse, heart disease, high blood pressure, or carbon emissions. They didn't get diabetes, or

27. See Goldberg, "Drug Runners."

depressed, or even old: fifty-year-olds could outrun teenagers, and eighty-year-old great-grandads could hike marathon distances up mountainsides.[28]

When describing Micha True's health after living a few years in the canyon, McDougall wrote that he never got injured and became the healthiest he'd ever been. While many of these details stem from cultural differences, community bonds, relative isolation, and nutritious food staples—all of which certainly do make the Rarámuri admirable in a number of ways—the implication here is that simply living in the canyon and eating pinole promotes some kind of magical healing and protection. Certainly, there is much we can learn. But none of this is to say that the Rarámuri don't face profound challenges both to their safety and survival.

The real and imagined collided in 2015 in the lead up to that year's Caballo Blanco ultramarathon, as documented by Ruiz. The day before the big race, an isolated incident involving members of one of the local cartels occurred in town; the sound of gunshots rang out, followed by a few hours of confusion, and eventually police from neighboring communities came in to secure the area. The situation created concern around the safety of the race. After some internal discussion that excluded the Rarámuri, the race was canceled. Van Duzer, one of the settler runners in Ruiz's documentary, was really upset. "I was ready for one of the biggest challenges of my life and suddenly that was being ripped away from me," he said, but he also expressed concerns about safety, saying nobody wanted to "run into a warzone." "They were jumping out of trucks, big guns, AK-47s or whatever they are. And I thought, oh wow, this is real now. This is the first time during the weekend when I thought, maybe this isn't as safe as I thought."[29] Cubesare, one of the most famous Rarámuri runners, commented on his surprise that the race would be canceled for the kind of violence that didn't just visit the city that day but had always been there: "At the time it was a normal thing for me." For the runners who came from out of town, the incident shattered the imaginary produced by McDougall's *Born to Run*, revealing the consequences of innocence. What was once a vague, abstract danger was suddenly very "real," and Ruiz's footage captured the look on setter runners' faces as they came to terms with a sliver of the daily reality the Rarámuri face. Because the food vouchers handed out at the end of the run were so important to the Rarámuri, with many counting on them, Cubesare said he was going to run no matter what. The next morning, the Rarámuri ran the race as planned. Because the canyons are their home and

---

28. McDougall, *Born to Run*, 14.
29. Ruiz, *Infinite Race*.

they had intimate knowledge of the location of cartel activity, they marked their own route for the run in areas they knew to be safe. But none of the visiting runners joined them.

"Going Native": Running Does Not Make Us Indigenous

Settlers who align themselves with Indigenous ways of knowing and being are part of a broader political practice that gives them the power to set the terms of Indigenous belonging. Many even go as far as falsely claiming Indigenous identity. Research into the "self-Indigenization" of white people in the United States and in Canada involves close attention to issues of "indigeneity, Indigenous identity, and/or Indigenous ancestry," but this work often reveals much more about "the shifting politics of whiteness, white privilege, and white supremacy."[30] Scholars like Kim TallBear and Darryl Leroux have at times been controversial within Indigenous discourses but have undeniably helped to expose individuals and groups who have profited in various ways through a falsely constructed Indigenous identity at the expense of Indigenous peoples.[31] Such people include academics (Ward Churchill, Andrea Smith, Gina Adams), artists (Buffy Sainte-Marie, Michelle Latimer, Joseph Boyden), and others typically in positions of power who knowingly delude the public and political and educational institutions in order to gain access, wealth, credibility, authenticity, or other forms of social benefit by performing Indigenousness. While these discussions unfold in Indigenous spaces, it is important for settlers to listen.

While certainly less egregious than those who falsely claim to be Indigenous to advance their careers, the discourses in trail and ultrarunning communities during *Born to Run*'s heyday were saturated with statements that range from appropriation to co-optation, and tread dangerously close to full-blown claims to Indigeneity through the "simplicity" and "universal" experience of running. Whether intentional or not, *Born to Run* created the circumstances that resulted in people wanting to be like the Rarámuri. This phenomenon takes Philip Deloria's historical accounting of settlers' "playing Indian" a step further, to an imaginary where runners feel they have been given an authentic experience that has allowed them to *become* Indigenous. McDougall writes, "like everything else we love—everything we sentimentally call our 'passions'

---

30. Leroux, *Distorted Descent*, 3.
31. Also see Audra Simpson's op-ed on the topic, "Indigenous Identity Theft Must Stop."

and 'desires'—it's really an encoded ancestral necessity. We were born to run; we were born *because* we run. We're all Running People, as the Tarahumara have always known." He continues: "Perhaps all our troubles—all the violence, obesity, illness, depression, and greed we can't overcome—began when we stopped living as Running People."[32] We should examine statements like this less in terms of the author's intention and more in terms of the effect this language has on his audience in settler colonial contexts. Shari Huhndorf further develops the compulsion among settlers to take on Indigenous identities through rhetorical practices in *Going Native: Indians in the American Cultural Imagination*: "*Going Native* articulates and attempts to resolve widespread ambivalence about modernity as well as anxieties about the terrible violence marking the nation's origins. A function of white supremacy, and central to recreational colonialism, "one of the primary impulses behind going Native" is "European Americans' desire to distance themselves from the conquest of Native America." Because of the anxiety around the violent history of colonization, Huhndorf argues that "going Native" functions to legitimate European Americans as "the proper heirs of 'Indianness' as well as of the land."[33] Recreational colonialism gives language to this phenomenon, naming this anxiety, distancing, and legitimation as it plays out in outdoor recreational discourses.

Critical and personal engagements with recreational colonialism also invite settlers to put their intentions on the back burner and recognize the effects of their rhetorical positionings. There is a moment in the 2016 documentary *El Chivo* ("The Mountain Goat," which refers to the name given to Will Harlan by the Rarámuri after he won the 2009 ultramarathon in the Copper Canyons) that illustrates this kind of tension between intention and effect as it relates to Indigenous belonging. At the start of the documentary, Harlan reflected on how the experience changed him: "After that race, it changed me into being more of a Tarahumara-like person."[34] Statements like this, though genuine in terms of how he feels the Rarámuri have positively influenced him in many aspects of his life, can also substantiate the troubling notion that one can "become" Indigenous. While this is not at all what Harlan likely means, there is tremendous possibility for misunderstanding and misinterpretation among those who admire him and aspire to run like the Rarámuri. They may see their problematic claims of belonging and kinship easily substantiated by such statements—that they may become more "Rarámuri-like" if they adopt the right attitudes, practices, and attire. This is especially likely considering how much trail and ultrarunning discourses were flooded with these kinds

---

32. McDougall, *Born to Run*, 93, 99.
33. Huhndorf, *Going Native*, 2, 3, 4.
34. R. Murphy, *El Chivo*.

of praises that don't get at the cultural and spiritual nuances, the historical knowledge and proximity to colonial violence that contribute to ways of
understanding and being in the world that settlers can never embody, no matter how hard they try.

In some ways, these co-optations reflect profound privilege. At the end of
The Infinite Race, Cubesare is shown a clip of McDougall running barefoot in
New York City, talking about the Rarámuri and what he learned about running form. His reaction was somewhere between laughter and confusion. "I
don't know what they are thinking why do they do this? Why do they want to
run barefoot, it seems strange. Why would they want to suffer? I think they're
crazy." Chávez reacted with anger. "Running barefoot is offensive, it's a mock-
ery of us. . . . The Rarámuri people do it because we lack resources," she said
and mentioned the double standard between white runners' co-opting Indigenous running practices and "making a business out of it" while the Rarámuri
face discrimination at home for running barefoot.[35]

Micha True's vision for his Caballo Blanco Ultramarathons in the Copper Canyons, an effort he described as an "intercultural exchange of ultrarunning people," always centered the Rarámuri; he spent a number of years
building relationships with the intention of giving back to this community he
loved and admired. Yet as this analysis demonstrates, there are challenges that
relate to the larger settler colonial context that can't be addressed alone with
good intentions. True would later talk about how uncomfortable he felt with
McDougall's portrayal of him as this eccentric hermit in the canyons, a portrayal that he didn't have any control over. Luis Escobar, who knew True well,
said he sometimes worries that as the race continues, now organized by the
City of Urique and True Messengers, a nonprofit inspired by True, it is becoming a business based on Rarámuri culture and image. "That's not what Micha
intended," he said. Before True died in 2012, he said he wanted to continue to
organize the marathon for "as long as it's bringing good," awarding prizes and
resources from his own pocket.[36] According to Escobar and those who knew
him, he never sought fame or attention; he never made money on the event.
It was always about celebrating the Rarámuri culture of running and using the
event to bring needed resources to the community.

One of the races I had considered running in 2015 was the Monument
Valley Fifty-Mile Ultramarathon in northern Arizona. I learned about a series
of events organized by Matt Gunn and his organization Ultra Adventures,
with races at Antelope Canyon, Arizona; Zion, Utah; and Monument Valley,

---

35. Ruiz, *Infinite Race.*
36. Ruiz.

Arizona, among others. Gunn, like True, infused his love of the outdoors with his respect and admiration for Indigenous peoples in ways that brought resources and support to those communities through which he forged meaningful relationships. Despite his work to use the race to educate settler runners about Indigenous cultures, using race profits to directly benefit Diné communities, what I read of individual settler runners' experiences indicated similar problems between intention and rhetorical effect. It was clear that participants in the Monument Valley ultramarathon began the race believing that they were prepared to view, understand, and experience the landscape in the same way a Diné person does. Andy Pearson, writing at *I Even Ran This Far*, admitted that before visiting Monument Valley he "didn't really know much about the Navajo Nation," but he quickly took on the surface-level identities of Indigenous people introduced to him. "My very favorite part of the race was any time I passed into the shadow of one of the huge mesas or buttes," he recalled in his race report. "It made me feel safe. Almost like I was being embraced by these giant, gentle ancients. The rocks were protecting me."[37] Cory Reese, writing as "Fast Cory" on his blog, spoke for the group, articulating the connection to mystical Indigenous landscapes he had been prepared for: "We all knew we were surrounded by something amazing, something spiritual, something special."[38] The blogger at *For Love of Trails* reported what it was like to "experience the sacred lands of the Navajo's" and noted that she understood what that meant. "While out there I could feel why they were sacred."[39] Race directors like True and Gunn—settlers who approached the organization of their event with care—were nonetheless limited in the ways they could use their positions to develop long lasting structures of accountability and awareness among their participants.

Paatuwaqatsi:
Running against Settler Colonialism

The ultramarathon I did sign up for and run in 2015 was the Paatuwaqatsi (Water Is Life) fifty-kilometer ultramarathon on the Hopi Reservation, which I had heard about for years. In my role as a journalist, I had come to know and respect the founder of the run, Hopi farmer and runner Bucky Preston, who had used running throughout his life to bring attention to injustices threatening what he describes as the "sanctity of water." In addition to his opposition

---

37. Pearson, "Race Report."
38. Reese, "Monument Valley 50 Race Report."
39. "Majestic Monument Valley 50K."

to the Arizona Snowbowl Ski Resort's use of reclaimed wastewater to make snow on the San Francisco Peaks, Preston ran to draw awareness to a number of other issues, such as the effects of uranium mining rendering water resources irreversibly contaminated and Peabody Coal's overuse of aquifers to draw water to run coal slurry from Black Mesa, a community of Hopi and Diné people whose houses lack running water. For thousands of years, for both practical and spiritual purposes, running has been an integral part of Hopi culture.[40] Preston, who grew up in Walpi, Arizona, a village on top of First Mesa on the Hopi Reservation, has been a runner his entire life.[41] He told me, "We ran everywhere; there are foot paths connecting the villages from all directions." After leaving the reservation to learn a few trades and returning to find many of those trails missing or in disarray, Preston organized the Water Is Life run fearing they would be lost forever. The Water Is Life run is a Hopi tradition first and foremost, a community event in which many Hopis, young and old, participate. "That's what I wanted to see for our people," said Preston of the event, "to get them back to long-distance running, because that's who we are."[42] The run is embedded in and embraced by Hopi communities in profound ways and is regarded as mutually beneficial to outsiders who seek both a recreational and cultural experience, and to the Hopi, in terms of sustaining and celebrating cultural and spiritual traditions.

At the start of the run, minutes before the sun rose, sixty-eight ultra-long-distance runners gathered around Preston, the sky clear and purple behind them. "These trails are like the blood vessels of our body—spread out—but all connected; they bring energy through our bodies," Preston told us. "When you put the footprints on the land, that's calling the rain, and it's calling the Kachina and the Cloud People. We're here, and we're asking for your help."[43] Unlike the marathons organized by Gunn and True, the Water Is Life ultra-marathon is entirely driven and embraced by the Hopi people, not organized by outsiders who want to "do good." And everyone who lives along the route is involved, often serving crucial functions—providing water and food under shade, or stationed at particularly dangerous places, warning weary runners to watch their step as they begin a steep decent. Many others are simply there to watch the runners, providing motivation, jokes, and high-fives along the way.

40. For more in-depth descriptions and illustrations linking running to Hopi culture, see Gilbert, "Hopi Footraces"; Nabokov, *Indian Running*; and Truglio, *Racing the Rez*.

41. Some observations about the run illustrated in this section come from my experience running this event on September 12, 2015. The quotes attributed to Bucky Preston came from an interview I did with him for my essay "Hopi Man."

42. Boggs, "Hopi Man."

43. Boggs.

At every stage of the run, participants, Hopi and settler alike, are reminded that their presence, their "footprints on the land," are not only welcome but necessary. "Kwakwhay!" yell the men. "Askwali!" yell the women. Both phrases are gender-specific ways of saying the same thing: "Thank you." The communities thank the runners because they help ensure the success of their crops.[44] In this way, the run is mutually beneficial to everybody involved—to traditional Hopi runners, to the community, and to settlers who still leave the reservation having run a "scenic" and "challenging" course, even as their experience as settlers is decentered. This is a Hopi tradition, and outsiders orient their expectations and experiences within the context of their identity as visitors.

While the Water Is Life run structurally emphasizes complex and multidimensional Indigenous ways of thinking and being in the world and invites settlers to participate and learn about their culture and politics on their terms, it is clear that the condition of settler colonialism and the systems of power upon which it relies runs deep. John McClung at *Barefoot in Arizona*, for example, reported on his experience at Paatuwaqatsi, explaining that he definitely wanted to run in his huaraches—Indigenous-inspired running sandals—because there is "something timeless" about them and "it's hard to find a more timeless place than Hopi."[45] So despite the fact that the run likely forced McClung to grapple with the Hopi as contemporary people, there is still a compulsion present in his language that prefers to internalize the Hopi as unchanging, as "timeless."

Meanwhile, after the blogger at *Flintland* ran Paatuwaqatsi in 2013, he felt such a kinship to the Hopi that he felt like he had "reunited" with his people: "I felt I had traveled here to reunite with more members of something greater than the sum of us all, the one tribe I feel I truly belong with."[46] That he felt their meeting was a reunion of sorts indicates his dissatisfaction, the disunity he feels in his day-to-day life. Here "Flint," as he refers to himself, echoes Huhndorf's notion of "going Native," where US Americans envision Indigenous peoples as "idealized versions of themselves, as embodiments of virtues lost in the Western world."[47] The sentiments expressed by McClung and Flint—like those race reports from the Monument Valley ultra—ultimately serve as a means of solidifying a definition of US American identity in relation

---

44. Boggs. Regarding this detail, one elderly Hopi man, a friend of Preston, joked with me during the run, which I mention here because I thought it was funny, but also because it actually strengthens Preston's point. He said, "Bucky is a smart man to design the run to go right through his cornfield; all your footprints make his corn grow. I think he put this whole thing together because he's a bad farmer."

45. McClung, "My First Ultra."

46. Flint, "Paatuwaqatsi."

47. Huhndorf, *Going Native*, 6.

to an other, and functionally distance that identity from culpability in past and present colonial violence. The two examples sustain settler colonialism as they "turn[ ] Native land and culture into an inheritance granting them knowledge and ownership of *themselves*."[48]

Yet it is also clear that others left Paatuwaqatsi with an enriched sense of responsibility. Chris Clemens left the reservation remembering something the Hopi announcer said at the conclusion of the run: "One day we will all leave this earth, but our footprints will stay." He said this "made me think about the kind of footprints I'm leaving in my life."[49] Another runner retraced the route, commenting on the stone steps that led to the village Walpi as having "been around longer than any of our White ancestors have been on this continent."[50] In their own way, both race reports appear to be grappling with history and the affective and situated colonial encounter produced by that experience.

Settler Innocence on the Trail

As I conclude this chapter and the first half of this book, I want to make one thing as clear as possible: I love long-distance running. Trail running specifically is something that I can honestly say has improved nearly every aspect of my life. I know many other runners feel this way too. I fully recognize that I'm privileged to live in a body that can even do it, and that this could change at any moment. The idea that McDougall centers through his book, that we as humans are inherently "born to run," makes sense to me when I consider my body in its current state and as I have known it, the way it has evolved to move and to sweat, how easy and natural it seems to me to be on the trail (at least, most of the time!), and how essential running has become to my life. But not everyone has a body that can run—we are not all biomechanically the same. And certainly, for those who do run, our cultures and histories as runners are vastly different.

Because I love running, this has been one of the hardest chapters for me to write. This difficulty is a reminder that when I critique trail and ultrarunning discourses, I am not critiquing the practice itself. This is true of critiques throughout this book; there is nothing intrinsically unethical about the practices of rock climbing, mountain biking, or skiing. There are, however, certain, deeply colonial modes of thinking that can arise through these practices because of the context from which they occur and the unacknowledged

---

48. Morgensen, *Spaces between Us*, 18.
49. Clemens, "Running with the Hopi."
50. Alene Gone Bad, "Paatuwaqatsi Run."

premises that precipitate their evolution. When those colonial modes of thinking are activated through outdoor recreation, they may show up in unexpected ways that demand interrogation. Settlers must recognize that there are different cultural understandings about what constitutes harm. When skiers demand infrastructure on sacred sites and dismiss Indigenous articulations of cultural survival, when mountain biking and camping sustain anti-Indigenous tropes of the frontier, when rock climbing infuses pioneer narratives into an otherwise healthy physical activity, settlers must examine the mechanisms that produce these outcomes. Settlers also must recognize what these phenomena reveal not only about them as participants but also about their relationships with the landscapes in which they engage, and how such predispositions may run contrary to commitments to social and environmental justice. As a trail runner who has spent thousands of miles mulling over my identity as a settler on stolen Indigenous lands, I want to end this chapter in the collective first-person, using "we" and "our" to implicate myself as I affirm my commitment to settler responsibility.

No doubt, throughout human history, there have always been runners. Running with this knowledge can be empowering. Running discourses can also produce problematic assumptions about kinship and belonging. Whether or not we acknowledge it, settler runners are benefactors of the ongoing colonial processes that both make our presence possible and simultaneously give shape to the trails we run on. It is perhaps the simplicity of running, the fact that one doesn't need to travel far or buy a lot of gear, combined with how widely running has been practiced for millennia across continents and cultures, that sustains a kind of unquestioned innocence that makes these assumptions possible. As the benefactors of colonialism in these spaces, what do we think about when we attempt to recall our human ancestors as we run on lands they never knew? When we allow our minds to stretch out across the landscape, what stories flood our imaginations of those places, of their histories, of the contemporary Indigenous peoples who hold ancestral claims there? When we participate in destination races, running events in lands unfamiliar to us, what is it that allures us, what provokes our imagination of those places? What do we import to those places and experiences? How have the cultures and landscapes of those places been narrated for us, and what contradictions in those stories might exist for us when we get there?

Even if one does unilaterally believe (which I do not) that humans are "born to run," we are not born to colonize, or to sustain settler colonialism through the recreational practices we have come to love. There is much I could have brought up in this chapter that is worth discussing, from the trophy belt buckles awarded at big ultrarunning trail races and what they represent to the celebratory and often incomplete historical framing of some of those races. The stories, told through promotional descriptions and elsewhere, might highlight the toughness of silver miners, for example, without recalling the way state, corporate, and military powers joined to quell worker strikes, occasionally with violence, or how those entities acquired that land to begin with and the effects of mining on Indigenous communities.

Many organized races, like Western States, a one-hundred-mile ultramarathon near Auburn, California, post land acknowledgments on their website, noting the original Indigenous inhabitants of the area. Such statements, which are increasingly common in a variety of venues and contexts, particularly those that involve public gatherings, can challenge assumptions of an empty landscape before European settlement and can productively complicate settler belongings. However, the experience of the frontier, the pioneer, the explorer, and the prospector still dominate the narratives of so many trail races, shaping the expectations and experiences of participants. Acknowledgments that do not confront settler legacies and inheritances in the present while accounting for past injustices, statements that do not invite ways of articulating commitments toward reparative futures, often function merely to preserve settler innocence.

There are also plenty of more casual forms of anti-Indigenous rhetoric in outdoor recreational discourses—from podcasts and social media forums to in-person conversations in group runs and trail running events. Individual expressions might seem inconsequential, but taken together they tell a story that demands recognition and confrontation. As someone who has been a runner most of my life, I must be honest and critical as I reflect on how settlers often talk about running, particularly long-distance running, and ourselves as runners.

When we talk casually about our "tribe" when referring to the running community (as the hosts of one of my favorite trail running podcast seem to do in nearly every episode), we are co-opting forms of belonging that are not ours, evoking language that settlers have historically used to dehumanize Indigenous peoples. While running ultra-long distances without a doubt produces mental effects from deep mindful meditations to hallucinations, when runners describe a long run as a "vision quest," we trivialize the nuanced spiritual role of running across cultures and the variety of ways Indigenous peoples use running as a cultural practice that is not ours. When we claim to tap into something "primal" or "natural" through the "universal" practice of running, when we say we can be like the Rarámuri or the Hopi or the Apache if we replicate their running practices, foods, and cultural running traditions, we pretend to embody Indigenous ways of knowing and being in the world that are not ours. This doesn't mean that we cannot learn from Indigenous peoples—certainly we can and should—but what we might consider replication, modeling, or inspiration could easily become co-optation, appropriation, and exploitation. These processes, often unconsciously embedded in the language we use, obscure our ongoing and inescapable position as colonizers on this continent. While the collective harm and exclusivity such rhetoric sustains may be unintentional, there is much we willfully leave unacknowledged in the preservation of our innocence.

Revealed in these everyday expressions are micro-attempts to universalize Indigeneity and remake it as something settlers can possess. While simple phrases and problematic word choices can easily be dismissed as innocent or waved off as unintentional, taken together and analyzed in context, they reveal how easily settlers may co-opt Indigeneity at the expense of Indigenous peoples. Deliberate or not, settler moves to innocence serve as a cover for this process. Such moves are not sustained only through language but by our very relationship to the material world, through the rhetoric of the outdoors, therefore preventing us from fully comprehending contemporary Indigenous lived experiences. It's a little embarrassing to write it out, but . . . running does not make us Indigenous. Nor does it distance us from our historical legacies and inheritances as settlers. Running does not allow us to imagine what it is like to be Indigenous. Running does not universalize our experiences. Running does not alleviate our complicity in the settler colonial systems from which we benefit. While I can be honest about how spiritual and meditative trail running is for me, how the ritual of it allows me to tap into something that is profound and personal to me—something many trail runners might even name as sacred—what I might feel and perceive as sacred is not comparable to what Indigenous peoples feel and perceive as sacred, embedded in the landscape and culture since time immemorial. The metaphorical trail I've been running all my life is unique to me; it is also undeniably tied to settler ways of knowing and being in the world, not Indigenous ways. And no amount of time on the trail will change that. But fortunately, the trail is long, and forms of resistance and solidarity present themselves in a variety of ways. Resisting recreational colonialism is multifaceted and complex, but we can start by recognizing and finding ways to resist those modes of thinking that tell us we can be like Indigenous peoples, that we can access Indigeneity through rhetorical practices like trail and ultrarunning.

The massive growth in the sport of ultrarunning in light of the *Born to Run*'s influence necessitates critical interventions into the often unarticulated relationship between trail and ultrarunning discourses and settler colonialism. There are, quite suddenly, a lot of people out there challenging themselves to go farther, beyond what they thought was possible—and I think this is wonderful and I definitely count myself among them. But it should also give us pause as we think about how those landscapes we enter have been narrated, and we should be prepared to recognize and confront that which may be uncomfortable and challenge our assumptions about who we are in these spaces.

In an interview discussion about his book *Do Hard Things: Why We Get Resilience Wrong and the Surprising Science of Real Toughness,* running coach and performance expert Steve Magness said something that stuck with me, something I took completely out of the author's intended context: "Running forces us to confront who we are, at the deepest level." What I am gesturing toward in this chapter and through the concept of recreational colonialism is that—for settlers—there are even deeper levels to confront beyond our immediate physical and mental experience, inviting us to embrace "resilience" and "toughness" in ways that bring us closer to ourselves by learning how to recognize our ongoing roles as settlers on stolen Indigenous land. "Who we are" is not only found in a deep slog up a rocky hill but through a reckoning of our historical and cultural presence on these lands, a confrontation of the privileges we inherit that allow us to run on those very lands, often at the expense of Indigenous peoples who used to inhabit them and continue to know them as their ancestral homelands. Resisting recreational colonialism is about being real with ourselves as settlers, reorienting our modes of thought away from constructions of authenticity that have been played out for us by deeply entrenched supremacist systems, and moving toward something new. It takes a different kind of resilience to do this work, to question deeply held assumptions, and it takes a different kind of toughness to shine a light on that which we are not meant to see, to meditate on our commitments, and find ways to make them actionable.

CHAPTER 5

The Ski Resort

(Re)Creating Space and Selling Recreational Colonialism

Skiing and the expansion of the outdoor recreation industry provide a curious inquiry into how space can be (re)defined through rhetorical practices, and how those practices privilege one racially hegemonic imagination. As the industry expands to make way for increasing numbers of participants, controversies pitting the interests of "outdoor enthusiasts" against what Indigenous peoples have referred to as their "cultural and spiritual survival" are becoming increasingly common. According to the findings of the outdoor recreation industry's annual report,[1] 74.4 percent of core participants identify as white, and the fastest growing outdoor recreational industries, such as skiing and snowboarding, are overwhelmingly white spaces, with a long history of exclusion of people of color.[2] Often reinforced through media representation, with regard to "participation in outdoor recreation in our forest and parks . . . African Americans and other nondominant groups are on the outside looking in."[3] Scholarship in leisure studies has increasingly focused attention

1. Outdoor Industry Association, "Outdoor Participation Trends Report." "Core participants," according to the report, are defined as regular participation, quantified by nine or more outings a year. The report analyzes data from 2015 to 2021 and notes that while diversity is up among new participants, core participation among white participants has increased, while core participation among BIPOC communities has actually decreased.

2. Spracklen, *Whiteness and Leisure*; Coleman, "White West"; and Coleman, "Unbearable Whiteness of Skiing."

3. Finney, *Black Faces, White Spaces*, 2.

on the racial disparities among participants of outdoor recreation,[4] and there remain numerous sites across the United States where this type of study could be applied.

In this chapter, I critically examine the way the space of the Arizona Snowbowl Ski Resort in what is now northern Arizona has been written by the resort and those who support its continued developments. The material-discursive theories of language I deploy in this book allow us to recognize those narrations that are based on what we think of when we typically think of texts such as ski maps, brochures, websites, but also and simultaneously those written on the physical land itself, such as ski runs, trails, snowmaking infrastructure. These narrations are also based on a kind of accumulation that forges belongings and propagates in the imagination over time. I situate this analysis by focusing on how Snowbowl and those who support its further development often defend continued proposals and development plans by describing the space of the resort as only existing on "one percent of the mountain." I argue that this articulation of the spatial confines of the Peaks is an argument that always already serves the interests of those who are pro-development and demonstrates how recreational discourses can limit the way settlers (even those who do not go there) are meant to understand the San Francisco Peaks. I analyze decades of promotional material from the ski resort to highlight the ways in which recreational colonialism is embedded in the physical and discursive landscape.

Settler Space: Beyond the One Percent

In the introduction to their edited anthology, *Making Settler Colonial Space: Perspectives on Race, Place and Identity,* Tracey Banivanua Mar and Penelope Edmonds begin their scholarly and creative intervention into settler colonialism from the view of Indigenous peoples with the transformation of physical spaces during the colonial era: "In geopolitical terms, the impact of settler colonialism is starkly visible in the landscapes it produces. . . . Land and the organized spaces on it, in other words, narrate the stories of colonization." While the authors list fences, roads, powerlines, gridded cities, dams, mines, and monocultural agricultural spaces as examples, they also include "carved and preserved national forest" and "wilderness parks," and they certainly *could have* included ski resorts. Outdoor recreation shapes (and is shaped by) social

---

4. Spracklen, *Whiteness and Leisure*; Long and Hylton, "Shades of White"; and Martin, "Apartheid in the Great Outdoors."

and cultural conceptions of physical landscapes; sacred Indigenous sites redefined through outdoor recreation, like ski resorts, also narrate the stories of colonization. Once the trees are cut for ski runs, lifts, lodges, and parking lots, once the allure of the resort enters the cultural imaginary through brochures, maps, commercials, and—importantly—experience, it becomes harder to disassociate the landscape from the resort, the material from the discursive. It is no small detail, therefore, that the Arizona Snowbowl Ski Resort continues to boast in its promotional material, "Established in 1938 . . . Arizona Snowbowl is one of the longest continually run ski areas in the country."[5] It is worth noting that in 1938, Indigenous peoples did not have access to the same rights and legal privileges that white US citizens did and therefore could not have legally resisted its initial development if they wanted to.[6] The resort's branding in this way suggests longtime status that naturalizes and normalizes its presence and its belonging as somehow predating any Indigenous resistance against it.

Through recreational discourses lies a particular construction of nature, where a specific, often narrow understanding and experience of the (use of the) environment is sustained. This construction underscores how "power and knowledge gain traction at the sites of affective investment" in some knowledges over others, "between and among those who are constituted through belonging."[7] Spaces of outdoor recreation exclude non-Western cultures and claims of sacredness but ironically limit the way even Western audiences are meant to relate to other cultures and the natural world.[8]

Linking this framework to the controversy over development on the Peaks is an interrogation of one of the most ubiquitous statements those in favor of development at the Arizona Snowbowl Ski Resort propagate, which is that its expansion and the use of reclaimed wastewater takes up "one percent of the mountain." While this line was used by the US Forest Service's legal team throughout its defense since 2006, it was a phrase echoed by many, including Flagstaff community leaders. One Flagstaff City Council member, Jeff Oravitz, wrote in a 2010 editorial, "Apparently 99 percent being preserved is not enough for some. Who's being greedy here? The people that want 1 percent, or the people that want 100 percent?"[9] Similarly, Snowbowl general manager J. R. Murray echoed these sentiments on camera to a group of children

---

5. Arizona Snowbowl Ski Resort, https://www.snowbowl.ski/media.

6. McDonald, *American Indians*.

7. Rowe, *Power Lines*, 3.

8. For an analysis on the many ways in which a discourse on the sacred has been deployed and the effects it has had on Indigenous peoples, see Tiedje, "Promise."

9. Oravitz, "Less Than One Percent."

in a 2006 documentary, *The Snowbowl Effect*.[10] He has continued to use the 1 percent claim in 2019 to justify even more expansions outlined in the $60 million dollar plan. "By offering limited night skiing on one percent of the mountain's skiable acreage, we'll be able to provide additional outdoor recreational opportunities for local youth," he said.[11] While the goalposts concerning what constitutes necessary developments to ensure the survival of the business continue to move each time the resort's ownership changes hands, claims that the resort's developments only affect a tiny fraction of the mountain persist.

This effort to frame the spatial dimensions of the controversy is also an effort to privilege the quantifiable material space over the lived social space, and animates a central feature of recreational colonialism, which is that it facilitates the erasure of Indigenous peoples and culture through redefinition of spatial terms. To question the physical, "real," or "material" space of the mountain validates those who use the 1 percent claim to make an argument about space. Such a narrow interpretation of space would enable questions like "1 percent of what?" Could it mean 1 percent of the Kachina Peaks Wilderness Area,[12] where the resort lies? Or is it 1 percent of the Peaks District, upon which the mountain range lies? Is it 1 percent of the entirety of the Coconino National Forest? Such questions would, however, evade David Harvey's observation of space as "relative," "relational," and always taking place in a "frame."[13] In other words, recognizing the *social* spaces in which lived practices are embedded is significant as they encompass social processes and interrelationships that foreground the actions that take place there and how they are to be understood in context.[14] According to Harvey, "Processes," including, I suggest, the long-term construction of ski infrastructure, "do not occur *in* space, but define their own spatial frame." Therefore, both processes and *practices* are spatialized. Important to the application of rhetorical exclusion in material-discursive spaces of outdoor recreation, Harvey notes the importance of asking who is defining that which is relative to the spatial frame.[15] Power and privilege, therefore, are always at work in the way material space is narrated, and whose stories are heard matters.

10. Benally and Cody, *Snowbowl Effect*.

11. Randazzo, "Arizona Snowbowl."

12. The ski resort predates the designation of the Kachina Peaks Wilderness area in 1984. In fact, archival research shows that there was some local confusion among some residents who were upset because they thought the San Francisco Peaks were going to be renamed the Kachina Peaks.

13. Harvey, "Space as a Keyword," 272–75.

14. Lefebvre, *Production of Space*; and de Certeau, *Practice of Everyday Life.*

15. Harvey, "Space as a Keyword," 273.

In this case, the contested space is controlled and managed by the federal government and run by a for-profit corporation that lies outside city limits. If "space and time lie within processes that define them," however, the *social* space of the resort is much more significant than the measurable acreage it takes up.[16] It is common for skiers in Flagstaff to say they are going to "ski on the Peaks." Indeed, the phrase "ride the mountain," and "ski the Peaks" are found in the resort's own promotional material; such phrases blur the distinction between the entirety of the Peaks and what occurs on the 777 acres of the resort.[17] Articulating the resort as social space reveals the larger tactic that privileges dominant discourses and obscures others; the resort's rhetoric has functionally "redefined the land in terms of leisure."[18] The social space of the ski resort is found not just on the mountain but in the city of Flagstaff—in ski rental businesses like the Ski Haus and in restaurants that cater to the aesthetics of skiing like Altitudes Bar & Grill, but also in the city's promotional material, colorful maps, and events like the Dew Downtown, an annual urban snowboarding festival.

To critically engage with the material-discursive spaces of outdoor recreation on the Peaks is to consider, all at once, the "material space" of experience, perception, and sensation as inseparable from the "representation of space," which is conceived, perceived, and represented, and "spaces of representation,"[19] or as Harvey explains, "the lived space of sensations, imaginations, emotions, and meaning incorporated into the everyday."[20] Such a framework therefore brings powerful new authority to Indigenous and anti-development advocates who seek to dismantle the established credibility of the 1 percent claim. For example, Caleb Johnson, former vice chairman of the Hopi Tribe, responded to the 1 percent claim, "You cannot divide spirituality into little pieces, you have to honor and respect the whole thing."[21] Yet when Mountain Capital Partners, a company that owns several resorts in the Southwest, took over in 2017, it listed Snowbowl on its website under the drop-down menu "Our Mountains." Other brochures deploy similar possessive rhetoric, such as "Do we have a mountain for you!" and "Your year-round playground."[22] The 1 percent claim is a rhetorical tactic designed out of a need

---

16. Harvey; and de Certeau, *Practice of Everyday Life.*

17. Snowbowl Vertical Files.

18. A. Wilson, "View from the Road," 22.

19. Lefebvre, *Production of Space,* 41–42.

20. Harvey, "Space as a Keyword," 272.

21. Benally and Cody, *Snowbowl Effect.* See also Glowacka, Washburn, and Richland, "Nuvatukya'Ovi."

22. Snowbowl featured this language in its brochure and website from at least 2009 until ownership changed in 2017.

to downplay the effects when the resort made the case for more development. Recreational colonialism transfers a false sense of belonging and ownership over stolen Indigenous land simply by operating a business on it. This spatial takeover is reminiscent of the language used at the height of colonial expansion as settlers attempted to justify genocide and Indigenous dispossession of their ancestral territories under the guise of productivity, assuming that they could morally lay claim to land because they would farm it, cultivate it, make productive use out of it in ways Indigenous peoples were not.

Through leisure, landscapes and cultures are commodified in gift shops, coded on maps, and written and rewritten in museums and wilderness supply stores.[23] Generations of discourse connecting the ski resort to the Peaks and to the city of Flagstaff have solidified the idea that the resort *is* the mountain, that the city is a "ski town." Such a synecdoche can only be created over time. As Cara Aitchison, Nicola MacLeod, and Stephen Shaw note, through representations and "(re)representation of the past within the present," the landscape can be transformed "for the purposes of leisure and tourism."[24] Indeed, the social space that the resort takes up, the representations of space, and the lived spaces of representation are far greater than 1 percent. It is a material-discursive interrogation of spaces of outdoor recreation that brings validity to such arguments and makes visible the way some narratives are privileged and accommodated through recreational colonialism.

Promoting Recreational Colonialism

Functioning discursively, recreational colonialism persuades skiers and snowboarders to see the mountain and the material space of the resort in a way that accommodates an inherently pro-development view: if one is pro skiing, they must support the resorts insatiable desire for more development. Time and again this was reiterated in city council meetings by the resort's owners: "If you enjoy skiing, and you want a ski resort, know that the Arizona Snowbowl will disappear without snowmaking." This section, however, uses the resort's historical promotional material to interrogate the way settlers are accommodated at the resort. Phrases pulled from the promotional material of the resort, such as "Do we have a mountain for you!" and "Your year-round playground," provoke inquiry into who they mean by "you." "You" refers to "skiers," but given the pervasiveness of whiteness in outdoor recreation, and

23. A. Wilson, "View from the Road"; and Rothman, *Devil's Bargains.*
24. Aitchison, MacLeod, and Shaw, *Leisure and Tourism Landscapes,* 11.

skiing specifically, those terms are also rhetorically coded as white. A casual observer on an average day at the Arizona Snowbowl Ski Resort would see that not only skiers but also personnel and managers—nearly everybody there—is overwhelmingly white. At the same time, I am mindful of Carolyn Finney's work, which resists dominant narratives that associate whiteness with notions of the environment, which she extends to outdoor recreation.[25] Certainly, my aim is not to reproduce assumptions about racial hegemonies by claiming that people of color don't participate in outdoor recreation like skiing—of course they do. Rather, I'm concerned about the way in which outdoor recreational industries and the discourses that produce and are produced by those industries—and sometimes by participants themselves—cater to, accommodate, and ultimately sustain the supremacist systems on which settler colonialism relies, including white supremacy. And of course, this isn't just an Arizona skiing phenomenon.

The modern ski resort, particularly in the West, is overwhelmingly a white and middle-to-upper-class space. "On a clear day, skiers might see blue sky above and green trees below, or flashes of brightly clad people whizzing by," writes Annie Gilbert Coleman in the first sentence of her article, "The Unbearable Whiteness of Skiing," "but mostly they see white."[26] Finney observes this same phenomenon elsewhere in the outdoors: "In outdoor recreation in our forest and parks . . . African Americans and other non-dominant groups are on the outside looking in."[27] Of course, people of color are not legally excluded from such places—the Arizona Snowbowl would gladly grant access to any paying customer, but such uncritical assertions allow issues of whiteness to remain "unspoken," an "uninterrogated norm, taken for granted, the way a fish takes water for granted."[28] Polite conversation would not label a ski resort as a white space, but that does not change the fact that what it means to belong or not belong is coded in that space. Therefore, it is impossible to talk about whiteness without also talking about privilege. Whiteness isn't just an identity but an imaginary with a privileged status that translates to unearned advantages based on race. "Whiteness theory" therefore "treats whiteness not as a biological category but as a social construction" that grants access and unearned advantages.[29] Longtime antiracist writer and activist Tim Wise elaborates: "To be white in the U.S., whether one is from the South . . . or from the North, West, or Midwest; whether one is rich or poor; whether

25. Finney, *Black Faces, White Spaces*, 2.
26. Coleman, "Unbearable Whiteness of Skiing," 583.
27. Finney, *Black Faces, White Spaces*, 2.
28. Wise and Myers, *White Like Me*, 2–3.
29. Thompson, "Summary of Whiteness Theory."

one is male or female; whether one is Jew or Gentile, straight or gay, is to have certain common experiences based solely upon race: experiences that are about advantage, privilege, and belonging."[30] That people of color are not *legally* excluded from the ski resort does not change the fact that racialized exclusion takes place.

There can be no doubt that skiing is a pastime for the privileged. Leisure scholar Karl Spracklen turned his attention to skiing in his book, *Whiteness and Leisure*: "Skiing is one of the most obvious exclusionary outdoor leisure pursuits. Participants need to have time and money to train to be competent. They need to be able to purchase expensive equipment and [have the time and money to take] holidays."[31] Similarly, Tim Edensor and Sophia Richards have noted that skiing is often characterized through an "elitist, exclusionary identity."[32] Here, whiteness can be obscured through its "limited participation to an affluent elite," though it is embedded in these characterizations. Despite its association with and "origins in youth, urban, counter-hegemonic subcultures," today snowboarders must "have money, time, and access," or in other words, privilege.[33] Illuminating the racial or class privileges associated with skiing—or linking the history of skiing in the West to whiteness as Coleman and others do—is simply another way to express the fact that "being white only means to be advantaged."[34] By pointing out that US "American ski culture continues to exist as an increasingly wealthy culture exclusive of minorities," Coleman demonstrates the profound ways in which the ski resort produces spaces of and for whiteness and, in turn, how whiteness produces the ski resort.[35]

One of these ways is through the cartoonish visual rhetoric of the ski map. Broadly speaking, Senda-Cook observes how maps "relay not only information but also a way of seeing,"[36] ways of understanding that produce ways of being through the function of symbols. As such, the map, according to Ben Barton and Marthalee Barton, is "quintessentially ideological," and "the visual signification serves to sustain relations of domination. . . . It privileges or legitimates certain meaning systems but at the same time dissimulates the fact of such privileging."[37] The ski map isn't the Peaks but a symbolic representation

30. Wise and Myers, *White Like Me*, 3.
31. Spracklen, *Whiteness and Leisure*, 182.
32. Edensor and Richards, "Snowboarders vs Skiers," 183.
33. Spracklen, *Whiteness and Leisure*, 182, 183.
34. Wise and Myers, *White Like Me*, 145.
35. Coleman, "Unbearable Whiteness of Skiing," 605.
36. Senda-Cook, "Materializing Tensions," 358.
37. Grabham, "'Flagging' the Skin," 50.

of the Peaks, the idea of a mountain divorced from any cultural context, history, or geography. The cartoon map of the Peaks is not radically different from that of any other ski resort on any other mountain in the West. In this way, the map and its aesthetics functions as a kind of flag, signaling to recreationalists a particular way of understanding the physical landscape, a space undisputedly *for* recreation, all of which feeds into and sustains settler belongings in contested landscapes.

Through the decades, each version of the Arizona Snowbowl ski map has further functioned to flag belongings. For Emily Grabham, "flagging" is a way to signal racial hegemonies, in this case through the visual representation of the resort. Because of the historic link between whiteness and skiing, "the resort" is a symbolic representation of white space. Following Grabham, this "flag" fosters a sense of belonging that both produces and regulates subjects. Grabham notes, "Belonging connects here to feelings of comfort, security, alikeness, acceptance and freedom to be oneself."[38] Shifting the focus from the most recent ski map to the history of promotional material, one can easily see the legacy of exclusion at work. For this kind of analysis, Foucault's notion of the "unsaid" becomes infinitely more revealing than what is said. At those sites of inclusion, therefore, the nuanced ways in which exclusion occurs can more easily be interrogated. The cartoonish map, in addition to the 1 percent claim and Snowbowl's promotion of itself as one of the country's oldest resorts, further functions through what Amanda Murphyao and Kelly Black refer to as "property regimes," which ultimately reflect settler anxiety in their attempts to naturalize settler presence on land that is not theirs. "This proprietary approach" to Indigenous lands "(re)inscribes settler belonging while concealing ongoing (dis)possession."[39]

Every person featured in every piece of promotional material from Snowbowl, dating back to the 1940s, is visibly white. While this fact provides further illustrative evidence linking skiing to whiteness generally, its function is even more profound in the context of recreational colonialism. In the white space of the Arizona Snowbowl, the phrase, "do we have a mountain for you!" or more recently, "Your year-round playground," implies a specific kind of "you."[40] Such representations indicate an intended audience but also articulate exclusion. "You," in the context of Snowbowl's intended audience, as evidenced by who is included—not just statistically but visually represented—on the resort's own promotional material, is not a person of color, not queer, and likely not financially privileged. This exclusion, based on what identities are

---

38. Grabham, 65, 66.
39. Murphyao and Black, "Unsettling Settler Belonging," 318.
40. Snowbowl Vertical Files.

prominently featured in the material, allows for white skiers to see both themselves and the resort transposed on many different mountains in the West. "Belongings," according to Grabham, "might have cultural force, linking an individual or a group of people to a geographically defined area," like a ski resort in Arizona, but also those in Colorado, Utah, California, or elsewhere.[41]

Recreational colonialism mobilizes outdoor recreational discourses to create settler spaces on physical landscapes that are historically Indigenous. As Dina Gilio-Whitaker observes in a chapter on appropriation and Indigenous surf culture, "In the context of settler colonialism, appropriation is always about the continual remaking of indigenous space into settler space, at both material and discursive levels of culture and politics."[42] Recreational colonialism is an articulation of the processes by which settler appropriation occurs on stolen Indigenous land in the context of outdoor recreation. As I interrogate in the next section, appropriation has many forms: outdoor recreational discourses like those found in the promotional material of the Arizona Snowbowl demonstrate how outdoor recreationalists appropriate not just land but Indigeneity, and Indigenous ways of knowing, and what follows is the trivialization of actual Indigenous peoples and cultures.

Settler Memory

While the Arizona Snowbowl Ski Resort is overwhelmingly a white space, those spaces still heavily rely on an often-unarticulated connection to and relationship with Indigeneity, what Philip Deloria refers to as "Indianness."[43] In settler societies, identity is inextricably linked in opposition to—and therefore also dependent on—Indigenous peoples. Scott Morgensen reiterates this association as interrelationships in the first sentence of his book *Spaces between Us: Queer Settler Colonialism and Indigenous Decolonization*: "We are caught up in one another, we who live in settler societies, and our interrelationships inform all that these societies touch."[44] Deloria describes how the image of Indigenous peoples of the historic past has been performed by white people who have "played Indian," either by dressing up as a generic idea of what it means to be "Indian," or through the rituals, customs, and cosmology co-opted by white-led, white-organized, and white-attended summer camps.[45]

41. Grabham, "'Flagging' the Skin," 66.
42. Gilio-Whitaker, "Appropriating Surfing," 228.
43. P. Deloria, *Playing Indian*.
44. Morgensen, *Spaces between Us*, 1.
45. P. Deloria, *Playing Indian*.

Leah Dilworth examines how reverence for Indigenous peoples and cultures is expressed by upper-class white people through the consumptive fetishization of Indigenous arts and jewelry, drawing rhetorical power through what Robert Berkhofer describes as the "White image of the Indian."[46] The shallow construction of this reverence is called into question when actual living and breathing Indigenous peoples are often met with distain when they speak out against injustices.[47] Former Navajo Nation tribal chairman Peter MacDonald best sums up this relationship. In 1974, in a hearing with Summit Properties, a company that sought to develop the San Francisco Peaks into a resort community called Snowbowl Village, he said, "if you wear your feather, make Kachina dolls, weave rugs and pose for tourists, you are a good Indian, but if you exercise your rights as a citizen, you are a bad Indian."[48] This coheres to a more contemporary statement made by Klee Benally regarding his relationship to the city in 2016. "It seems like, in Flagstaff, sometimes our culture . . . is only accepted if it is a commodity, if it's on a shelf, in a book, behind glass. But we're here," he said. "Our voices matter. Our cultures matter. Our ways of life matter."[49] This relationship has been theorized by Kevin Bruyneel as "a process of remembering and disavowing," which he calls "settler memory":

> The way in which a settler society habitually reproduces memories of Indigenous people's history and of settler colonial violence and dispossession and in the same moment undercuts the political relevance of this memory by disavowing the presence of Indigenous people as contemporary agents and of settler colonialism as a persistent shaping force.[50]

The work of settler memory is found in many different examples across the culture and landscape, from Indigenous place-names, trail and state names, to Indigenous sports teams and mascots, consumer products, literature, and more. According to Bruyneel, in all of these examples, the work of settler memory refers to "a process of remembering and disavowing Indigenous political agency, colonialist dispossession, and violence toward Indigenous Peoples." Setter memory, in all its forms, works as a "shaping force on the story of the nation that calls itself America."[51] Recognizing the ways settler

---

46. Dilworth, *Imagining Indians*; and Berkhofer, *White Man's Indian,* xiv.
47. Sanchez, Stuckey, and Morris, "Rhetorical Exclusion."
48. Coconino County Planning and Zoning Commission, "In the Public Hearing Reference."
49. Benally quoted in Boggs, "Replacing Columbus Day."
50. Bruyneel, *Settler Memory,* xiii.
51. Bruyneel, xiii.

memory is at work in outdoor recreation helps us understand how tightly the activities we enjoy and the landscapes in which we engage are bound up in colonial relationships.

Annie Coleman's historical research on white ski culture in the West recalls a particularly dry winter in the northern Rockies in 1963, when a ski resort brought in some Ute tribal members to perform a "snow dance." The tribe agreed to perform a rain dance and let it be referred to by the white skiers and marketed by the resort personnel as a "snow dance."[52] Because "it worked," and it soon snowed two feet, the Ute dancers found themselves as a tourist attraction, their ceremonial traditions co-opted to benefit the resort. This contradictory relationship also expressed itself during this time period on the San Francisco Peaks. There are many examples that point to the ways the Arizona Snowbowl Ski Resort has used Indigenous place-names, ideas of sacredness, and even iconography—such as the Hopi Kachina—in order to promote the resort. For example, in a brochure from the 1960s, within the same section that Snowbowl promotes local tourist attractions such as the Grand Canyon, Lake Powell, and Meteor Crater, the resort also directs tourists to the accessibility of "the Hopi Mesa Villages, and Navajo-Land." Turn the page in this same brochure, and in full color, a skier is posing alongside a human-sized wooden cutout of a Hopi Kachina (figure 5.1).[53]

In that same brochure, the Kachina—a Hopi deity that brings snow—is further co-opted as part of the Snowbowl logo, portrayed as a skier (figure 5.2). Similarly, a 1950s version of the Skyride brochure reads, "The Arizona Snow Bowl is on 12,200-foot Mt. Agassiz, second highest peak in Arizona, part of the San Francisco Peaks. The Peaks are the base of an extinct 26,000 foot volcano," and then after an em dash, appearing almost as an afterthought, "—A sacred mountain to the Navajos and legendary home of the Kachinas."[54]

Racializing Indigenous peoples is also central to the settler colonial project. All of these visual and textual examples suggest some of the ways that Snowbowl has historically cashed in on the aesthetic appeal of Indigenous culture, an appeal propagated and controlled by and for a settler audience. This is what recreational colonialism looks like at its most egregious in spaces of outdoor recreation. The caricatures of Indigenous peoples in the historic Snowbowl brochures appear in an era not far removed from a time in Flagstaff when some business owners were said to have posted signs that read "No Dogs or Indians Allowed."[55] In Flagstaff today, Indigenous peoples face extreme

52. Coleman, "Unbearable Whiteness of Skiing," 583.
53. Snowbowl Vertical Files.
54. Snowbowl Vertical Files.
55. For "No Dogs or Indians Allowed" quote, see Boggs, "Replacing Columbus Day."

FIGURE 5.1. This image of a Hopi Kachina was featured in the pages of an Arizona Snowbowl brochure from the 1960s. Northern Arizona University Special Collections and Archives.

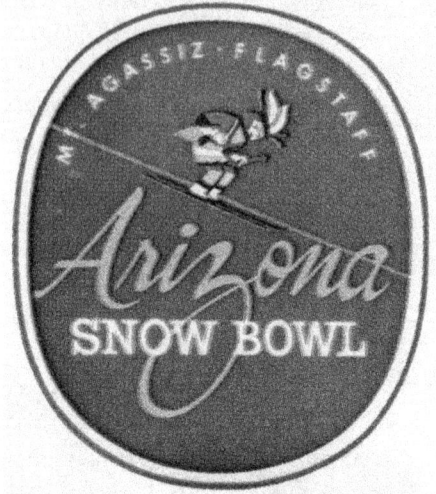

FIGURE 5.2. In this same brochure from the 1960s, a Hopi Kachina is depicted in the resort's logo as a skier. Northern Arizona University Special Collections and Archives.

racial profiling; they make up less than 11 percent of the population but make up the majority of arrests. The wooden cutout of the Kachina, the Snowbowl logo featuring a cartoon skiing Kachina, as well as some of the other racial markers discussed in this chapter recall what Elizabeth Abel refers to as the "enigmatic signs" of visual markers of race. They are "enigmatic" because they are subtle within the context they are deployed, which makes it is easy for them to go unexamined and become part of harmful racialized hegemonies.[56] In the case of the Kachina, this hegemony results in co-optation and trivialization of Indigenous culture, which has significant impacts for Indigenous peoples, who face unique challenges as they seek self-determination on their own terms amid a settler society. But its exploitative capitalist legacy should put the resort's anti-Indigenous racism into focus: past owners of the resort literally made money from co-opting Hopi spiritual deities, and that profit was absorbed each subsequent time the resort was bought and sold, bringing us to the present, where it is used to implement projects that the Hopi oppose and claim desecrate a holy place where those deities are believed to live.

The trivialization of Indigenous culture and spirituality is dramatically displayed in the use of the Kachina as a decoration, or a cartoon, or a mascot.

56. Abel, *Signs of the Times.*

The Kachina becomes an accoutrement to the skier's experience of the mythic West, at the expense of Indigenous dignity, culture, and spirituality. As Hal Rothman, Philip Deloria, and others have demonstrated, the view of nature held by settlers in the West includes mountains, canyons, great expanses of undeveloped land, and specific representations and ideas of Indigenous peoples. At the same time, the cartoonish caricature of the Hopi Kachina— Indigenous culture trivialized and co-opted by white supremacist capitalism— reduces any potential for cultural understanding. All forms of representation must be accompanied by questions that extrapolate *how* Indigenous peoples and their cultures and landscapes are represented, and to what effect.

The Kachina cutout reinforces settler hegemony in a way not radically different from the view of Indigenous peoples in the Southwest as famously promoted by the Fred Harvey Company, which set up restaurants, hotels, and other tourist destinations alongside the railroad in the late nineteenth century. According to the Fred Harvey Company ethos, reproduced in classic Western films and elsewhere, in settler societies, Indigenous peoples are exoticized as closer to and therefore part of the landscape; they are stoic, they create art, they share stories.[57] There is great disdain for Indigenous peoples in settler societies who do not live up to that caricature. During the most heated moments during the controversy over development on the San Francisco Peaks, this disdain was clear.[58] While comment sections in newspapers and public comments in city council meetings and other venues do not typically offer productive examples on their own, they do begin to narrate a story when patterns emerge. The pattern that emerges here tells a story of unapologetic anti-Indigenous racism that dismisses intergenerational settler colonial trauma. It doubles down on commitments to the colonial project by claiming Indigenous peoples should have no say on what happens on federally controlled land, described by settlers as "our" land, "public land." The story demonstrates that settlers are willing to come up with the wildest and most absurd ways to dismiss Indigenous dissent when it threatens their entitlement to stolen Indigenous lands.

As unproductive as these vitriolic comments are, again, they offer a window into what Indigenous peoples, especially in a so-called border town like

---

57. Howard and Pardue, *Inventing the Southwest*; Mullin, *Culture in the Marketplace*; and May, "'Little Taste.'"

58. In earlier drafts of this chapter, I included several quotes from the comment section from the *Arizona Daily Sun* to illustrate this point for those who might want my "evidence" of widespread and rampant anti-Indigenous racism, but I don't think it's productive to highlight those quotes in this way. The racism is so bad that in 2015, CBC, one of the biggest news outlets in Canada, completely cut comments out on any story involving Indigenous peoples. Given what I read during this time, however, I personally have no reason to believe the *Arizona Daily Sun* moderated these comments at all. See CBC News, "CBC Closing Comments."

Flagstaff, experience every day, and analyzing the language produced by settler colonial contexts can highlight settler efforts to manage and control discourses about Indigenous peoples; when Indigenous peoples challenge those
constraints, they are mocked or met with verbal, even physical assault.[59]

Promoting False Equivalencies

Recreational colonialism creates distance between outdoor recreational practices and the settler colonial contexts in which they occur on stolen Indigenous land. Removed from their nuanced Indigenous contexts, landscapes are
reframed and rearticulated in promotional material through their relationship
to settlers, through heroic mining or pioneer narratives, but also in ways that
privilege other forms of settler orientations. This chapter has already touched
on some of these ways, such as Snowbowl's promotional phrase "your playground," which trivializes Indigenous cultural connections and even obscures
more nuanced settler connections to the Peaks. Additionally, in promotions
for the Skyride (a ski lift that carries visitors up the Peaks during off seasons
to take in the views or hike), the phrase "ride the volcano" appears on several brochures for the resort throughout the 1980s, 1990s, and into the first
decade of the second millennium. The 2014–15 brochure highlights, "'The
Peaks,' as the remains of an eroded, extinct 'stratovolcano' that was formed
between 500,000 and 1,000,000 years ago."[60] This sentiment is then followed
by "Snowbowl mountain facts," the rhetoric of which again suggests that the
resort *is* the mountain, but the "facts" themselves—a hodgepodge of elevation
data, skiable acres, and the number of runs—together with the promotion of
the mountain as a volcano, highlight a particular way of perceiving and representing the mountain. Through this perception of the mountain, which puts
geological and otherwise quantifiable data at the forefront, recreational colonialism effectively devalues other potential ways of seeing, experiencing, and
engaging with the mountain.

The apolitical "fun" articulated in outdoor recreational discourses, captured in the promotional material for the resort, renders any comparison
between that fun and colonialism as unfounded. To put it another way, when
those who oppose the development of Snowbowl yell, "No Desecration for
Recreation!" two seemingly incomparable ideas are juxtaposed: those conjured

---

59. See Indigenous Environmental Network, "Court Rules."
60. Snowbowl Vertical Files.

by notions of religious desecration and associations of fun, healthy exercise, and being in nature. This disconnect, however, is carefully exploited as a practice of recreational colonialism, one that ensures that control over stolen Indigenous land is not questioned, that any connection between recreation and settler colonialism is simply made unintelligible. When it is questioned, this framing elicits shock and often intense defensiveness at the suggestion that recreational activities have anything to do with colonialism. The shielding this provides against critique is yet another rhetorical effect of what Tuck and Yang have theorized in terms of "settler moves to innocence." In this case the preservation of innocence sustains and accommodates positions that are inherently pro-development regardless of Indigenous peoples' challenges. This is achieved in many subtle ways throughout the resort's history of promotional material. Nearly all Snowbowl's brochures highlight how the resort accommodates "families," situate the resort as part of "family vacations," and emphasize ski instruction for children. After the most recent round of developments, the 2014–15 ski map also features a "kid's adventure area."[61] All of these details paint a picture for settlers that is far removed from anything remotely recognizable as "desecration."

Recreational colonialism creates false equivalencies between the importance of recreational needs and Indigenous cultural connections to place. For example, the 1982–83 brochure describes the Arizona Snowbowl as situated within access to a number of other popular tourist destinations: "Northern Arizona stretches out beneath the chairlift all the way to the glittering international casinos of Las Vegas, breathtaking Grand Canyon," within driving distance of "the glittering international casinos of Las Vegas, breathtaking Grand Canyon," Lake Powell, as well as the "Hopi Mesas" and "Navajo-Land."[62] Within this framework, outdoor recreation (skiing) is couched within a number of other sites as if, somehow, they were all the same, as if ancient villages and ancestral lands are just another attraction, no more or less significant than gambling or a dip in a man-made reservoir.[63] This situation recalls a different version of the adage "if you have a hammer, everything looks like a nail" that is important to the promotion of recreational colonialism: if the purpose of language is to appeal to tourists, then everything is a potential tourist destination.

---

61. Snowbowl Vertical Files. Arizona Snowbowl Promotional Brochure, Winter 2014–15, 6.

62. Snowbowl Vertical Files.

63. It's worth noting as well that the outdoor recreation created by Lake Powell, a reservoir formed when Glen Canyon was dammed, comes at the expense of countless ancient Indigenous cultural sites, now drowned.

Indigenous Erasure

The settler aesthetics that recreational colonialism relies on often reinforces the idea that Indigenous peoples do not exist today,[64] a trend that continues, though more subtly, in the promotional brochures closer to the present day. In a section titled "Plan Your Trip" in the Arizona Snowbowl brochures for 2014–15,

> the cultural heritage of Flagstaff reflects centuries of Native American history. To learn more about diverse Indigenous cultures in the surrounding areas, visit the Museum of Northern Arizona, Wupatki, and Walnut Canyon National Monuments, all located just minutes away from the downtown.[65]

The excerpt suggests at least two points of inquiry worth examining: that the way to learn about Indigenous culture is by visiting museums and ruins, both of which are federally operated sites. But important Indigenous cultural sites like those at Wupatki and in the cliff dwelling sites of Walnut Canyon offer tourists little if any perspective on the present-day lived experience of regional Indigenous peoples and cater to a view of Indigenous peoples and cultures as only existing in the past. And both sites, as national monuments, are controlled by the US Forest Service, so the message tourists get is not only that Indigenous peoples do not exist as contemporary peoples but also that their stories are best told by settler governments and institutions.

The global story of settler colonialism follows a similar path as "extinction narratives colluded with stadial theories of human development to locate Indigenous peoples in other times, or out of time, in ways that legitimized and naturalised spatial displacements."[66] While museums have made great strides in the last several decades on the part of museums to be more inclusive, often collaborating with Indigenous peoples instead of presenting their culture and history through the narrow lens of anthropology and ethnology—where the ubiquitous white curator controls all—museums can be "very painful sites for

---

64. See Krawec and Estes's "Replacement" and "Eradication," in *Becoming Kin: An Indigenous Call to Unforgetting the Past and Reimagining Our Future,* for a better understanding of this wider belief and the implications of this myth.

65. Arizona Snowbowl, Promotional Brochure, Winter 2014–15, 6.

66. Mar and Edmonds, *Making Settler Colonial Space,* 3. As Mar and Edmonds make clear in a footnote, stadial theory was popularized by Adam Smith as a way of making sense of human progress in successive hierarchical stages, from hunters, pastoralists, and agriculturalists to commerce. This logic not only tied Indigenous peoples to the past but naturalized white European dominance.

Native people, as they are intimately tied to the colonization process."[67] Tra-ditionally, museums have been a place where cultural objects became valued because of the perception that they were "either already or soon to be scarce."[68] Emphasis on preserving cultural objects in this way extends easily to support the myth that Indigenous peoples themselves are becoming scarce. Therefore, the role of museums in perpetuating the myth that Indigenous peoples do not exist anymore lies at the heart of the colonization process. That the Arizona Snowbowl would even put this information in its brochures highlights how useful Indigenous erasure is for the resort.

Snowbowl's production of Indigenous erasure is further illustrated con-temporarily by a popular bumper sticker promoted during the 2006 lawsuit *Navajo Nation v. United States Forest Service.* The Navajo Nation, together with seven other tribes and three environmental groups, sued the US Forest Ser-vice over its decision to allow the Arizona Snowbowl to make snow artificially with reclaimed wastewater, citing that the move would detriment Indigenous rights to meaningfully practice their religion. To counter the "Save the Peaks" bumper stickers all over northern Arizona, the resort came up with one of its own: "Reclaim the Peaks." The sticker has a double meaning: it promotes the use of reclaimed wastewater to make snow on the one hand, but on the other it implies that the Peaks must be "reclaimed" from Indigenous peoples, a rhetorical reenactment of Indigenous dispossession from their own ancestral lands in the context of outdoor recreation. Recreational colonialism is power-ful in the way it functions to trivialize the ongoing colonial processes of con-quest perpetrated by settlers against Indigenous peoples, but as a function of settler colonialism, it also denies the lived experiences of Indigenous peoples in northern Arizona today.

When Mountain Capital Partners, the biggest ski resort chain in the Southwest, bought the Arizona Snowbowl in 2016, the company soon filed a new master development plan that included new lifts and ski runs, build-ing additions, and infrastructure to support night skiing and summer activi-ties, like mountain biking and a zipline.[69] The web page announcing these plans ends with frequently asks questions, which have been edited over the years. Initial versions included the question, "Does Snowbowl have a strat-egy for improving tribal relations?" While that question, or any mention of tribal relations at all, has been scrubbed from the site, I grabbed a screen-shot, so from here you'll have to trust me. The answer contained four bullet points; the first two were not answers but arguably false statements presented

67. Lonetree, *Decolonizing Museums,* 1.
68. Dilworth, *Imagining Indians,* 128.
69. Arizona Snowbowl, "Next Chapter."

objectively: "prior to legal action challenging snowmaking in recent years," the resort and local tribes "enjoyed a positive relationship," and "Snowbowl continues efforts to restore" those relationships. Other than a point about providing employment opportunities to tribal members, the resort's main answer to this question centered on a plan to work with tribal communities to "tell the story of the cultural significance of the landscape." "Woven into each recreational offering will be an interpretive narrative" that, among geological and biological information about the area, "communicates the immense spiritual power of the mountain." These collaborative narrations were not only going to include "interpretive signage" but would be integrated into "the fit and finish of materials, and the naming and messaging associated with the recreational amenities."

While the question and the resort's answer no longer appear on Snowbowl's website, and presumably are no longer part of the company's vision for the resort, it's amazing that they ever believed this was a good answer to the question of how to improve tribal relations. The plans mirror much of my analysis in the first two chapters of this book: settler entitlement to Indigenous knowledge and the appropriation of Indigenous aesthetics to sell the resort, which includes marketing tactics designed to construct belongings and authenticity on stolen land. Inasmuch as there is a difference this time, the company did pledge to consult Indigenous peoples in doing so. But what would even be Snowbowl's process for that? Did the owners really think that if they found a few people willing to participate in their own exploitation, maybe add a few Kokopellis to the designs, that everyone else would call it good? Even though these ideas—lofty as they were—were apparently scrapped, they reveal an utter lack of imagination or will to do anything differently than previous generations of Snowbowl ownership had done. This is a resort that has done nothing but demolish "tribal relations" for a generation, and its first response to an important question regarding reconciliation was to list several things that only benefit the resort and do nothing for Indigenous peoples. Nowhere does the site even acknowledge the harm the resort has caused. While relationships with this resort and regional Indigenous peoples are perhaps irreconcilable, there is a cautionary tale here for others across the outdoor recreational landscape.

PART 2

"PROTECT THE PEAKS" AND RESISTING RECREATIONAL COLONIALISM

CHAPTER 6

"No Desecration for Recreation!
Save the Peaks!"

An elderly woman who identified herself as Diné but wished not to disclose her name approached the microphone slowly, clutching the arm of a man who steadied her steps. As she pulled the microphone down to meet the reach of her voice, the reverberation of her silver rings against the metal of the microphone echoed throughout the chambers; all eyes were on her.

She paused before she spoke, mumbled something indecipherable, and paused again. Members of the city council glanced back and forth at each other before one told the woman that her words would be translated if she wished. And it wasn't until she spoke about Dook'o'oosłííd, or the San Francisco Peaks, in her own language, that she started to cry.

She went on well past her allotted time limit, speaking about sacredness, about desecration, about how the creator had entrusted the mountain to her people and in return how the mountain had looked after her. She spoke of shrines on the Peaks, ceremonial plants, and medicinal herbs. She told the people present that day about how generations of her clan had buried the umbilical cords of newborn babies beneath the soil of the Peaks in a specified location she did not wish to disclose. "To me, to us, that mountain," she pointed to the north side of the room, "is alive just like me or you."

Many other Indigenous peoples, community leaders, and environmental activists, as well as those who are pro-development, made public comments also. When the skiers, snowboarders, and Arizona Snowbowl Ski Resort personnel spoke up in favor of the expansion, one at a time, their messages were clear: "What is the big deal?" "It's skiing; it's all about having fun." "Why are you trying to ruin people's fun?"[1]

I witnessed the exchange recounted above at a Flagstaff City Council meeting in 2005, and other than some previous casual conversations and observations, it was really my first introduction to the controversy that would come to define the next decade of my journalism. Three years before this event, in 2002, the city entered into a contract with the Arizona Snowbowl Ski Resort to sell 1.5 million gallons of reclaimed wastewater per day to the resort during the winter months so they could make artificial snow, ensuring more consistent and profitable ski seasons. In 2004 the Coconino National Forest released its draft environmental impact study for public comments—in the months that followed, they received nearly ten thousand comments, overwhelmingly against the developments, with particular attention paid to the use of reclaimed wastewater to make snow. Given the backlash against the city's deal with the resort and the number of negative comments on the draft, the city's contract with the resort apparently made it back to the agenda that evening. I had just recently moved to Flagstaff, I ran a blog, I had just started a graduate program, and I aspired to do freelance journalism. It was an evening that quite honestly changed my life.

The pro-development skier and snowboarder reactions to the Diné woman indicate more than the obvious and complex contrasts between Western and Indigenous views of nature. Indeed, indicative of generations of Indigenous resistance since the late 1960s, the controversy over development by a ski resort on the San Francisco Peaks speaks to the notion that the land is regarded in different and often contested ways. The long-standing controversy over the San Francisco Peaks highlights "the power that institutional entities possess over indigenous people."[2] It also underscores the powerful role that outdoor recreation plays as part of an ongoing production of settler colonial entitlement to traditional Indigenous lands.

There are elements of this moment I saw play out over and over again in the years to come, at other meetings with the city council, the water commission, and planning and zoning boards, but also in Forest Service "listening sessions" for which Havasupai elders traveled the hard road out of Cataract Canyon, an offshoot of the Grand Canyon, to go on record against the resort's developments. Other Indigenous peoples from the Colorado Plateau to the US-Mexico border joined them. Pro-development skiers and snowboarders

---

1. This excerpt also appears in Boggs, "Material-Discursive Spaces," 184.
2. Bauer, "Protecting Indigenous Spiritual Values," 343.

showed up as well, each group prepared to engage in extremely different conversations that boiled down to religious and cultural survival versus the mostly white kids and their parents who just wanted to have "more fun." For me, the disconnect was both fascinating and absurd. For so many Indigenous folks, it was clearly a matter of life and death. As a community writer, I was not only drawn to the complexity but also motivated by the challenge to communicate this complexity to a regional audience.

In this chapter, I revisit a historic moment in the controversy over Snowbowl's development on the Peaks, punctuated by four court cases beginning in 2006 and ending in 2014. This period ends with the courts' siding with the ski resort and the Forest Service, as snowmaking infrastructure was eventually installed despite unwavering Indigenous opposition and over a decade of fierce, creative, and collaborative resistance to those developments. While much of that resistance is detailed in chapter 7, here I focus on the structural challenges imposed by state, corporate, and legal entities, often working together to limit the influence of Indigenous peoples and dilute the power of their arguments in matters of land-use decisions. This distillation of power dynamics working against Indigenous peoples points to a story that is, of course, older than the United States itself, but its unfolding in the context of outdoor recreation often goes unrecognized. What follows are the exhaustive ways in which Indigenous peoples have tried to "work within the system" to resist development on the Peaks. From closed-door government and corporate collaborations consolidating power and the forced compartmentalization of legal arguments to the grift of "public participation" processes, this chapter considers the variety of ways rhetorical exclusions occur. In the end, each moment in this story reveals itself as yet another strategy deployed to ignore what Indigenous peoples have been consistent and clear about for decades and—if we're really listening—since the beginning of time: that the Peaks are sacred, and their ecological integrity is indispensable to cultural and spiritual survival. "No desecration for recreation!" points to the profoundly absurd, if not condescending framings Indigenous peoples are forced into in these circumstances, made to defend the very essence of who they are against those who just want to "have fun"—within a system that treats these two positions as somehow fundamentally equal when they are not.

Rhetorical Exclusion

Recognizing "the outdoors" as a discourse—where physical space is implicated by language, history, and culture as well as material reality—allows for an understanding of how privilege and oppression are constructed in the

arrangements of those spaces. This process has been termed rhetorical exclusion, one of the many communicative tactics "designed to foreclose debate
without appearing to engage in undemocratic action," and "a strategy used
by members of the prevailing power structure to conceal any antidemocratic
consequences of its actions."[3] Much of the scholarship on rhetorical exclusion points to the nuanced ways in which it occurs through the language of
governmental policy and procedures, whereby Indigenous peoples' voices are
excluded from deliberation. Prominent works in this area have included studies of the American Indian Movement of the 1960s and 1970s and of Indigenous peoples rejection to proposals to store nuclear waste at Yucca Mountain
in Nevada.[4] Many of the ways Indigenous voices were systematically excluded
from public deliberation over development on the San Francisco Peaks mirror
those that were analyzed in these previous studies, including exclusion from
the public participation process and development of environmental impact
statements.[5] While much of the scholarship on rhetorical exclusion interrogates government procedures, like the environmental impact statement draft-
ing process, as mere democratic performance, there are even more subtle ways
in which rhetorical exclusion is at work in the controversy over development
on the San Francisco Peaks, particularly in the spatial arrangements that foreground the terms of the debate.

In the controversy over development on the San Francisco Peaks, Indigenous peoples have little say or influence in decision-making processes because
the Peaks lie on federally owned land rather than reservation land. This is
an example of the material-discursive arrangement of space functioning as a
"strategic silence," or a type of rhetorical exclusion including practices meant
to "continue silencing an already silenced group."[6] As John Sanchez, Mary
Stuckey, and Richard Morris have argued, "rhetorical exclusionists are unable
to see outside of their frames, unable to question their ideological predispositions"; therefore, the way those boundaries were defined, the history of colonial violence that resulted in the delineation of reservation land from federally
owned land, is systematically erased from acceptable deliberation over land-
use policy.[7] Indigenous opposition to development on the Peaks is not just
resistance to development but also a rejection of these frames. As Hopi Tribal
Chairman LeRoy Shingoitewa remarked in 2010, "It is our duty to protect

---

3. Sanchez, Stuckey, and Morris, "Rhetorical Exclusion," 27–30.
4. Sanchez, Stuckey, and Morris; and Endres, "Rhetoric of Nuclear Colonialism."
5. Killingsworth and Palmer, *Ecospeak*, 166.
6. Endres, "Rhetoric of Nuclear Colonialism," 52.
7. Sanchez, Stuckey, and Morris, "Rhetorical Exclusion," 28.

what has been given to us by the creator long before Flagstaff even existed."[8] The Peaks lie on Forest Service land, which is partitioned into districts; the resort itself lies within the Kachina Peaks Wilderness Area. While these designations legally silence Indigenous peoples' contentions to land-use policy, statements like Shingoitewa's serve as a reminder that all decision-making bodies—the resort, the Forest Service, and the City of Flagstaff—make their claim and authority on stolen Indigenous land.

Resisting Frames

At least thirteen tribes, spanning from the four corners region of the Southwest to the US-Mexico border, hold the Peaks sacred in different ways. The details as to why are varied and complex, and they reflect how the Peaks are woven into creation stories, songs, and ceremonies; mark the boundaries of ancestral homelands; are home to deities, shrines, and burial sites; are a place where medicinal herbs and plants are cultivated; and more. For each tribe, as I learned, the Peaks mean something different, but all too often reference to "the tribes" was deployed to actively dismiss this diversity of connection. This is reflected more broadly in settler culture, including outdoor recreational cultures, which often refer to "the Native Americans" as a kind of monolith. This framing works to trivialize the profound nuance that exists within the hundreds of distinct and diverse Indigenous cultures on this continent.

In 2014 the principal owner of the resort at the time—Eric Borowsky—told me that I had been unfair to the resort in my coverage and that I was the "only one listening to the activists anymore."[9] He told me on the phone, "You think a handful of activists are more important than 300,000 citizens of Arizona [who go to Snowbowl annually]? The activists have cost the tribes a lot of good will and created a lot of unnecessary disruption for the city, for the tribes, and for the Snowbowl."[10] Borowsky's distortion, mostly accommodated by mainstream media accounts, would have the public believe that a mere "handful of activists" who are out of sync with their communities are just trying to cause disruption to get attention. Major media outlets and government officials also took up Borowsky's language when referring to "the tribes," affectively distilling the nuanced cultural connections of thirteen tribes into a

---

8. Flagstaff Planning and Zoning Commission meeting, July 29, 2010, Sinagua High School auditorium, Flagstaff. These quotes come from my personal recording of this meeting. To my knowledge, no official transcript was recorded with the City of Flagstaff.

9. Boggs, "Borowksy," 11.

10. Boggs, 11.

single position. This framing served the interests of Snowbowl by simplifying the diversity of objections expressed by members of individual tribes.

"The tribes" rhetoric works toward an ongoing process of erasure. A "handful of activists" further obscures the way in which Indigenous activists against Snowbowl are part of the larger story of resistance to settler colonialism that continues today in northern Arizona and around the world. While Indigenous communities, not just "activists" but tribal leaders, elders, and other members of these communities, were diverse in their articulations of cultural and spiritual survival, others—Indigenous peoples and settlers—focused on the local environment as well. These concerns ranged from conservation to preservation to ecological ones, including red flags raised in local studies on hydrology, toxicology, and biology over the use of reclaimed wastewater and the idea of dedicating scarce water resources in this way.

Borowsky's hand-waving dismissal of these diverse perspectives as a "handful of activists" is neither honest nor accurate. Scores of tribes were consistent and unified in their opposition to the resort's expansions, specifically the use of municipal reclaimed wastewater to make snow. While thirteen regional tribes hold the Peaks sacred, many took legal action alongside social justice and environmental organizations. In 2006 the Navajo Nation, together with the Hopi Tribe, the Havasupai Tribe, the Hualapai Tribe, the Yavapai-Apache Nation, the White Mountain Apache Nation, the Sierra Club, the Center for Biological Diversity, Flagstaff Activist Network (a now defunct coalition of several Flagstaff area environmental and social justice groups), and individual tribal members from Hopi, Navajo Nation, and Havasupai tribes sued the US Forest Service over its decision to approve the resort's expansions.[11] The Hopi Tribe also brought two separate lawsuits, one against the Forest Service[12] and another against the City of Flagstaff.[13] In 2009 the Save the Peaks Coalition, together with nine concerned citizens, sued the Forest Service in another lawsuit citing the unexplored human health concerns of using reclaimed municipal wastewater for snowmaking.[14]

Opposition was also expressed in widespread appeals outside of court cases, regionally and internationally. According to a 2010 letter to the City of Flagstaff, the Inter Tribal Council of Arizona (ITCA)—representing twenty different tribes—said, "We are reaffirming our opposition to the expansion of the Arizona Snowbowl and reaffirming our opposition to any actions

---

11. *Navajo Nation et al. v. USFS*, 2006.
12. *Hopi Tribe v. USFS*.
13. *Hopi Tribe v. City of Flagstaff*.
14. Save the Peaks Coalition, "U.S. Government Ignores."

that would further desecrate the San Francisco Peaks."[15] That same year, the Navajo Nation's former president Dr. Joe Shirley Jr. similarly stated, "Navajos are united in their opposition to the use of any water source to make artificial snow for the purpose of skiing."[16] In 2011 the International Indian Treaty Council wrote to the United Nations Convention on the Elimination of all forms of Racial Discrimination, referring to the situation, including what it described as "violent reaction of police against peaceful protesters," as an "urgent and important human rights issue."[17] The Navajo Nation Human Rights Commission told the United Nations special rapporteur on the rights of Indigenous peoples that "the United States frequently allows for the desecration and economic exploitation of Indigenous Peoples' sacred sites, including the San Francisco Peaks located in Flagstaff, Arizona[18] for the benefit of non-Indigenous peoples, business owners, and the non-Indigenous public to the detriment of Indigenous peoples," and the special rapporteur used the issue as one of the animating examples in their final report.[19]

While Borowsky's "handful of activists" narrative works to his benefit as a wealthy and politically connected businessman with a vested financial interest in limiting the scope and depth of media coverage against the expansions, he perceived me as being unfair because my coverage honestly reflected the full range of opposition. Just because the courts were ruling in his favor doesn't erase this opposition.

The False Promise of "Public Participation"

Borowsky expressed to me his frustration that "the tribes" were so unwilling to compromise on this issue.[20] What becomes clearer in this section, however, is how the privileges afforded through rhetorical exclusion rendered Borowsky incapable of seeing how much legal and recreational discourses on so-called public lands were already working in his favor. The rhetoric of "public comments" and "listening sessions" seems to imply that if enough people voice opposition, if people show up and speak from the heart against

---

15. Inter Tribal Council of Arizona, letter.

16. Shirley, "Sanctity."

17. International Indian Treaty Council, letter.

18. United Nations, "Rights of Indigenous Peoples," 12. Source correction: the San Francisco Peaks and the Arizona Snowbowl Ski Resort in fact lie outside the city limits of Flagstaff.

19. United Nations, "Rights of Indigenous Peoples," 12.

20. Boggs, "Rhetoric of Exclusion." As of 2017, the majority owner of the Arizona Snowbowl Ski Resort is James Coleman.

the use of reclaimed wastewater on their sacred mountain, a project will be halted. However, my experience covering this controversy showed that public participation—though the only real avenue to get comments on the public record—is institutionally necessary to move a project forward. In Klee Benally's 2005 documentary *The Snowbowl Effect,* Forest Service Ranger for the Peaks District Gene Waldrip noted that the Forest Service recognized in its environmental impact statement that the expansion at Snowbowl, particularly the use of treated sewage effluent to make snow, was "an adverse action."[21] It was well-documented in the environmental impact statement that Snowbowl's expansion, and the use of reclaimed wastewater to make snow, was extremely offensive to Indigenous peoples who hold the mountain sacred, the natural integrity of the mountain integral to their cultural and spiritual survival.[22] Benally asked Waldrip how it would be possible to go through with an action if it were recognized as being "adverse," to which Waldrip responded on camera, during an information session at a Forest Service office: "Well, the law doesn't say that we can't go through with it; it just says that we have a process and a consultation process that we have to go through. At the end of that, the land management agency can still make a decision even though it's an adverse action. It's just that you have to document it as an adverse action."[23]

It quickly became clear that the intention behind public comment periods and listening sessions was never about deciding whether to approve Snowbowl's expansions and developments—they'd already been approved. The Forest Service's focus was not *if* but *how* to implement Snowbowl's plan. And in order to do that, they needed to document the effects of that plan, no matter how terrible they were. So by showing up, and sitting around for hours waiting to voice their opposition, Indigenous communities were ironically part of the process that enabled that which they sought to stop. These observations are not unique to this situation or my analysis of it. In his book *Red Skin, White Masks: Rejecting the Colonial Politics of Recognition,* Glenn Sean Coulthard discusses this same dynamic beginning when the Dene, Inuit, and Métis people overwhelmingly rejected a gas pipeline proposal and supporting infrastructure through their ancestral lands in Northwest Territories of Canada. What ensued was a decades-long battle between the Canadian government over how the state should recognize the political rights of Indigenous peoples, the terms by which they might express those rights, and that eventually established territorial boundaries that limited their land and a government that

---

21. Benally and Cody, *Snowbowl Effect.*

22. Coconino National Forest, "Environmental Impact Statement"; and Save the Peaks Coalition, "U.S. Government Ignores."

23. Benally and Cody, *Snowbowl Effect.*

limited their power in land-use decisions.[24] In both examples, participation in the process helped enable that which was originally resisted.

Waldrip's statement reflects the structures by which Indigenous voices are institutionally excluded from public discourse and decision-making processes. His comments animate the larger problems of marginalization within the public participation process, but specifically they reflect the problem of rhetorical exclusion for Indigenous peoples.[25] At the level of policy and procedure, rhetorical exclusion is always already[26] at work in the limited structure of decision-making processes, all while appearing not to engage in antidemocratic actions. Public comments, though required to comply with the National Environmental Policy Act (NEPA), do not necessarily affect the decision-making process; the Forest Service can ultimately approve anything it wants. Even though public comments were overwhelmingly against development,[27] the Forest Service legally approved Snowbowl's proposal regardless. As the rhetoricians Jimmie Killingsworth and Jacqueline Palmer have argued, though decision-making processes

> may draw upon the conventions of a democratic discourse that is open to information from diverse sources, the aim of instrumental documents is never to treat deviant discourses with respect but always merely to take note of them, to record them, and ultimately to treat them as "noise" in the system, which needs to be ignored or expunged.[28]

In this case, they were ignored. It was clear the developments, particularly the use of reclaimed wastewater, negatively and disproportionately impact regional Indigenous peoples in terms of their cultures and spiritualities, which

---

24. See Coulthard, *Red Skin, White Masks.* See specifically chapter 2, "For the Land: The Dene Nation's Struggle for Self-Determination."

25. Killingsworth and Palmer, *Ecospeak*; and Endres, "Rhetoric of Nuclear Colonialism."

26. The phrase "always already" was popularized by Heidegger, though it can be traced back to Marx, and back even further to Kant's *Critique of Pure Reason.* It became important to Derrida and other poststructural theorists of discourse (see Spivak's introduction to Derrida's *Of Grammatology* for an expansive use of this term). The phrase is often used to articulate a relationship between language and ongoing processes, for example, the way ideology constitutes subjects. I use the phrase in this chapter to describe the way Indigenous peoples are often forced to navigate a system that was never designed to accommodate their ways of knowing and being in the world.

27. Coconino National Forest, "Environmental Impact Statement."

28. Killingsworth and Palmer, *Ecospeak,* 166. Also see chapter 7 in Depoe, Delicath, and Elsenbeer's *Communication and Public Participation in Environmental Decision Making* for a lengthier discussion of marginalization within the process for creating environmental impact statements and the structural problems of public participation.

are tied intimately to the landscape. The fact that they lost lawsuit after lawsuit in settler courts doesn't negate this reality for Indigenous peoples.

Redefining Water for Recreation, Part 1: Reclaimed Wastewater

In June 2010, the US Supreme Court refused to hear the case the Navajo Nation and other tribes brought against the Forest Service claiming the decision to use reclaimed wastewater on the Peaks violated Indigenous religious freedoms. The case went back and forth in the courts with wins on both sides—with the Ninth Circuit Court of Appeals in San Francisco ruling in favor of tribal opposition to snowmaking. However, after a rare *en banc* appeal in 2008 that reaffirmed the lower Arizona court's decision in Snowbowl's favor, the Supreme Court's refusal to hear the case marked the end of that legal argument. But the potential impacts of reclaimed wastewater ran even deeper than religious freedoms and also raised serious and unanswered questions about human health. This was on the minds of plaintiffs all along, but the courts proved structurally incapable of accommodating an argument that articulated religious freedom and human health simultaneously.

In 2009 the Save the Peaks Coalition and nine citizens brought a new lawsuit against the Forest Service, calling upon the agency to take seriously the growing public health concerns regarding the safety of using 100 percent reclaimed wastewater to make snow.[29] By not testing the water directly to ensure safety and instead deferring to the Arizona Department of Environmental Quality (ADEQ), the lawsuit claimed, the Forest Service was not complying with the NEPA process when it drafted its environmental impact statement. According to the Save the Peaks Coalition, "The use of reclaimed sewer water to make snow, however was not only repulsive to people who hold the San Francisco Peaks sacred, it raised concerns from skiers and the community over the safety of being immersed in, and even ingesting, snow made from non-potable treated sewage effluent."[30] This different group of plaintiffs included concerned citizens and parents who wanted assurances that when their kids inevitably ingest the snow or fall into it, they would not be harming themselves.

The confluence of science and water policy is complicated and often contradictory. Since proposing its plan to the city, the ski resort had been engaged

29. *Save the Peaks Coalition et al. v. U.S. Forest Service*, 2011.
30. Save the Peaks Coalition, "U.S. Government Ignores." Also in Boggs, "No Really," 12.

in a deception campaign, claiming with zero evidence that reclaimed waste-water was cleaner than natural snow, often citing ADEQ's rating of the water as A+.[31] Northern Arizona University hydrology professor and then director of the School of Earth Science and Environmental Sustainability Abraham Springer observed that "according to the Arizona Department of Environ-mental Quality's own regulations, treated sewer water can be graded A+ even when it contains fecal matter in three out of every ten samples. The treated wastewater can meet all applicable water quality standards, but still not be as high of quality as precipitation."[32] Studies of wastewater across the country have revealed the persistence of industrial wastes such as antimony, mercury, chromium, cadmium, lead, dioxins, flame-retardants, anti-freeze, insecticides, and pesticides. When the 2009 lawsuit was brought against the Forest Service, one of Flagstaff's two wastewater treatment facilities was cited by the Environ-mental Protection Agency because of high amounts of cyanide and selenium, and the city was accused of lying about this in the years that followed.[33]

ADEQ also doesn't require tests for pharmaceuticals often found in reclaimed wastewater. The only rigorous tests performed on the water dis-charged from Flagstaff's reclaimed wastewater plants then had been conducted by Northern Arizona University biological sciences professor Catherine Prop-per, whose research revealed more about the content of the water than what ADEQ requires of the city. "In the last 100 years, humans have introduced hundreds of new, synthetic compounds into the environment," she wrote in a 2005 study on endocrine-disrupting compounds,[34] which "disrupt physiologi-cal processes including development, reproduction, general metabolism and behavior."[35] In 2009 I interviewed her, and she explained her research to me in a way that a broader public audience could understand. Her studies have exposed compelling evidence of skewed sex ratios present among aquatic ani-mals exposed to reclaimed wastewater in their habitat, in which 100 percent or nearly 100 percent of a given population is female. She has also observed dramatic increases of newborn species in testing areas born hermaphroditic, that is, male fish with evidence of eggs developing in their testicular tissue or male fish that produce female yolk protein. The City of Flagstaff is not required to test for pharmaceuticals, but these findings suggest high levels of

31. Though this was repeated by a lot of people over the years, it was captured on camera in Benally and Cody, *Snowbowl Effect*, when Snowbowl general manager J. R. Murray said this to a group of children.

32. This quote appears in multiple articles I wrote from 2009 to 2012, including Boggs, "Arizona Testbowl"; and Boggs, "Storm Clouds."

33. Cole, "ADEQ."

34. Propper, "Study of Endocrine-Disrupting Compounds," 194.

35. Boggs, "No Really," 12.

estrogen in the water.[36] The challenge of using this kind of research to make an argument about water safety is based on the invisibility of long-term effects of exposure, though the endocrine system impacts everything from fertility to intelligence.[37] "You're not going to see folks dropping dead because of endocrine disruption," she told me, "but you do see, the way I put it is, you see 'quality of life outcomes.'"[38]

While many resorts make snow, even with mixtures that in whole or in part use reclaimed wastewater—the quality of which varies greatly from state to state and country to country—Snowbowl was on track to be the only resort in the world to use 100 percent reclaimed wastewater, so answering questions of safety was important. Propper reminded me that it would be unethical for scientists to conduct experiments on humans to demonstrate causation (rather than her correlative evidence) but wouldn't go so far as to align herself with Peaks activists who asserted exposing humans to snow made from 100 percent reclaimed wastewater is tantamount to such a human experiment. Howard Shanker, attorney for the Save the Peaks Coalition and the nine citizens who filed the lawsuit against the Forest Service, says, "By approving treated sewage effluent for snow making without adequate analysis, the government essentially turns the ski area into a test facility with our children as the laboratory rats. That is unconscionable."[39]

During court hearings, Shanker stood against a team of lawyers representing the United States Department of Agriculture, in addition to the lawyers representing Arizona Snowbowl Limited Partnership, who joined the lawsuit against the Forest Service as a "voluntary intervener."[40] Eager to start construction, the intimidating merger between state and corporate power to defend the expansions of a ski resort against the objections of thirteen Indigenous tribes and citizens with valid and unanswered questions about human health revealed how badly the resort and the Forest Service wanted the lawsuit to go away as quickly as possible. As exposed through correspondence I obtained through Freedom of Information Act requests, the language of settler entitlement to Indigenous land and political support for the resort extended far beyond the courtroom.

---

36. Boggs, 12.

37. For explanations of these concerns written for a public audience, see Colborn, Dumanoski, and Myers, *Our Stolen Future*; and Baker, *Body Toxic*.

38. Boggs, "Our Water Systems," 10.

39. Save the Peaks Coalition, "U.S. Government"; and Boggs, "Arizona Testbowl."

40. The fact that Snowbowl joined the Forest Service voluntarily, mobilizing state and corporate power against Shanker and his clients, is a detail often lost in conversation. Snowbowl spokespeople repeatedly voiced frustration about how much money they were spending and losing in court, but nobody made them join this lawsuit. The plaintiff's complaint was with respect to the Forest Service's failure to comply with its own policy in approving this project.

Redefining Water for Recreation, Part 2: Recovered-Reclaimed Water

Months before the 2009 NEPA case was even decided, it was revealed that the United States Department of Agriculture, under the new Obama administration, including then secretary of agriculture Tom Vilsack and Deputy Secretary of Agriculture Kathleen Merrigan, were engaged in secret talks with the City of Flagstaff and Snowbowl. Their goal was to secure a new water source for snowmaking that would be "less offensive" to the tribes, who consistently rejected the use of reclaimed wastewater on the Peaks but might be okay with making snow from another source.[41] The motivation was based on assumptions that all Indigenous cultures affected by the resort's plans to make snow thought about it in the same way. The Hopi Tribe, for example, had always been against the idea of humans making snow, from any source of water. For the Hopi, the Peaks are the home of the Kachina, spiritual deities that bring rain and snow. Their position, that the Kachina make snow, not people—let alone people doing it to make money—was clear and consistent from the moment the idea was proposed. Nonetheless, from the end of June 2009 to the end of the year, everyone else was kept in the dark, including area tribes like the Hopi that the USDA claimed to be consulting.

During this time, Arizona political leadership, including senators John McCain and Jon Kyl and representatives Ann Kirkpatrick and Trent Franks, in addition to Snowbowl's lawyers, the resort's principal owner Eric Borowsky, and manager J. R. Murray, wrote several letters urging the USDA to give the Snowbowl "notice to proceed," the first step in the process toward construction. The first round of letters to Vilsack expressed frustration that the federal government was trying to accommodate Indigenous concerns at all, given that the Navajo Nation lost its religious freedom lawsuit against the Forest Service. To Merrigan, Snowbowl lawyer Clayton Yeutter said it was "obviously troubling to our clients who feel that the tribes have had their day in court."[42] Representative Trent Franks dismissed the current NEPA lawsuit as an attempt "to circumvent the court's ruling through questionable tactics."[43] To Merrigan, Borowsky and Murray said, "It is extremely frustrating to learn that others are now challenging this final decision of the U.S. Supreme Court," never mind that the Supreme Court declined to hear the religious freedoms case and the 2009 NEPA lawsuit was an entirely separate one.[44] Meanwhile, Representative Franks reminded Vilsack that although it is acceptable to "invite tribal input

41. Cole, "Secret Snowbowl."
42. Yeutter, letter.
43. Franks, letter.
44. Borowsky and Murray, letter.

and participation," tribal leaders are of "no authority or decision making."[45] And McCain, Kyl, and Kirkpatrick sent joint letters to Vilsack in support of Snowbowl, one of which ended by telling Vilsack that McCain would go so far as to "maintain my hold on," or block, "all USDA nominees over this matter."[46] It's worth pausing here to reflect on the weight of this moment. Powerful political figures vehemently defended a for-profit corporate entity, reminded the federal government that Indigenous peoples should not have a say in decisions that impact sites held sacred, and the "Maverick" himself, John McCain, threatened to hold up the normal operations of the federal government until they greenlighted ski resort developments while a court case against those developments was ongoing.

At the end of January 2010, Vilsack's office began contacting all concerned parties as to the reasons for their delays and lack of communication:

> USDA will work with the City of Flagstaff to expand the City's water resources so that it can better serve the people of Flagstaff and provide an alternative water source to Snowbowl for Snowmaking. . . . I am pledging a commitment of USDA's own resources to help build the remaining infrastructure needed to bring more water to Flagstaff and make it available to Snowbowl for its use.[47]

The USDA's plan, though vague in these initial letters, was—as it turned out—proposed by officials working for the City of Flagstaff. The plan articulated an option that was neither reclaimed wastewater nor potable drinking water but an apparent third option, a classification that had never existed before: "recovered-reclaimed water" or "stored water." During a crowded city council meeting, city officials explained: after unused reclaimed wastewater is discharged into a local stream known locally as the Rio de Flag, it mingles with existing water from storm drains and snowmelt and eventually recharges the Coconino Aquifer; that water is recovered-reclaimed water. Audible confusion ensued among those in attendance, as citizens began whispering and looking at each other because Flagstaff's potable drinking water comes from that same aquifer. In combination with surface water collected from nearby Lake Mary, any water "recovered" from the Coconino Aquifer is the same water that Flagstaff treats and delivers to residents as potable water. As citizens in attendance connected these dots, the city read the rest of the proposal from Vilsack's office at the USDA.

---

45. Franks, letter.
46. McCain, Kyl, and Kirkpatrick, letter, November 20, 2009.
47. Vilsack, letter.

The city also announced that the federal government would commit $11 million in urban development funds to support the project, essentially using taxpayer funds to subsidize snowmaking at the Arizona Snowbowl. It was not until March of 2010 that the existence of any of these talks were known, let alone the USDA's proposal, and not until August that the city discussed this publicly. McCain, Kyl, and Kirkpatrick, also left in the dark during these talks, blasted the decision in a final letter to Vilsack, claiming that it was an irresponsible use of taxpayer dollars that would take from projects intended to receive funds like this, and demanding that Snowbowl be immediately allowed to start construction under the original proposal to use reclaimed wastewater.[48] In Vilsack's response, he said they are not required to issue a "notice to proceed" while "a second case remains pending in Federal district court," referring to the 2009 NEPA lawsuit with respect to human health and reclaimed wastewater. He also said that "at the request of Tribal Governments" the USDA was "trying to resolve their concerns about snowmaking." If "recovered-reclaimed" water was acceptable, the NEPA lawsuit would be moot, and construction could immediately begin. But, as it came to light, "recovered-reclaimed water" was a lie concocted by the city to move the project forward. They knew that the use of wastewater was unacceptable to area tribes who hold the Peaks sacred, and they knew there would be resistance among citizens if the city committed what would become their drinking water, given ongoing drought and water scarcity in the region.

As the city's water manager in cooperation with Snowbowl and the Forest Service tried to sell this idea, the public raised a lot of questions. Why were US senators so invested in seeing this unpopular and divisive project move forward? Why would the federal government want this project to move forward so badly that they were willing to subsidize its implementation? How could a third water option suddenly be available in a two-pipe system? Why did the federal government seem to believe it was reasonable to use potable drinking water for snowmaking in Arizona? And, finally, were Flagstaff residents currently drinking water contaminated with reclaimed wastewater?

In the meantime, the owners of Snowbowl offered to sell the resort to the Navajo Nation, valued at between $4 and $6 million, for $49 million.[49] The Navajo Nation obviously declined. Because of this extremely inflated price, many people assumed it was offered as a joke.

In the months leading up to the city council's vote on whether to amend its contract with Snowbowl to deliver potable water (a.k.a. "recovered-reclaimed" water) option instead of their previous promise to deliver reclaimed wastewater,

---

48. McCain, Kyl, and Kirkpatrick, letter, March 8, 2010.
49. Shirley, letter.

the USDA insisted that there was Indigenous support for the new plan to use potable water, when there was not. City officials also claimed they received letters of tribal support for the new water option but declined to say who wrote these letters or what they said.

It was suspected that one letter was sent to the USDA in support of the project by Scott Canty, the Hopi Tribe's general council, a white attorney the tribe had just fired. According to Hopi Council members, Canty had a long history of disregarding ethics and tribal laws; council member Leroy Sumatzkuku was paraphrased in *Native Times* as saying that Canty had advocated positions to the federal government that were not approved by the council, likely referring to his letter to the USDA supporting the new water option without approval by the tribal council.[50] Andy Bessler, then Sierra Club's Southwest regional representative for their Tribal Partnerships program, corroborated this suspicion when he said to the city council, "The Hopi Tribe's general counsel, Scott Canty, who most likely wrote and sent the letter to the City on the Tribe's behalf was fired in part because of sending that letter"; he also said the Obama administration did not do its homework and consult with the over thirteen tribes who have opposed snowmaking for years. They would have learned that the Hopi have had a resolution since 1972 opposing any development on the Peaks.[51]

"Tribal support" was manufactured, creating confusion and doubt for everyone, that is, except Indigenous peoples whose opposition had been clear, consistent, and unwavering. Leigh Kuwanwisiwma, director for the Hopi Cultural Preservation Office, told the council, "The Hopi Tribe's position at this point has not changed. . . . We are clearly opposed to snowmaking entirely, from any source of water," a position he had told the USDA when they met in the previous fall. Hopi farmer Bucky Preston agreed, saying, "snowmaking on the San Francisco Peaks would interfere with sacred instructions passed down through Hopi generations about the proper roles of humans and natural forces on the Peaks. It's against the creator to make snow. That's not humans' job." Similarly, Havasupai councilwoman Carletta Tilousi rejected the USDA's proposal: "Making artificial snow for economic purposes is still steps toward abusing sacred mountains. Whatever process they use to make artificial snow is still unacceptable to us Havasupai people."[52] The Inter Tribal Council of Arizona, made up of twenty Arizona tribes, passed a resolution denouncing the use of any source of water to make snow artificially.[53] In a separate statement to Vilsack, Navajo Nation President Joe Shirley wrote, "The Navajo Nation recognizes that clean drinking water is sacred and essential for all living

50. Fonseca, "Hopi Lawmakers Drop Top Attorney."
51. Boggs, "Storm Clouds," 10–11.
52. Cole, "Tribes."
53. Inter Tribal Council of Arizona, letter.

beings, especially in the arid Arizona climate, and should not be wasted on non-essential recreational activities such as snowmaking for a limited skiing population."[54] The reaction was clear as well among advocacy and conservation groups like the Sierra Club, Friends of Flagstaff's Future, Black Mesa Water Coalition, and Grand Canyon Trust, who said in a joint resolution, "We do not believe it is prudent to use potable water to aid a private business outside city limits in their effort to provide limited recreation opportunities to those who can afford them. The City of Flagstaff has a responsibility to its citizenry to provide a long-term, clean drinking water source for essential survival." In trying to find a "less offensive" water option, the USDA simply made matters more confusing by replacing one offensive option—reclaimed wastewater—with another offensive option—recovered-reclaimed water, which was proved to be a made-up term for Flagstaff's drinking water. The fact of these backdoor dealings and manipulations in light of such strong resistance was a reminder of what Indigenous peoples are up against when settler colonial structures consolidate power, in ways that obscure even the clearest of positions.

On August 30, 2010, close to eight hundred people packed into a local high school's auditorium, where the city council held a special meeting to vote on whether to allow Snowbowl to use Flagstaff's drinking water (i.e., "recovered-reclaimed" water) for snowmaking. The meeting lasted over seven hours, ending after midnight. Borowsky, Snowbowl majority owner, said he preferred "any other alternative [source of water] that allows construction to start immediately."[55] Overwhelmingly, those engaged in public comments were not just against the use of drinking water for snowmaking but urged the city to completely cancel its contract with the resort. Ultimately, the city decided against the manufactured alternative and reaffirmed its commitment to sell reclaimed wastewater to the resort as planned. In attendance was a representative from the USDA, Alan Stephens, who reminded those in attendance that the proposal to use drinking water for snowmaking did not originate from his office, which many still believed, but with undisclosed staff members of the City of Flagstaff. The decision visibly upset Borowsky, who referred to those who spoke—Indigenous elders and leaders, conservationists, concerned citizens—as "uninformed and mostly illiterate people," stating that he was "offended that the mayor allowed five tribal officials to talk about no snowmaking for 10–15 minutes each . . . wasting everybody's time allowing these people to talk about something the federal courts already decided."[56]

The 2009 NEPA case was decided at the end of the year in favor of the Forest Service, allowing the resort to continue their plans to make snow from

54. Shirley, letter.
55. Boggs, "Storm Clouds," 10–11.
56. Boggs.

reclaimed wastewater. The decision was made on a technicality,[57] and the merits of the case were never heard. During a key moment, there was discussion over what constitutes "immersion." While it is an illegal use of wastewater to immerse oneself in it, like swimming in ponds filled with it, eventually the court concluded that the inevitable faceplant in snow made from reclaimed wastewater did not constitute "full immersion." According to Howard Shanker, the attorney representing the plaintiffs in the case,

> This court found that the Forest Service does not have to do a thorough analysis or include a reasonably thorough discussion of the impacts associated with the potential ingestion of snow made from reclaimed sewer water in the Final Environmental Impact Statement because Arizona Department of Environmental Quality approved the use of reclaimed sewer water for snowmaking.[58]

The agency approved using reclaimed wastewater to make snow but not for skiing, leaving several questions unanswered in terms of the human health effects of ingestion or the impact of reclaimed wastewater on the local environment. In May 2011, construction crews were given the green light to break ground and start laying the pipeline deep in the dirt along the road to the ski resort.

There were two other short-lived lawsuits brought by the Hopi Tribe, the first of which was a civil case filed in 2011 against the United States Forest Service,[59] arguing that snowmaking with reclaimed wastewater would threaten the San Francisco Peaks groundsel, a small flowering shrub that grows nowhere else in the world.[60] Ultimately, this case was settled out of court. In 2013 the Hopi Tribe filed a different lawsuit against the City of Flagstaff, claiming that

---

57. The claim was barred by a legal concept called "laches," which deals with the timeline in which merits can be heard. In this case, one of the judges said that the merits over NEPA violations should have been raised in the previous lawsuit brought by the Navajo Nation et al., also represented by attorney Howard Shanker, even though that case was strictly about religious freedoms.

58. Boggs, "Resistance Continues," 10.

59. *Hopi Tribe v. USFS.*

60. An interesting detail about this moment in the controversy is that, despite the common name, San Francisco Peaks groundsel, the Forest Service began referring to the plant as the San Francisco Peaks ragwort. The agency refers to Arizona Fish and Game, who claim that the plant was originally misidentified as being in the *Senecio* family (*Senecio franciscanus*) and then in the early 1980s was identified as actually being in the *Packera* family (*Packera franciscana*), thus technically it is a ragwort, not a groundsel. The timing of this public discussion, during the Hopi's lawsuit, is curious. While the timing could be a coincidence, it is also easier to motivate people to protect something called "groundsel" than "ragwort." When I inquired about the timing of this reclassification, I was told it was done so that reporting would be more "accurate." Further digging on my part revealed that the taxonomic change had been widely accepted—though both terms are listed as correct.

snowmaking, facilitated by the city, constitutes a "public nuisance."[61] In Arizona, a public nuisance claim is valid only if one can demonstrate "special damage," or damage different from that endured by the general public. The Arizona Court of Appeals ruled that the Hopi Tribe could claim that Snowbowl's use of treated wastewater to make snow did cause "a special injury" to the tribe in terms of their cultural and spiritual practices, but in a 5–2 decision, the Arizona Supreme Court ruled that the "tribe's graphic descriptions of reclaimed wastewater and its effects strongly suggest that anyone and everyone who visits the Peaks, not just the Tribe, will suffer substantial environmental harm," wrote Justice John Pelander in the court's opinion.[62] This means that the injury is not specific to the tribe, which invalidates a public nuisance claim. In a problematic precedent to future cases, the ruling also concluded that "environmental damage on culturally important public lands is not special injury." In their 2018 dissent, Chief Justice Scott Bales and Justice Clint Bolick argued that the court's ruling "largely ignores the distinctive harms alleged by the Hopi" and "fails to appreciate that the wastewater will affect the Hopi's use and enjoyment of ancestral lands that have played a central role in the Hopi culture and religion since before the Coconino National Forest was of concern to the broader public."[63] Snowbowl had already been making snow with reclaimed wastewater at this point for nearly five years.

The centrality of outdoor recreation in the culture of this community, and the perception that the resort is a significant driver of the regional winter economy, which it is not,[64] in addition to the obvious political connections between state representatives and Snowbowl owners, all constitute a kind of settler colonial collaboration that works against consistent and clear objections from Indigenous peoples. The internal political wrangling, the teams of corporate and government lawyers, the dismissal of solid scientific debate, and the sudden crafting of new rhetorical classifications of water reveal the lengths these collaborators will go to secure their possession of stolen Indigenous land. The settler colonial context produced a political, legal, and corporate consolidation of power capable of raising suspicion when there is conviction, making dirty water appear clean and clean water appear dirty.

61. *Hopi Tribe v. City of Flagstaff.*
62. Woods, "Hopi Lose Arguments."
63. Woods.
64. Multiple economic analysis have proved that, contrary to the popular perception that the Arizona Snowbowl Ski Resort—which lies outside of the city limits—is crucial to the economy of Flagstaff, is wrong. A study by Bioeconomics, "Economic Significance of Arizona Snowbowl," shows that the resort's expansions would not have a measurable or significant economic impact on the Flagstaff area. There is also a scene in Benally and Cody, *Snowbowl Effect*, that features a Flagstaff city clerk coming to the same conclusion.

"What Part of Sacred Don't You Understand?"

On February 11, 2011—just a few months before construction began on the thirteen-mile reclaimed wastewater pipeline from Flagstaff to the Snowbowl ski resort—I interviewed Indigenous writer, farmer, and activist Winona LaDuke before she gave a talk at Northern Arizona University. In the years that preceded this moment, Indigenous peoples had tried to communicate why the Peaks are sacred in their individual cultures and how the sacred status of the Peaks meant the Snowbowl project was unacceptable. From city council meetings to court rooms to Forest Service listening sessions, many expressed complex feelings of frustration because (1) Indigenous spirituality is really nobody's business: Indigenous peoples were forced into a position where they had to explain their religion and culture because of the threats to the ecological integrity of the mountain, and what that means to their cultural and spiritual survival. And (2) the metaphors often deployed to appeal to settler audiences, such as likening the use of reclaimed wastewater on the Peaks to "peeing in a church," simply did not resonate. I later heard a more useful metaphor, that wastewater at the resort was like injecting poison into one's body; the injection site is small, but the poison can affect the whole body. While the metaphor reflects other Indigenous articulations of the Peaks as being alive, as having a body, there exists inherent problems with metaphors. When the metaphor is deployed, suddenly the speaker is talking about something they're not really talking about—urine and needles—instead of desecration of a sacred site and spiritual and cultural connections to landscape.

When I sat down with Winona LaDuke, I had been drawn to the challenge of bridging this disconnect in understanding. I thought if I could learn as much as I could about why and how the San Francisco Peaks were sacred that I could convey it to my largely white audience and that that would make a difference. I thought of this as a strategy that leveraged my privilege by appealing to other settlers through my platform as a community writer. I was self-aware enough at the time that I never pretended I was capable of understanding sacredness the way a Diné elder does, and I was careful never to articulate Indigenous cosmologies in my own words. But I thought if I dedicated enough column space to Indigenous explanations of sacredness, gleaned from interviews and archival research, that I could reach this audience where metaphors failed. Looking back, it's clear that anyone kind enough to speak to me about sacredness fell into a similar trap, as they had been made to believe that if they explained in depth why the Peaks are sacred and I wrote about it, then maybe the desecration would stop. As a journalist and researcher, I thumbed through hundreds of pages of archival material going back a hundred years on a variety of issues that plagued Indigenous peoples on the Colorado Plateau. I read accounts of Indigenous folks speaking about sacredness, not necessarily because they wanted to, but because they felt like they *had to* in order to stop something: Snowbowl Village and ski resort expansions on the Peaks, mining operations on Black Mesa, theft of water resources on the Little Colorado, and construction of a telescope on Mount Graham. I wrote a lot about it, and having made use of Winona LaDuke's books in articles and in invited talks related to the Peaks, specifically *Recovering the Sacred: The Power of Naming and Claiming* and *All Our Relations: Native Struggles for Land and Life,* I knew I wanted to ask her about it, and—if she would—give me some advice on how to better communicate sacredness to settler audiences.

When I did ask her, she gave a long sigh, and then proceeded to give me a thoughtful response, which I deeply appreciated but never used in an article, and here's why. During her talk that evening, she recounted her participation in defeating the construction of a golf course outside of Duluth, Minnesota, on Spirit Mountain, which is held sacred to the Ojibwe. She said, "It is time to quit discussing what is sacred; I got asked that a lot today," and I immediately assumed she was talking about me.[65] When she continued, I saw myself within a long pattern of settler prodding:

> It is ironic to be an Indigenous person who has an eight-thousand-year-old relationship walking on this land to be hauled into court in northern Minnesota to explain why it is sacred, how sacred it is. If, in this case, it is okay for the Indians to pray between the sixth and seventh hole? That is absurd. But that is what is going on. In the end, it is actually institutional and systemic. We are in courts that were created by Christian doctrine and the King's law. That's where your judicial system came from. So we are brought into a court of an entirely different paradigm and asked to justify our existence.[66]

By asking Indigenous peoples to explain sacredness to me, I learned that I wasn't doing anything radically different from what city and government officials had been doing for decades, across multiple contexts, in asymmetrical systems of power. It reminded me of some old transcripts I had read during my archival research during a moment in the mid-1970s, when Indigenous and environmental activists resisted a plan to turn what is now Hart Prairie Nature Preserve—characterized by its breathtaking meadows and brilliant aspen groves—into Snowbowl Village, which would have had given wealthy

65. LaDuke, "Environmental Justice."
66. LaDuke.

residents direct access to the ski resort, modeled on cities like Aspen or Vail, Colorado. On January 29, 1974, during a city council meeting that drew no fewer than two thousand people into Flagstaff High School's gymnasium, Forest Service Supervisor E. H. Weigel interrogated Herbert Lewis (Hopi). When "you describe the Peaks area, at what level? How low down on the mountain do you go or how high up do you go"?[67] Lewis responded in a similar fashion as the others who were asked that same question that day: "When I meant the Peaks area, I didn't just mean half of the San Francisco Peaks or just the bottom of the San Francisco Peaks. Like my father indicated over there, he says the San Francisco Peaks has roots and this could go out for miles. We have shrines around the adjacent area."[68]

Indigenous sacredness, in these frameworks, becomes a kind of object that settlers seek to poses and then wield over Indigenous peoples. The implication is that if sacredness can be broken down into little bits and pieces, corporate and government entities can then move projects forward more easily by simply developing around those parts.

My focus on trying to explain sacredness as it had been recounted to me from Indigenous peoples that I then presented to a largely white settler audience had unintended consequences that still haunt me. Feedback I received from some of my articles in those days, specifically from skiers and snowboarders, confirmed that my intention did not produce the effects I had hoped. They told me, and often used this line to retort to Indigenous peoples in real time in public spaces, that "skiing is sacred to me."

On July 29, 2010, during a Flagstaff Planning and Zoning Commission meeting addressing the source of water the city would sell to the Arizona Snowbowl, a meeting that drew so many people it was moved to a local high school's auditorium, at least five members from the public who spoke up in favor of the expansions remarked, "skiing is sacred to me" during public comments. The phrase was also seen on pro-Snowbowl counterprotest signs in front of city hall during this time.

Bron Taylor has written about recreational activities like surfing as a spiritual practice, and others like Dolores LaChapelle have written directly about backcountry skiing as a way to connect with nature. Both of these examples, in different ways, complicate the relationship between religion and recreation.[69] While acknowledging the validity as well as the growing popularity

---

67. Coconino County Planning and Zoning Commission, "In the Matter of Public Hearing." This also appears in Boggs, "Material-Discursive Spaces," 184.

68. Coconino County Planning and Zoning Commission, "In the Matter of Public Hearing."

69. See B. Taylor, *Dark Green Religion*; and LaChapelle, *Deep Powder Snow*.

of nature religions and their associated activities, those "religious perceptions and practices that are often characterized by a reverence for nature and that consider its destruction a desecrating act," the context of skier's claims of sacredness in terms of the Snowbowl controversy trivialize the thousands of years of Indigenous cultural and spiritual connection to landscape.[70] While it may prove challenging to distinguish the sincere from the insincere, in this case it is important to note that the multiple individuals in Flagstaff who proclaimed their spiritual connection to skiing only did so after Indigenous peoples described their spiritual connections to the land; particularly during this public meeting, "skiing is sacred to me" was a reaction to the many sincere comments from Indigenous peoples that linked the natural integrity of the mountain to their tribe's cultural and spiritual survival—the tone and intention of which is incomparable.

As Sanchez, Stuckey, and Morris have described, "Rhetorical exclusion is often a reflexive rather than calculated strategy," and thus such reflexive claims for the sacredness of skiing is a clever way of elevating recreation to the level of Indigenous cultural and spiritual identification with natural landscapes.[71] Strategies of rhetorical exclusion, particularly "strategic silencing," are at work here again: elevating skiing simultaneously devalues Indigenous identities in this comparative structure.[72] And this is important to the settler colonial situation, in which "disavowal is directed at denying the very existence and persistence of Indigenous presences and claims."[73] While I cannot take credit for the pervasiveness of "skiing is sacred to me" as a settler comeback, I have to be real with how my line of questioning and focus on sacredness are part of a long story of frustration to Indigenous communities, and perhaps how some settlers learned a new language from which to further entrench their entitlement to stolen Indigenous land.

At best my approach was cliché, and at worst it was counterproductive and damaging to the communities that trusted me. But worst of all, my approach was prescriptive, based on what I thought would be effective. It was extractive, in the sense that before some of these interviews, I had already decided what I wanted to write about; I mined for Indigenous knowledge that fit my narrative. Despite my "good intentions," my approach was not what those Indigenous communities needed or wanted from me, and ultimately those articles

---

70. B. Taylor, *Dark Green Religion*, 5.

71. Sanchez, Stuckey, and Morris, "Rhetorical Exclusion," 28.

72. Endres, "Rhetoric of Nuclear Colonialism," 52–53. This is not radically different from how environment-versus-economy arguments always work in favor of pro-development stakeholders, as discussed in Killingsworth and Palmer, *Ecospeak*.

73. Veracini, "Settler Collective," 368.

did not produce the effects I had hoped. Even if misguided at times, however, my coverage was always rooted in spaces of trust that I had built through community relationships. I was therefore open to criticism and motivated by doing right by those relations. This experience radically transformed my community listening praxis—a concept I develop further in the last chapter of this book—and my approach to researching and writing those articles immediately shifted.

Through this experience, I learned to write in such a way that takes sacredness as a given, as matter of fact that is not up for debate; sacredness shouldn't demand explanations, translations, or settler accommodations. In his chapter that deals with the kinds of and nuances of sacred sites, Vine Deloria Jr. describes some places that transcend articulations of something as sacred *to* a tribe but are sacred "in and of themselves." Ceremonies associated with such places, those that must occur at certain times of the year to maintain healthy life for all living things, are not mere philosophy or moral code, says Deloria, but a moral responsibility commanded by the holy places themselves.[74] As a settler these are ideas difficult enough for me to understand, let alone explain to others. One thing I know for sure though: it is not my place to explain Indigenous sacredness, but to listen. Discussions with Indigenous activists like Klee Benally also helped me steer my writing away from lingering on the question of sacredness. In a 2017 essay, Benally explained, "What part of sacred don't you understand? Essentially, we're saying why isn't it enough for us to say a site is sacred and should be set aside and protected and respected because it's integral for our spiritual practice to be continued."[75] I found that proceeding from this premise freed me to work more creatively and collaboratively with Indigenous peoples in ways that turned the focus back on the audience. This shift invited my audience to question and resist the colonial logics—both personal and institutional—that compel their entitlement to Indigenous knowledge and land. Instead of asking Indigenous peoples about why, how, and in what ways the Peaks are sacred, I interrogated settlers instead, with questions like why, how, and in what ways are skiing and snowboarding more important than Indigenous cultural and spiritual survival?

Attempts to "work within the system" ultimately failed those who tried every legal strategy they could think of to defend the Peaks. These systems enabled collaborations that consolidated state and corporate power and limited the ways in which Indigenous peoples could be understood. In the end, what we can learn from these experiences is to simply believe Indigenous

---

74. V. Deloria, *God Is Red*, 85.
75. K. Benally, "San Francisco Peaks," 99–100.

peoples when they link sacredness, their cultural and spiritual survival, to the landscapes in which we engage, to infuse dignity and respect into our relations, and to not be surprised when nonlegal means of persuasion become the next step when all other available means of persuasion have been exhausted. Or to put it in the way, as Klee Benally did: "Respect existence or expect resistance."

CHAPTER 7

The Pipeline as a Site of
Indigenous Resistance and Solidarity

Throughout this book, I've tried to find ways to invite the larger public to understand and learn to recognize and reckon with the ways their identity as settlers on stolen Indigenous land shows up in discourses of outdoor recreation. In this chapter, I interrogate the pipeline as a site of Indigenous resistance and alliance. Of these sites, one that garnered widespread national media coverage and elicited many forms of Indigenous and settler solidarity is the Standing Rock Sioux Tribe's historic stand against the Dakota Access Pipeline in 2016. Another site, I argue, is the summer of 2011, in which more than fifty people were arrested in a series of direct actions and occupations on the San Francisco Peaks during the construction of the Arizona Snowbowl Ski Resort's reclaimed wastewater pipeline. In this chapter, I cement this moment as part of the same legacy of resistance and solidarity exemplified by the 2016 stand at Standing Rock. In doing so, I return to my coverage of the controversy on the San Francisco Peaks, focusing on the inspiring Indigenous-led resistance to snowmaking with reclaimed wastewater that, like at Standing Rock, occurred at the very site of cultural and environmental harm: the pipeline.

Separated by 1,300 miles, two pipelines cross stolen Indigenous land, and the physical sites of their construction marked the location of Indigenous-led resistance. Though one pipeline, which the Sioux named the Black Snake, carries crude tar sand oil, and the other carries municipal reclaimed wastewater through green pipes buried six feet deep, both were made possible by a merger between state and corporate power and a settler court system; both were enabled by the narrow argumentative frame of "environment versus economy" that is inherently anti-Indigenous and always pro-development; both sites were offered "less offensive solutions" that looked good on paper but did nothing to address the underlying issues;[1] both threaten important Indigenous cultural sites and the sanctity (and safety) of water. Also, both sites mobilized creative and collaborative Indigenous-led resistance that included a convergence of Indigenous tribal members and settler allies who camped on-site to contribute in demonstrations and direct actions but also to make food and provide other forms of necessary support.

While the stand at Standing Rock marked a pivotal moment in the long history of Indigenous resistance to settler colonialism, mobilizing more than ten thousand people to the site of the pipeline, the stand on the San Francisco Peaks is part of that same history. In terms of the larger and ongoing project of settler colonialism, which in simple and complex ways replaces and writes over Indigenous ways of knowing, being, and existing in the world, the difference between an oil pipeline and a reclaimed wastewater pipeline are not all that significant—a black snake and a green snake. Both are egregious efforts to transport resources, despite staunch and overwhelming Indigenous opposition and notwithstanding the clear threats to sacred sites and other important cultural places, to benefit settlers to the detriment of Indigenous peoples. The oil translates to profits for Energy Transfer Partners, and the reclaimed wastewater translates to profits for the partners who own the Arizona Snowbowl Limited Partnership, though both parties convinced the larger public that the projects would lead to larger economic benefits. At the same time these projects primarily benefit the corporate interests that own them. Both pipelines, culturally and historically, are meant to sustain settler belongings; they both constitute settler placemaking practices, the very sites where Indigenous land is written over through the language of the pipeline. It is no wonder, therefore, that the sites of pipeline construction become the battleground for Indigenous-led resistance and solidarity.

The next several pages document the demonstrations and direct actions Indigenous peoples and settler accomplices took to protect the Peaks, beginning with how annual protests of the resort unfold today. What also continues today is a chasm of misunderstanding between ski resort patrons—everyday skiers and snowboarders—and Indigenous agitators who continue to work to bring attention to the harm the resort brings. Some of what is recounted here might be hard to read, especially for those who were there, whose ears likely still ring with the sounds of industrial saws near their heads and the

---

1. On November 2, 2016, Obama said in an interview that the US Army Corp of Engineers is "examining whether there are ways to reroute this pipeline in a way . . . that I think is properly attentive to the traditions of the first Americans." Hersher, "Key Moments."

callousness of police. Recounting these moments—fierce and harrowing as they were—is important for a few reasons. It should be widely understood that those who put their bodies on the line for the Peaks, for the sanctity of water, for the ecological integrity of the Peaks, did so with the same dedication, determination, and commitment as those at Standing Rock. For settler skiers, snowboarders, rock climbers, trail runners, mountain bikers, race directors, and more, this simple recognition should give us pause.

Many so-called outdoor enthusiasts approach their love of the outdoors with a strong environmental ethic; they want to do right by Indigenous peoples, and many voiced their solidarity with those resisting the pipeline at Standing Rock. Yet when Indigenous people resist developments meant to expand outdoor recreation opportunities, that solidarity appears to vanish. For most, this isn't intentional or from a place of malice but the consequence of a conditioning that prioritizes some forms of colonial harm over others when they are part of the same story, simply different expressions of settler entitlement to Indigenous lands. I begin this chapter from the assumption that when outdoor enthusiasts understand the lengths people went to protect the Peaks, how land-use decisions are infinitely more consequential for Indigenous peoples, it will be impossible to look the other way when it happens elsewhere. To that end, it is my hope that recounting these moments will promote greater solidarity across Indigenous-led efforts to protect land and sacred sites, from resource extraction to recreational colonialism.

"Our Action Is a Prayer"

As the unseasonably warm winter sun pierced the horizon, meandering slowly through bare aspen branches and sharp ponderosa pine needles to illuminate the northwest slope of the San Francisco Peaks, a strange sight emerged: one long strip of yellow-tinged snow in a sea of otherwise dry forest.[2] On this November morning in 2017, the Arizona Snowbowl Ski Resort finally opened for the season after two previous attempts. Due to the warm weather, the resort—determined to open this time—ran its snowmaking equipment through the night to keep its promises to season pass holders that the resort would be open in time for Thanksgiving break.

---

2. The title of this section, "Our Action Is a Prayer," comes from a press release written by Indigenous land protectors on the day of the August 2011 action that can be found at Indigenous Action Media, "Direct Action." It was also cited in K. Benally, "San Francisco Peaks."

Much of this large section comes from edited excerpts from Boggs, "Anti-Snowbowl Direct Actions"; and Boggs, "Direct Action" (this article first appeared in *The Noise,* July 2011, but was later published by *Earth First! Journal* in March 2012).

While skier and snowboarder attendance was sparse, recreationalists and Snowbowl employees were met with more than a dozen "sacred sites protectors," whose presence drew the public's attention back to what has been a multigenerational, Indigenous-led resistance against past and ongoing development at the resort—most recently and most contentiously, the resort's use of municipal reclaimed wastewater to make snow.

Demonstrators gathered at the base of the run and performed a mock "quarantine" action in hazmat suits with banners and caution tape to reaffirm their stance that the resort's development—approved by the Forest Service and sanctioned by the City of Flagstaff, who entered into a contract with the resort to sell them the water—remains unacceptable.

"Even though I knew about the treated sewage used to make snow at Snowbowl, I was shocked when I looked at the snow and saw this yellow tinge," said demonstrator Crystal Zevon, who observed the yellow tint on the snow when the sun hit it. At this point, the resort had been using the City of Flagstaff's municipal reclaimed wastewater to make snow for the previous three ski seasons. Since snowmaking began in 2012, the first time the resort turns on the system at the start of the season, the snow has a yellow tinge, which the resort claims is from rust in the pipes. The yellow tint, however, is a visual reminder that the snow is not natural, that it does potentially contain harmful compounds, and that the resort, skiers and snowboarders, the city, and the Forest Service have all prioritized skiing no matter the cost to human health, ecological integrity, and their relationships with regional Indigenous peoples.

"No desecration for recreation!" the demonstrators yelled in unison as police approached. Such demonstrations have occurred every year on opening day since 2002, when the Snowbowl first proposed its expansions and appealed to the City of Flagstaff to sell the resort treated wastewater for snowmaking. Each year a similar sort of disconnect occurs. Indigenous-led activists have shown up condemning the expansions as desecration, as cultural genocide, a perspective so obvious in Indigenous communities that the former Navajo Nation president described it using those same terms[3] Stressing the importance of this case to the Hopi people, LeRoy Shingoitewa, the chairman of the Hopi Tribe, said, "The health and safety of the Hopi people is indistinguishable from the health and safety of the environment—protection of the environment on the San Francisco Peaks is central to the Tribe's existence."

And then there are the skiers and snowboarders, mostly white folks from Phoenix, who stare with blank faces as they coast by to get back in the lift line. Some, clearly aware of the controversy, are combative, if not overtly racist in their confrontations. But most appear to be genuinely dumbfounded. How can

---

3. Shirley, "On the Sanctity."

a ski resort be racist? How is outdoor recreation desecrating the mountain? How is any of this related to colonialism, to genocide? Some, not many, actually ask these questions, and hopefully some go home wondering about the answers. But it is safe to assume that if the tribes had won the previous decade of lawsuits and the resort had not been able to produce this snow and had not opened on this day, no skier or snowboarder would protest as if their cultural survival were on the line.

"This mountain is our church, Snowbowl's opening today and the threat of arrest for 'trespassing' was another reminder that we do not have religious freedom as Indigenous peoples in our own lands," said Klee Benally. Benally and other Indigenous activists had been arrested for trespassing on the Peaks before. The very notion of "trespassing" on ancestral lands recalls Scott Morgensen's observations that the biopolitics of settler colonialism construct any Indigenous presence in places claimed by the settler society as a threat in need of elimination.[4] During this time, Snowbowl rallied security and called police to monitor protesters every time they were anywhere near the resort. Nonetheless, this occurrence reaffirmed what Benally already learned in 2006, when the courts ruled in favor of the Forest Service against the Navajo Nation on the grounds that the developments did not constitute a "substantial burden" to the tribe's religious freedoms. That court decided, "the only effect of the proposed upgrades is on the Plaintiffs' subjective emotional religious experience," and said their "damaged spiritual feelings" were not enough to constitute any religious freedoms violation. These descriptions of Indigenous religion as based on emotionally subjective experiences and feelings is not a description courts would likely use to describe other religions, which is why when the Supreme Court denied a petition to hear the case, Howard Shanker, the attorney representing the Navajo Nation, in addition to several other tribes and three environmental groups, said, "In a country that supposedly values the free exercise and accommodation of all religion, it is unconscionable that Native American religious and cultural beliefs have essentially been relegated to second-class status by the federal government."[5]

---

4. Morgensen, "Biopolitics." Morgensen's analysis here is also referenced in Barker and Ross, "Reoccupation and Resurgence," 208.

5. *Navajo Nation et al. v. USFS*, 2006; and K. Benally, "San Francisco Peaks." As a matter of accuracy, after the 2006 lawsuit was decided in an Arizona court, the plaintiffs appealed the case and won at the ninth circuit court of appeals in San Francisco, California (*Navajo Nation et al. v. USFS* 2007). This was regarded as a huge win for regional Indigenous communities; however, that win would be legally erased less than a year later. In a rarely granted form of appeal called *en banc*, in which all the judges of an appellate court rehear a case regarded as especially complex, those judges ruled against the ninth circuit decision, thus reaffirming the lower court's ruling in favor of the Forest Service (*Navajo Nation v. U.S. en banc*, 2008). Plaintiffs then appealed to the Supreme Court, who refused to hear the case.

"This is a clear example of continued colonialism," said demonstrator Maile Hampton. "What's happening is Dook'o'oosłííd, a sacred mountain to many Indigenous peoples in this area, is being desecrated by this Snowbowl company." Recreation has escaped critique because it is often regarded as apolitical and innocent, yet the controversy over development on the San Francisco Peaks constitutes the process of theft, exclusion, and marginalization that often mirrors cultural genocide in other contexts. "We were there to try to stop the desecration of our sacred mountain where our prayers and ceremonies are held," stated Dustin Wero. "Being Diné, our instinct is to defend the sacred."

•

A prayer gathering was held at the base of the San Francisco Peaks a few days after construction began in May 2011. Navajo Nation President Ben Shelly addressed the crowd, "We've got to stop the construction." Kelvin Long, director of ECHOES (Educating Communities while Healing and Offering Environmental Support), stated, "We're going to protect our mountain, we're not going to allow snowmaking to happen." Steve Darden of the Navajo Nation Human Rights Commission and former Flagstaff City Council member added a specific message to youth: "In our Hogans and sweat lodges we are offering our prayers, we're relying on you young ones to step up." On June 16, land defenders engaged in the first of several actions that would eventually result in the arrests of over fifty people.

On the morning of the action, as the full moon faded and the sun rose, two men, Evan Hawbaker and Kris Barney chained themselves to the wheel wells of a large excavator (figure 7.1) while two other protesters, Hailey Sherwood and Ned del Callejo, sat back-to-back deep inside the six-foot-trench, bound to each other by the neck with U-locks (figure 7.2). The action occurred a few miles up Snowbowl Road where construction had been in progress since May 25.

The first to respond to the scene was Snowbowl. The security vehicle, a blue Mercedes, screamed up and down Snowbowl Road, apparently trying to locate those involved in the action. By 6:00 a.m., more than fifteen armed agents had arrived on the scene, as well as the Coconino County Sheriff's Department, City of Flagstaff Police, and the FBI.

At the same time a group of at least eight demonstrators gathered at the bottom of Snowbowl Road, blocking access. Five demonstrators wore white hazmat suites in a symbolic quarantine of the resort, stretching banners across the road that read, "Protect Sacred Sites" and "Danger! Health Hazard—Snowbowl." Caution tape was stretched across the width of the road along with other objects to form a makeshift blockade.

FIGURE 7.1. Evan Hawbaker and Kris Barney chained up to the wheel well of a towering excavator, stopping construction on June 16, 2011. Photograph by the author.

The demonstrators engaged in a multivariate approach to what is very much considered a multilayered issue. The complexity of the controversy was illustrated in the diversity of demonstrator's shouts, echoing from the base of the mountain, from those locked to construction equipment, and from voices deep from within the pipeline trenches. "Protect sacred sites, defend human rights!" "No desecration for recreation!" "Stop the cultural genocide! Protect the Peaks!" "Human health over corporate wealth!" "Dook'o'oosłííd, we've got your back!" Another mantra that rang throughout the forest that morning—a phrase associated with Standing Rock though it was a hallmark among protests against Snowbowl in Flagstaff for the previous decade—is, "Water is life!"

Police first concentrated their efforts on the men chained to the excavator giving Hailey and Ned some time to talk in anticipation of what was to come. Hailey said to Ned, "Don't you feel kinda small in this deep trench?" Ned paused, then responded, "Not when I'm doing big things."

By 7:30, assisted by county sheriffs, the Flagstaff Fire Department began aggressively cutting demonstrators from their various lockdown devices. To the excavator, the police brought muscle and saws. "The police's use of excessive force was in complete disregard for my safety. They pulled at my arms and forced my body and head further into the machine, all the while using heavy-duty power saws within inches of my hand," said Evan.

Rather than negotiate, as the demonstrators were cut, it was clear that the police and firefighters preferred to use scare tactics. "We don't want to cut

FIGURE 7.2. Ned del Callejo and Hailey Sherwood at the bottom of a deep wastewater pipe trench, locked back-to-back by the neck with a U-lock, pausing construction on June 16, 2011. Photograph by the author.

your arm off," repeated one of the firefighters several times, to which Evan finally responded, "I don't want you to cut my arm off either!" Evan said the fireman looked dead serious when he said, "Well, we will if we have to."

Evan and Kris were chained to the same excavator. The device that bound them to the machine is referred to as a lockbox. Both arms go through a PVC pipe and from the outside, that's all anybody can see. Inside, however, their hands gripped a metal rod; a chain around their wrists was also connected to the rod with a strong carabiner. There are many variations of this design, which is commonly seen in nonviolent direct actions around the world.

Evan said after holding on to the rod for a while that his hand became numb. The firefighters used a Sawzall to cut the PVC pipe lengthwise. When the blade hit the metal rod, it rattled the chain violently and Evan described a warm feeling that trickled down his arm. "I thought it was blood; I thought they cut my fingers," he said. "Those who cut us out endangered our well-being, ignoring the screams to stop. They treated our bodies the way they're treating this holy mountain."

"I've done this quite a bit and never have I feared for my safety like this before," said Ned. "The whole thing was disorganized and dangerous. There was no communication."

A demonstrator locked to another in a similar fashion as Hailey and Ned described how one police officer attempted to stand them up while another officer moved the other demonstrator a different way. Because U-locks bound the demonstrators by the neck, they were choked.

"Nobody even bothered to ask what it would take to get us out voluntarily. Finally, they just started hurting us," said Ned. "I'm here to protect the mountain, I said, and you're hurting me. You're choking me." The police responded in a way that did not sugar-coat their lack of experience in dealing with non-violent demonstrators: "That's your own fault."

"Our safety was prioritized second to Snowbowl's demands. I was not aggressive. My lock was sawed through, inches away from both of our heads, secured solely and recklessly by the hands of a deputy. During the process, we were repeatedly asked to chant to reaffirm our consciousness. The police's response was hasty, taking about ten minutes in total—it was dehumanizing," said Hailey.

One at a time, as demonstrators were removed from their locking devices, they were treated by paramedics and arrested for trespassing. Two demonstrators who had been bound to minors were also charged with "contributing to the delinquency of a minor," and another was charged with "endangerment."

"How can we be trespassers on our Holy Site?" questioned Kris. "I do not agree with these and the other charges; we will continue our resistance."

•

After the June 16 action, affinity groups began to arrive, setting up self-sustained base camps on the San Francisco Peaks. An affinity group is a small group of activists, united under a common cause, who work together on direct actions and other forms of resistance on-site. Scholarship describes protest camps "as distinctive material and mediated spaces where people come together to imagine alternative worlds and articulate contentious politics, often in confrontation with the state." Protests camps, and the strategic and imaginative work done in them, are also spatial, meaning "the sites of protest camps are chosen because they are strategic—they draw attention to an injustice."[6] By mid-August, twenty-six known basecamps had been established within the legal camping area of Forest Service land on the San Francisco Peaks in an area between the pipeline's construction and the resort itself. Said one activist who wished to remain anonymous: "The notion is clear: if you want to protect the mountain from further expansions, don't write letters,

6. Brown and Feigenbaum, *Protest Camps*, 1, 11.

don't sign petitions, stop asking yourself 'why government agencies, from the city to the Feds, are fighting so hard for an unpopular project' and take action!"

While at least half of those groups are from Flagstaff, other supporters, both Indigenous and non-Indigenous, reside elsewhere on the Colorado Plateau and in the state. Eight people who had spent nearly one hundred days and nights to protect Glen Cove, a burial site held sacred to several tribes near Vallejo, California, arrived in early August. The occupation of the cove, called Sogorea Te, resulted in a "cultural easement" that set a legal precedent guaranteeing that the Yocha Dehe and Cortina tribes will have legal oversight in all activities taking place on the site. Motivated by the success of their own victory, they came to support those taking similar action on the San Francisco Peaks.

In mid-July the Peaks CookShack was established in a legal camping area near Snowbowl "to support other encampments and affinity groups by providing access to available food, gear, first aid, information, and other supplies being offered and dropped off by supporters and community members." At the time, those running CookShack were committed to remaining on the mountain indefinitely.

"A few folks from Tohono O'odham came and hung out with us for the first weekend we were here," said Ned, speaking on a beautiful Sunday morning at CookShack toward the end of July. "They did a prayer for rain and protection on the mountain. Literally right when they left, it hailed for two days straight. Construction had to stop because there was a foot of hail on the ground. In July."

Sitting on a large downed log, looking up toward swaying aspens, Ned continued, "There are moments like that up here; regardless of the kind of hopelessness folks feel. Up here, you just can't feel it. I mean, you see the destruction every day and it does get to you, but there is also this other part of it, where you understand fully how important it is to do the work and to find a way."

•

August 4–9, 2011, was organized as a "Week of Action," which included multiple marches throughout Flagstaff, with protests and rallies in front of city hall, the Coconino County Forest Service Office, and High Desert Investment (the construction company contracted by Snowbowl). On August 7, police aggressively disrupted the Protect the Peaks march, which drew more than one hundred people, arresting six people, including several known organizers.

FIGURE 7.3. Mountain protectors engage in a road blockade, blocking construction, on August 8, 2011. Photograph by the author.

The next morning, nine people formed a blockade across Snowbowl Road (figure 7.3). Adam Barker and Russell Myers Ross have written about the function and historical role of blockades, specific to Indigenous resistance to settler colonialism:

As settler states have relentlessly driven railways and roads through Indigenous homelands, while restricting Indigenous nations onto reserves, fractions of their former land-bases, direct actions to violate those colonial spaces can be a powerful act of resurgence for Indigenous Peoples. In response, blockading has become an important tactic through which Indigenous communities reassert their traditional forms of place-based culture and governance.[7]

Some demonstrators locked themselves to steel drums full of concrete, while others were bound to each other. More than fifty armed agents showed up and used industrial saws, toxic chemical degreasers, and a jackhammer to break apart the blockade. The human blockade delayed construction that day for eight hours, animating other blockades at Standing Rock and elsewhere, where a blockade has been "explicitly erected to impede the power of state

---

7. Barker and Ross, "Reoccupation and Resurgence," 199.

and capital from entering and leaving Indigenous territories respectively."[8] It also quelled any preconceived ideas that opposition to development would go away.

Snowbowl General Manager J. R. Murray appeared a few hours into the action. The sound of industrial saws pierced the quiet at nine thousand feet, and he stood on the side of the road with his arms crossed, watching police drag demonstrator after demonstrator away from the scene. The look on his face could only be described in one way: he was dumbfounded.

It could be compared with the same facial expression of pro-development factions during the last forty years of Flagstaff City Council meetings concerning development on the Peaks—when Indigenous elders spoke about desecration, with tears running down their cheeks. That dumbfounded look, the look that forces us to ask, *If skiers and snowboarders had to make do without expansions, without the pipelines and the clear-cuts, would the prospect of that reality bring tears to their eyes? Would they put their lives on the line to defend their perceived right to ski?*

"The only choice for us is to take action against those who threaten Indigenous cultures, the environment, and our future. It's frustrating that we had to do this in order to make this point clear," stated Jenna Tomasello, who took part in the action.

Stephen Zavodnyik, also arrested during the blockade, elaborated: "We decided to take matters into our own hands, and you can too. Whatever you feel is sacred, defend it with all your heart and take a risk, because our future generations will not forgive inaction."

"For us, our actions are self-defense," said Ned after they were arrested for the third time that summer. "And everyone has that right. I am not afraid of what will happen to me if I protest, what I am more afraid of is what will happen if I do not stand up."

Many of the people who chained themselves up alongside Indigenous peoples in all of these actions, including other demonstrations and protests not mentioned here, were settlers who made the decision to stand in solidarity with Indigenous peoples and risked their personal safety and freedom alongside them because of their commitment to Indigenous struggle. Another example of someone who made this commitment is James Kennedy, who occupied a large ponderosa pine tree that summer near Thorpe Park in Flagstaff. The tree was scheduled to be cut down to make way for the reclaimed wastewater pipeline. Kennedy, a snowboarder who used to be a Snowbowl

---

8. Coulthard, *Red Skin, White Masks*, 118. This reference is also used in Barker and Ross, "Reoccupation and Resurgence," 201.

season passholder, had changed his mind after intimate conversations about the resort with a Hopi woman he worked with. "It's just recreation, you know? It's not something that takes precedence over someone else's culture and life," he said.[9]

The courageous stand at Standing Rock is now legendary and has inspired other similar pipeline protests around the world. Important contextual reflection and analysis of this important moment in Indigenous resistance should be read widely, specifically Nick Estes's *Our History Is the Future: Standing Rock Versus the Dakota Access Pipeline, and the Long Tradition of Indigenous Resistance,* Dina Gilio-Whitaker's *As Long As Grass Grows: The Indigenous Fight for Environmental Justice from Colonization to Standing Rock,* and Joyce Rain Anderson's chapter "Walking with Relatives," among others.[10] Resource extraction projects, like the Dakota Access Pipeline, and outdoor recreation developments, like Snowbowl, that are unacceptable to Indigenous peoples and cause disproportionate harm dot the landscape in the United States, Canada, and elsewhere. In an area not far from where the Ktunaxa Nation has resisted development by the Jumbo Glacier Ski Resort in northeastern British Columbia, the Wet'suwet'en First Nation organized a similar stand against the Coastal GasLink natural gas pipeline. In all these cases, Indigenous peoples were not properly consulted, were locked out of decision-making processes and criminalized when they resisted, and settlers often inspired by Indigenous leadership and a sense of moral obligation stood in solidarity. Though the green wastewater pipe buried deep in the soil from Flagstaff to the Arizona Snowbowl Ski Resort does not transport oil, it still represents the context of settler entitlement to Indigenous land, and resistance to it is part of the long history of Indigenous resistance to settler colonialism.

---

9. Boggs, "Tree Sit."
10. Anderson, "Walking with Relatives." Also see Todrys, *Black Snake.*

CHAPTER 8

Community Listening, Relationality, and the Public Art of the Peaks

On a chilly mid-September morning in 2011, the city of Flagstaff woke up to something unexpected and disorienting. At Heritage Square, the center of Flagstaff's downtown, cornstalks stood upright, carefully placed in a pile of mud on the pavement. Written in the same dirt around the cornstalks were illustrations of mountains and the words "Protect Dookʼoʼoosłííd." Similar installations were found in front of Cline Library on the campus of Northern Arizona University and other locations. The headline in the local paper described it as "mud mayhem." Even though the completely organic installations would wash off, Thomas Greyeyes and Elizabeth Mills faced criminal charges of vandalism. According to the police report, when an officer asked them why they did this, "Greyeyes replied that he was Native American and that the land belonged to him."[1]

At this point, twenty-eight people had been arrested throughout the summer while taking part in Indigenous-led direct actions on the Peaks and demonstrations in Flagstaff. The "mud mayhem" incident was many things at once: public art, direct action, and (allegedly) vandalism. As an art installation, in my reading, it was provocative and confrontational, reasserting that the land under the city—where the dirt is—is Indigenous. It drew attention to the ways the land has been written and claimed by and for settlers, and how the everydayness of such spaces obscures settler colonialism in the present. It disrupted

---

1. Betz, "Mud Mayhem Draws Charges."

ideas about the location of the Peaks controversy, the space in which it occurs being not just the mountain itself but on all stolen ancestral Indigenous lands. It was a material-discursive installation that reinscribed Indigenous ways of knowing and being in areas where they are no longer supposed to be, forcing Flagstaff citizens to reckon with that contradiction. This installation seemed to cycle out of local news and public discussion quickly, but I bring it up a lot in my community writing classes because of how powerfully and directly its meaning is tied to the historical, cultural, and linguistic context of that place. Not only do unconventional forms of advocacy like public art function as a kind of community writing, but public art can often reach audiences in ways that text on paper—the form of community writing I engaged in as a journalist—is structurally incapable of doing. The confrontational nature of public art holds infinite potential to affect audiences in myriad ways that command attention in unexpected places. Like writing, public art speaks to audiences and invites us to listen; through that listening we come to know ourselves and our community in ways we couldn't have before.

There are many ways to be a community writer. One can do this work individually or collaboratively, across a broad range of genres, and can effect change, deepen understanding, and provoke engagement and action in a multitude of ways. As a result of my journalistic coverage, I developed a personal stake in the ecological integrity of the Peaks and a commitment to local environmental and Indigenous activists who trusted me to do whatever I could to bring more attention to this issue. In doing so, I came to understand my responsibility in this role but also a sense of connection to the work of others. I saw myself as one part of a larger collective of people, deploying whatever communicative tactics we had to write as a community. And this looked like a lot of different things. There were filmmakers, musicians, web designers, novelists, poets, photographers, muralists, cartoonists, dancers, screen printers, banner droppers, and a variety of other print and digital visual artists.[2] While I wrote, many others were engaged in composition all around me. The role of art in the public's perception of this controversy has been profound, reflecting a range of human expression and emotion.

As community writers, creators, and publishers, all of us in our own way composed together, creating a diverse yet unified voice in support of the ecological integrity of the Peaks. During moments when many of us were together, at a demonstration, a workshop, a teach-in, I observed a kind of collaboration

---

2. In earlier drafts of this chapter, I listed people and examples of their work as a way to honor the breadth and diversity of expression, and this went on for a full two pages. In the end, I have decided to shorten the discussion to protect people's names and get to my point more quickly. But when I think back to all the creative forms of expression in support of the Peaks against Snowbowl, it truly was amazing.

at work that was grounded in listening and relationality. All of us were committed to producing different kinds of texts that leveraged our skills, talents, and positions toward a common goal. It was hard for me to square this with the community writing theory I was reading at the time, which seemed to limit what "counted" as community writing. In terms of intention and affect, the work I've been describing is all in the orbit of creative and collaborative community writing and publishing, composing in the context of Indigenous solidarity and protection of the Peaks. The process they went through to create these pieces were not radically different from what I was doing as a community writer; both involved deep community listening, self-reflection, and building trust, all of which were necessary to become accountable, complicit, and implicated. Not only that, but these forms of visual art had the potential to reach audiences in ways that revealed the limitations of the written word.

At its core, this chapter focuses on community writing and public art as a vehicle for understanding the process of relational accountability, and part of that process involves deep community listening. But I take the long way getting there, beginning first with further reflections on what I've learned as a community writer before I turn toward a larger analysis of public art—specifically the work of Chip Thomas, a.k.a. Jetsonorama.

I analyze the visual and material rhetoric of his photographic murals to emphasize the necessity of community listening as both a process-oriented and relational practice and something that shows up in the work, revealing structures of accountability to the communities in which they appear by reflecting back to them their own experience and shared struggles. After introducing Thomas and demonstrating these relationships in his work generally, this chapter analyzes several examples of his work, both in the ways it communicates Indigenous resistance to development on the Peaks and how it exemplifies the profound relationship between community listening, visual art, and meaningful public engagement.

In representing Thomas in his own words, I rely primarily on film and print interviews and profiles; I also weave in moments from my own interviews with him when I was a journalist and more recently. The result is a personal reflection of his work over many years, which exemplifies my observations about community listening as a process built from long-term commitments. Thomas's murals further emphasize new ways that a community that is listened to can speak through the work, where the art—like all meaningful community writing—speaks *with* and not *for*.[3] While Linda Alcoff calls for more research into practical ways to speak *with*, or at least "lessen the

---

3. With this phrasing, I am recalling Alcoff's discussion of the problems of speaking *for* and speaking *about* in her 1991 essay, "The Problem of Speaking for Others."

dangers" of speaking *for* or speaking *about*, this chapter constitutes one of the ways community listening, particularly through public art, can contribute to this larger ongoing discussion.[4] Ultimately, for anyone engaged in the work of representation—whether through writing or art that represents other cultures, ways of being, ways of understanding that are not one's own—there will be lessons here, guidance aimed at opening new pathways toward better relations.

Community Writing against Extractive Listening

In my teaching and research in community writing I often weave in lessons that I learned through my time as a community writer. These lessons draw on moments when I felt like I got it right, when my coverage was not only in the public interest but also honored those I interviewed by representing their experiences on their own terms. Based on community feedback, those were moments when I was successful at drawing meaningful attention and support to communities that needed it. But more notable were lessons drawn from the times I made mistakes or would have done things differently in hindsight. By being honest about those moments when the outcome of my coverage did not always line up with my intentions, I position myself as particularly useful to students who are eager to "get it right," knowing that they won't always and that those are often the most valuable lessons. I try my best in these conversations to emphasize the value of community listening before, during, *and after* writing, allowing students to recognize the work they produce as more than isolated pieces but as part of an ongoing conversation with the communities in which they engage. There will be many extrapolations of community listening throughout this chapter, but as a point of entry, the practice requires a willingness to reflect, to question our assumptions, and most importantly, to be vulnerable, to lean into those moments when we are told our work could have been better. Community feedback provided in good faith is evidence ultimately of support for the work, an acknowledgment of its necessity. I always tell my students to think of these moments not as failings but as opportunities that invite us to grow in new ways.

These experiences have prepared me to further define community listening by also describing what it is not, and cannot be, even under the best of intentions. For example, a journalist might deploy deep listening strategies in the moment of an interview through verbal and nonverbal cues that communicate comprehension and empathy, relying on a recording device to be more present, and they might take care in composing and organizing questions that

---

4. Alcoff, "Problem of Speaking," 24.

feel more conversational than interrogational. These strategies tend to result in stories that are meaningful and engaging. However, if the journalist enters a community in which they have no relationship only to get quotes for a story reflecting positions they think they already know, listening only for what they want to hear, these deep listening strategies may also be transactional, and the exchange or transaction may be more valuable to the journalist than the interviewee and their community. This kind of listening, known as "extractive listening," results in stories that are not just inaccurate or based on misrepresentations but that reinforce false narratives and partial perspectives. Community listening in service of diverse public collaborators must resist extractive listening to understand "what a community wants and needs."[5] Community listening refers to the process by which a writer negotiates their positionality and defines their goals in relation to what a community needs on terms that community helps to define. As such I aspire toward community listening as a practice that honors the lived experiences, histories, and cultures of the communities in which I engage, and by putting these commitments into practice through a deep listening practice, the community writer is in a better position to establish lasting trust through systems of accountability and relationality.

Further, when journalists engage in extractive listening within an Indigenous community or in conversation with an Indigenous person, they risk reproducing colonial structures and power dynamics in a place where extraction already occurs in many ways. Extractive colonialism extends from the historical subordinating processes of racial capitalism that exploit the often resource-rich lands held by Indigenous peoples and bring dramatic "material changes to social and ecological life" to people who live there; listening that is based on an extractive model also produce troubling outcomes.[6] The work produced under this framework can ultimately help sustain attitudes and beliefs that are harmful and have material and social consequences. Affect is profoundly more important than intention. A journalist can enter an interview with good intentions but still work from structures that can sustain harm rather than challenge it. The adage of content-driven engagement and engagement-driven content doesn't necessarily make for better relations, produce trust, or challenge existing power structures or meaning-making systems. I've worked with journalists who simply believe that showing up and doing the story is enough, but the *how* of that story is just as important.

I certainly found this to be true of writing, which—like public art—is the result of a listening process that engages many modes of perception, openness,

---

5. Goins, "Embodying Key Principles." Goins also uses the phrase "extractive listening" in this essay, which I found instructive, however not grounded in the colonial framework I deploy in my understanding.

6. Gómez-Barris, *Extractive Zone*, xvii.

and honesty with one's positionality. As a journalist who often visited the Navajo Nation, I bore witness to the effects of coal extraction by seeing it for myself. I came to understand the relationship between culture and landscape by walking dusty footpaths that led to springs, I reveled in the way sheep smell in fresh morning snow among pinion, sage, and juniper, and I read the look on the faces of those I interviewed to gauge understanding and interest. It is through this kind of deep listening that I learned the difference between experiencing Diné culture on the Navajo Nation and recognizing and reflecting instead on *my experience of that experience.* In other words, I found my integrity as a writer through perceiving myself honestly as an outsider, affecting how I listen in that space. This distinction allowed me to recognize my own misconceptions, biases, preconceived ideas, and privileges, putting me in a better position to be more present, engaged in modes of perception that enrich our understanding of what listening is. Further, all of this constitutes forms of community listening that are placed-based and thus invite us to confront our own positionality in those places. In the process, forging our own community listening praxis becomes integral to holding ourselves accountable to our own commitments.

Community Writing and Community Listening

Independent newspapers, chapbooks, newsletters, broadsides, zines, and more remain crucial for their interventions into public discourse, their articulations of identity and sense of place, and their capacity to provoke public debate and challenge institutional dominance over the public sphere through radical and democratic action. Public art has also been established as a meaningful form of advocacy, a valid form of community writing. It catalyzes a particular kind of community listening that is expressed uniquely through the mediums of art that reflect community and its values, goals, lived experiences, histories, and identities; it has the power to translate the community's needs and struggles as well as its joys. These characteristics, expressions, and orientations are made visible in public art that is engaged in community listening and in turn produces a viewer that becomes a listening audience. Whether the viewer engages or ignores the work's provocations, those provocations nonetheless persist, perhaps long after the viewer returns home.

Community listening as a practice/process is fundamental to how I understand the formation of accountability and relationality, and it is central to cultivating what Shawn Wilson calls "relational accountability," a means of building solidarity and provoking action that focuses on the process of *how.*[7]

---

7. S. Wilson, *Research Is Ceremony,* 99.

When I think of relational accountability in public art, I'm recognizing how listening is communicated visually and what that reveals about the artist's process of representation and their relationships with the community. When public art appears in shared community spaces, when people or their cultures, practices, and histories are depicted or reflected in the work, it is the community that ultimately decides whether the work will continue to stand. This measure of community listening, foregrounded by accountability and relationality, is not something that can be achieved overnight. However, community listening practices and processes can also be meaningful in a particular moment. For example, recall "the people's mic," or the "community microphone," as it was also called, which became the signature form of amplification during the Occupy Wall Street protests in 2011. The practice refers to a large group of people gathered around a speaker with no microphone. Each line shouted by the speaker is promptly repeated by the group, thus amplifying the message of the speaker to those in the back. As each listener moves back and forth between roles as listener and speaker, their relationship to each other extends from their shared participation and solidarity with the message.

Focusing on community listening scholarship on community writing and public art has helped me find ways to recognize, contextualize, and process the ways we are implicated by our research and by those we interview, how we are situated in the topic, and it allows us to articulate difference in terms of consequence: what is at stake for those we engage with might be vastly different from what is at stake for us or to our readers. Public art, especially that which is unconventional and unexpected, may similarly provoke this kind of reflection. While scholarly work on visual rhetoric has long maintained that the production and rhetorical effect of images can certainly do the same persuasive work that written texts do,[8] I also understand what visual texts like public art can do to produce forms of community listening that activate and engage the public in ways that are dynamic and meaningful. I understand this claim as synesthetic in nature, as community listening works across senses synergistically, producing new forms of engagement as it participates in complex sense-making processes that are folded into the work.

The View from the Road

Around 2009 I noticed Chip Thomas's murals when driving up 89, the road that goes north from Flagstaff, Arizona, through the Navajo Nation. One

---

8. See Foss, "Rhetorical Schema"; DeLuca, *Image Politics*; Dobrin and Morey, *Ecosee*; Hill and Helmers, *Defining Visual Rhetorics*; and Robins, *Into the Image*.

installation, then a few months later another, would pop up, breathing new life into a structure I had hardly noticed before. In the years that followed, they were everywhere: large-scale photographs, most of them black and white with splashes of accent color. I saw images of a woman herding sheep, a close-up of a man's face laughing, a toddler with eyes inquisitive and mischievous, children laughing hysterically, grazing sheep, a child's eyes gazing up toward a big piece of raw coal, a woman on a swing smiling with her head upside down, a close-up of hands, a man standing proudly next to stalks of corn (and lots more sheep!). Sometimes the work featured text, sometimes written on subjects' faces and other times below, off to the side, or overlaid. At the time, I recognized how this text often worked in tandem with the image to convey meaning that would not otherwise be possible through either the image or the text alone. Because of the contrast between the landscape, quiet and still, and the vibrancy of the images, I found myself compelled to pull over, to turn off my engine, and to listen. The images clearly had something to say, stories to tell and communicate about that place and the community it represented; they quite literally animate the landscape, making it talk, making it move.

Thomas is a Black physician, photographer, public artist, and activist originally from North Carolina. While he has recently retired and moved to Flagstaff to concentrate on his art full-time, he had lived and worked on the Navajo Nation in northern Arizona practicing medicine since 1987. After finishing medical school in the mid-1980s, Thomas came out to Arizona to serve as a physician on the Navajo Nation through the National Health Service Corps, a program that connects physicians to places around the country with limited access to healthcare. Although he finished his obligation in 1991, he had fallen in love with the people, the culture, and the landscape of northern Arizona, and he decided to continue to live and work on the reservation as both a physician and an artist. In the latter role, he is part of the Painted Desert Project, where he works with other artists to create works across the region. As many of the examples here show, he often draws inspiration from his relationships with patients and coworkers, most of whom are Diné, who have shared stories with him about their lives, their struggles, and their joys.

Having grown up admiring the photojournalism of people like Eugene Smith and Gordon Parks, whose work regularly appeared in *Life* magazine and *Look* magazine in the 1960s and 1970s, Thomas became a photographer. "I just loved turning the pages and looking at the images and seeing how people lived in other parts of the world," he said. "People who were being documented and photographed weren't necessarily famous people, but just everyday people; so I came away with a sense that everyone has a story to tell."[9] He

---

9. New Mexico PBS, "NMPBS ¡COLORES!"

often asked people on the reservation if he could photograph them, and his work appeared in some regional exhibitions, but as a street artist himself, he always wanted to "go bigger," to create art "where the people in the work got to see themselves represented," to "create work that reminds people of the beauty they've shared with me over the last thirty years."[10] Between the craft of his photography, his interest in street art, and the relationships he has cultivated with the Indigenous communities with which he lives and works, he asked, "Is there a way that I can bring that medium to a place that has never had it, and can I do it in a way that is respectful and appreciated by the people whom I am representing?"[11]

The work of Chip Thomas brings the concept of relational accountability into focus as a useful framework for community listening. In his own words, Thomas is an "artist, activist, and physician," "a visual storyteller."[12] He's an "intentional provocateur, putting work out that people might not expect to see in a particular space."[13] I met Thomas and wrote about his art when I was a journalist in northern Arizona; his work is primarily situated where he lives and works on the Navajo Nation. I found that Thomas's visual work not only constitutes community writing, but in a lot of ways it transcends what I was able to do as a journalist.

Relational Accountability and Listening

In *Research Is Ceremony: Indigenous Research Methods*, Shawn Wilson articulates an Indigenous research framework assembled by traditional Indigenous practices that center relationality and relational accountability. One who is accountable to their relations recognizes the ways they are implicated in the consequences of the work. For Wilson, relational accountability refers to the process by which one becomes accountable to and respectful of all relationships, including relationships between individual people, human and non-human communities, ideas, and land. It's a process that should feel organic, less like prescription and more like building a relationship. Accountability in this framework refers to the process by which one forges meaningful relationships and establishes trust through working together, collaborating, and learning from one another. The effect of becoming accountable to one's relations

---

10. KQED Arts, "Street Artist Portrays Navajo Life."

11. Bell, "Outside Magazine."

12. Bell, "Outside Magazine." Jetsonorama is Thomas's street artist name, associated with his work with the Painted Desert Project and other past and ongoing collaborations and installations.

13. KQED Arts, "Street Artist Portrays Navajo Life."

creates the conditions from which work that is wanted, needed, and celebrated by that community is imagined; it means one is open to criticism because they want to do right by that community, to find ways to connect on deeper levels, to forge stronger connections that provoke, inspire, and challenge. These practices and processes scaffold structures of accountability over time and are intimately connected to community listening.

I am invested in community listening that mobilizes public engagement against settler and white supremacist systems. What does it mean to be a settler on stolen Indigenous land? I am interested in new rhetorical approaches that find ways to articulate the landscapes in which we engage as the palimpsests of culture and history that they are. This requires modes of thinking that disrupt and complicate what we see as anything but simple physical spaces but rather as an amalgamation of stories, competing histories, and contested spaces. The view from the road on the Navajo Nation, a view that is vast and made to feel empty, reflects colonial logics that sustain silences that are strategic and systemic. Thomas's work proves that a rusty old silo or abandoned building can be reclaimed and transformed into something that works against these silences. Listening, when it attends to culture and relationality, when nurtured by the kind of intention exemplified by the words of Shawn Wilson when he wrote, "I come to you with a good heart," can indeed be translated into a language that is visual, responsive, and has the power to provoke action.[14]

The work of Chip Thomas and, more specifically, the process through which he creates his work, which he described to me as an "evolving dialogue," applies the same responsible relational engagement that has been articulated through Indigenous research paradigms as articulated by Wilson. Relationships, for Wilson, are themselves an "ongoing process," within which "all intelligible action is born, sustained, and/or extinguished."[15] But Wilson also doesn't view us and our practices as "being *in* relationship"; he writes that "we *are* the relationships that we hold and are a part of."[16] Community artists and writers literally embody the relationships reflected in their work as they recognize how they are implicated and intimately connected in ways that are unique to them. "I identify as a visual storyteller," says Thomas.[17]

Emphasizing Thomas's public art on the Navajo Nation as a form of visual storytelling, I agree with Rachel Jackson, who based on conversations with Dorothy DeLaune understands stories "as a kind of community listening" that "call[s] us to consider the ways in which community writing occurs beyond the colonialist implications and limitations of printed text." As an Indigenous

---

14. S. Wilson, *Research Is Ceremony,* 7.
15. S. Wilson, xv.
16. S. Wilson, 80.
17. New Mexico PBS, "NMPBS ¡COLORES!"

scholar, Jackson is concerned with the ways that Western academic discourses impose a "rational order on otherwise organic ideas and spontane-
ous meanings," and I'm drawn to her understanding of community listening
as a praxis that "invites us to listen without limitations." For Jackson, storytelling "depends on community listeners for collaborative meaning making,"
asking listeners to "imagine possibilities," attend to "potential meanings" and
"actions," and to examine the "relationships between the past and present situation, between peoples and places, between 'then and now' and 'us and them.'"
While considering visual stories in the same light, I am drawn to Jackson's
analysis of Kiowa storytelling in that it "invites us to listen differently, *with* a
community rather than *to* a community or *for* a community." Jackson's analysis of Kiowa storytelling not only challenges our understanding of community
writing itself but mobilizes it toward Indigenous solidarity and resistance to
settler colonialism. By focusing on the visual storytelling of public art, this
chapter is invested not only in expanding our understanding of what "counts"
as community writing but mobilizes community writing to work against settler colonialism by using visual storytelling in ways that move "historical legacies into the present."[18] And when those legacies are thrust into the present,
they demand to be listened to and reckoned with in the present.

By listening to Thomas and observing his work, I learned to be a different kind of listener, one more attuned to the multiple stories and converging relations a work can communicate. Thomas's visual storytelling reflects
these commitments in ways that depict the intensive listening moments that
he experienced so that others may experience them too. As a journalist, I
learned to think of myself as a community listener as well. My responsibility
as a storyteller necessarily relies on community listening, and the work produced through a deep community listening process is also better positioned to
challenge systemic colonial structures. A storyteller who engages in community listening that is relational, that is focused on building long-term connections, and that creates spaces where the community can speak to each other
can clarify needs that can then be pursued via more stories that the community wants, that will benefit them, and through which they can see themselves
accurately represented.

Public Art and Relational Accountability

What follows are three visual stories, examples of Thomas's work spanning
nearly a decade from 2011 to 2020. I refer to them as visual stories, not only

---

18. Jackson and DeLaune, "Decolonizing Community Writing," 40, 42, 38.

FIGURE 8.1. (above and facing) Panoramic photo of an installation in an alleyway in Flagstaff in 2011. Photographed by John Running and printed with permission from the artist, Chip Thomas.

to animate Thomas's self-identification as a visual storyteller but also to draw attention to the fact that each of these examples is the culmination of a process that begins with community listening—building meaningful relationships, community belonging, accountability, and trust, before responding visually and artistically in a way that is public and provocative. Community listening is embedded in the work itself, through visual cues that reflect relationality: private moments captured through smiles, home settings, family intimacy, and daily practices—all of which typically reside outside public view. This is community listening that is evidence of a healthy relationship, one built on trust cultivated over many years. That these private moments are displayed publicly and embraced by the community as evidenced through the overwhelmingly positive feedback Thomas has received is further evidence of community trust and relationality. As a matter of affect, work produced through community listening, in turn, encourages an audience to listen further and listen differently, both to themselves and to those depicted. Thomas's articulation of his work as an "evolving dialogue" is also a useful way of thinking about community listening as a back and forth between listening and reflecting. When he is installing a piece, Thomas said that it is common for people to stop and talk about their reactions to it, how it made them feel, why they decided to stop. This indicates a strong and meaningful level of engagement that first requires listening to trigger a reflective process. And that process continues after that person has driven away, within and among their home communities.

There are many installations that easily put Thomas's work in conversation with Indigenous activists resisting development at Snowbowl, and the use of reclaimed wastewater to make snow. Those installations are foregrounded by

messages like "water is life" and "defend the sacred," but one installation from 2011 confronts this issue directly.

"What We Do to the Mountain We Do to Ourselves"

In 2011, during a year of Indigenous-led nonviolent direct actions, road block-ades, and demonstrations against the City of Flagstaff and the US Forest Ser-vice's approval of reclaimed wastewater to make snow on the San Francisco Peaks, I wrote articles while Thomas worked with area activists, photogra-phers, and artists to create a large-scale installation that combined black-and-white photography with text drawn on subject's faces (figure 8.1). While I was aware of Thomas's work, this was the first time I met him and encountered his work in the city in which I lived, centered on an issue I covered extensively.

The installation appeared in a public walkway in downtown Flagstaff at the height of this controversy, featuring several Indigenous and non-Indigenous people together, with writing scrawled across their faces that they each com-posed. John Running, a long-celebrated regional photographer, wrote, "Con-sider the San Francisco Peaks are Sacred to Natives and to Non-Natives," a message positioned in solidarity with Indigenous peoples, literally pictured alongside non-Indigenous peoples. One man, "Sam," wrote, "faces are sacred, faces are beautiful. We walk on the face of the Earth. The Mountain is a beautiful sacred place that needs to be protected. In beauty I walk." Another woman, Stephanie, connected the protection of the Peaks with global issues of concern, bridging the concern over contaminated snow with climate change

FIGURE 8.2. Klee and Princess Benally. "What we do to the mountain we do to ourselves" is scrolled in black across their faces. Printed with permission from the artist, Chip Thomas.

and the poisoning of our global environment. She writes: "I am the change. Industrialization, pollution, and drought. Water, air, earth. Fake snow. CO_2." This installation is a great example of writing *with,* community writing that is foregrounded by concerns and connections that the community wants and needs—messages they literally wrote themselves—that transcends the limitations of traditional ink on paper. This is achieved by literally and figuratively attaching these messages to bodies, to identities, reflected in body language, expression, and emotion. Writing *with,* and thinking through what that process looks like in different ways according to the needs of a community, is therefore integral to the practice of community listening.

One part of the larger installation featured Princess Benally and her husband, Klee Benally. In this photo, they are forehead to forehead. His eyes are closed, while her hands cradle the back of his head (figure 8.2). A message is scrawled directly across their faces in thick black letters: "WHAT WE DO TO THE MOUNTAIN WE DO TO OURSELVES." The message is written across both of their faces as if it were on canvas. This choice visually connects Klee and Princess, as they express this statement together. It is a powerful message that illustrates the idea of sacredness, skipping over any need to define it, and instead homes in on effects and consequences, declaratively. It conveys a deep cultural and spiritual connection that cannot be denied or dismissed. Both Klee and Princess's faces are covered by bandannas, which were often

FIGURE 8.3. Installation in Flagstaff of a woman, Raechel, eyes closed while it snows around her, with "Keep it Real" scrawled on her face. Reprinted with permission from the artist, Chip Thomas.

worn during the Indigenous-led direct actions and demonstrations against the resort, ongoing at the time of the installation—the bandannas signal this moment of quiet reflection during the resistance as it unfolded in real time. As I've noted throughout this book, skiers, snowboarders, and others who support the resort's developments would often stand annoyed and confused at such demonstrations against ski infrastructure, asking, "Why are you trying to ruin people's fun?" Listeners of this image are asked to weigh their love of outdoor recreation against the cultural and spiritual survival of regional Indigenous peoples who hold the mountain sacred. Complementing the actions happening in the streets, characterized by signs reading, "defend the sacred" and "no desecration for recreation," Thomas's work deepens a kind of cognitive dissonance that is productive and provocative. The disconnect between recreation and desecration forces outdoor enthusiasts to reckon with the ways they are caught up in colonialism in the present, that one can help to sustain colonialism without a conscious commitment to it.

The same installation stretched across town to a historic neighborhood where another subject tilts her head upward with her eyes closed as the snow falls around her (figure 8.3). On her face are the words "Keep it Real." The message was simple and direct, simultaneously appearing elsewhere during this time on protest signs and stickers. The image and the message in context of the controversy articulate the gift of snow that gives so much more than skiing opportunities. The image depicts the snow, lightly falling in the arid Southwest, as something that cannot be taken for granted. It infuses dignity and respect for natural snow, which cannot be replicated and cannot be bought and sold. And certainly, the installation in context reveals how unacceptable it is to make snow with reclaimed wastewater. Here, Thomas's installations write against the narratives pushed by the rhetoric of this place, the ski town. Embedded in the images is a deep listening process, revealing the profound possibilities of art to engage with communities in ways that infuse a deeper understanding of culture, history, and place. In doing so, Thomas's work inserts counter-stories that position outdoor recreation within the context of settler colonialism, that give language to Indigenous solidarity, that complicate outdoor recreationalists' idea of the developments at Snowbowl.

While Thomas has produced installations in cities like Flagstaff, Telluride, and even much larger ones like Phoenix, Los Angeles, and Brooklyn, most of his work has been scattered throughout the Navajo Nation. This is certainly where I first encountered his murals from the road, where the work animated an otherwise immense landscape with an endless sky. Here, the art and the landscape mingle, where the art writes the landscape and the landscape writes the art, producing meaning in context that is inextricably material-discursive.

"Art Challenges the Way We Perceive the Ordinary"[19]

In his 2017 analysis of graffiti writing, Charles Lesh calls for broader understandings of community publishing that "include a wider range of texts, rhetorical strategies, and communities" that have been "historically unrecognizable" to the disciplinary mainstream.[20] While unconventional, even illegal, forms of community publishing like graffiti writing may have been historically dismissed by scholars, they have nonetheless functioned as "an inventive rhetorical-material process by which networks are produced, sustained, or challenged by the specific genres of writing that move through them."[21] In other words, despite the lack of attention by scholars and the practice's status as mostly illegal, graffiti writers and street artists have been doing the rhetorical work of community publishing anyway, work that has constituted

---

19. Quote in context: I like to think that art challenges the way we perceive the ordinary" (New Mexico PBS, "NMPBS ¡COLORES!").

20. Lesh, "Writing Boston," 64.

21. Lesh, 70.

FIGURE 8.4. Rose Hurley with her great-grandson. Installation by Chip Thomas. Photograph by Chip Thomas, 2018. The work appears on a roadside stand on the Navajo Nation.

place-based belongings in ways that are meaningful, unexpected, and at times, confrontational in the sense that "encountering public art is not entirely elective. . . . We go to private art, but public art is come upon."[22] Thomas's work is certainly "come upon" in this way, and it coheres to Lesh's articulation of street art as a form of rhetoric that depends as much on discourse as it does the physical, material world. But there is a relationship between Thomas's rhetorical-material work that engages audiences in community listening.

Thomas's photographic murals often adorn small structures positioned within a sea of red desert and blue sky, a landscape that is otherwise quiet and vast. Thomas revises these quiet places, creating small interruptions that invite audiences to listen in new ways—curated by him and the culture and community in which he engages. In a landscape that is riddled with colonial myths and misconceptions, the photographs disrupt and demand to be listened to. They radiate a dignity of being, an honesty, a vulnerability that invites an empathetic response, and they resonate a powerful sense of shared humanity and relationality.

---

22. Hein, *Public Art*, 55.

This is achieved by depicting people and their relationships as they are yet in unexpected places, where the image and the landscape cohere and necessarily constitute one another. Figure 8.4, which depicts Rose Hurley with her great-grandson, seems like a simple family picture, but against the backdrop of open high desert, the photo works against the colonial logic that would prefer passersby not see or recognize the experience, the presence, and the dignity of Diné people. Further, the candid image itself, which represents not a photo shoot where everyone might be dressed up and smiling for the occasion but rather a regular, everyday occurrence, communicates to me that the photographer is a trusted friend with whom the son and his great-grandmother are sitting comfortably and at home.

The art itself also produces a kind of reciprocity in that the work is for those settler visitors like me who pass by, but it is also embraced as a gift to the communities depicted. This speaks to the affective possibilities of rhetoric, which is to say that the art is produced through years of ongoing listening interactions between the artist and the community, but the art also potentially affects those who see it, like me, from outside of the community. For passersby, the cultural connection to the landscape is brought into focus, potentially harmful myths are challenged, and a greater sense of accountability is activated. For those who live there and are accustomed to viewing Thomas's work displayed in the landscape, "his murals reflect back our everyday life; I know that he gets it, he understands it."[23] Not everyone who passes by will see it operating in this way, however. While the rhetoric of the mural against the backdrop of the desert does intervene, interrupt, and provoke, the work itself constitutes a mere invitation for engagement, not the promise of it.

"Share Their Story in a Way That Honors Them"[24]

Thomas elaborated on how other aspects of his life, his career as a community physician and his activism, are connected to his identity as a storyteller: "In medicine, you know, we start with a history, and we hear people's stories; as a photographer and an activist, I'm attempting to tell stories as well."[25] As a physician Thomas describes his careful attention to his patients, and over time he has begun to unravel the ways that medical history is woven into the

---

23. KQED Arts, "Street Artist Portrays Navajo Life."
24. Quote in context: "It's really a matter of developing a relationship, a trusting relationship with people such that you cannot only hear their story, but you can present their story, and share their story in a way that honors them" (New Mexico PBS, "NMPBS ¡COLORES!").
25. Bell, "Outside Magazine."

cultural history of the patients and communities he serves, a colonial history that continues to structure the present.

As a function of settler colonialism, historically the view from the road—where Thomas's art often appears—has rhetorically silenced Indigenous peoples. While the occasional billboard might advertise an attraction, those images often rely on and sustain settler colonial logics through Indigenous caricatures, such as ads for a casino or a trading post, for example. One of the challenges Thomas confronts in his work is how to represent voice, or how to visually reclaim voices from the settler colonial structures that prevent them from being heard on their own terms. To do so he must work in and with the absences and silences produced by settler colonialism. Thomas's public art exemplifies community listening as described by Romeo García, that it "pushes us to both take up the traces left behind of the past and people and work toward creating presence from absence and sound from silence."[26] Thomas's work answers the absences and silences with images of Indigenous peoples in the present on their own terms. Those images demand viewers reject false caricatures of Indigenous peoples trapped in a mythic past. Krista Ratcliffe discusses the ways in which James Phelan and Andrea Lunsford theorize listening as relating to "voices speaking or not speaking within written texts."[27] This is useful for this analysis as it positions listening within a similar framework of inclusion/exclusion that Thomas's public art addresses. Thomas proves that public art has the potential to disrupt this silence, that listening is a means of reclaiming the voices of Indigenous peoples living under the spatial, material, and cultural conditions of settler colonialism in the every day. Thomas's visual storytelling challenges the terms of those conditions by placing Indigenous peoples in those spaces on their own terms, unexpectedly, and in ways that demand to be seen. In the same way that a rhetorically "loud" billboard wants to be heard, the struggles, joys, and everyday experiences of Indigenous peoples portrayed in Thomas's work also demand to be heard. Through this work as a storyteller, Thomas has recognized how his own role as an artist and physician on the reservation is an identity bound up in the lives of the community in which he lives, loves, and works.

As I gesture toward this chapter's conclusion, I return to some of my initial observations about the synesthetic qualities of public art, and how this analysis of Thomas's work maps out new pathways toward understanding the broader possibilities of a community listening praxis. Public art is a "hybrid" of material and discursive elements that cut across "a variety of polarities,"

---

26. García, "Creating Presence," 7.
27. Ratcliffe, Rhetorical Listening, 18.

allowing it to transcend boundaries of perception, specific sensory receptors, or mediums.[28] While it is certainly true, as Wendy Hinshaw observes, that "the sounds of a place and space orient us, teach us and help us connect," the emphasis on sound obscures the multitude of ways cultural and community knowledge can be transmitted and received, how places and spaces themselves can orient, teach, and connect us in a myriad of ways that don't rely on the ability of our ears.[29] Our understanding of what counts and what doesn't count as community listening need not be limited to one way of perceiving the world. Public art scholars have also noted the dynamic relationship between the artist and the public that improves community relationships through the work: "Public art compels both artists and public to refine communicative skills."[30] To describe the communicative process as a simple back and forth between speaker and listener obscures other ways we can be present as we listen to and show up for each other, how we acknowledge our understanding and misunderstanding, how we process and communicate cultural knowledge. When it is rooted in building trust, reflecting a relational process that establishes structures of accountability, community listening becomes a mode of perceiving, reflecting, and responding that is personal and situational.

A community that is heard is a community that is first listened to. In order to be a responsible and effective storyteller, to tell stories that demand to be heard yet are not one's own, the process of listening must necessarily come first. Thomas lingers on this notion of process and community listening: "It's really a matter of developing a relationship, a trusting relationship with people such that you can not only hear their story, but you can present their story, and share their story in a way that honors them."[31] His observation echoes Wilson's assertion that "the relationship with something (a person, object, or idea) is more important than the thing itself."[32] Thomas's art, while aesthetically stunning, is itself a reflection of a relationship, a move toward cultivating other relationships, and therefore more stories. Without the relationship, the art loses its meaning and productive power, therefore, relationality takes precedence over the "thing itself."[33] "It's all about the process of creating with good intention and with love," Thomas told PBS, which I understand as another way of articulating Wilson's idea of relational accountability.[34] Deep, intensive

28. Hein, *Public Art*, 50.
29. Hinshaw, "Writing to Listen," 64.
30. Hein, *Public Art*, 55.
31. New Mexico PBS, "NMPBS ¡COLORES!"
32. S. Wilson, *Research Is Ceremony*, 73.
33. S. Wilson, 7.
34. New Mexico PBS, "NMPBS ¡COLORES!"

listening is necessarily part of this process, and for community writers, work like Thomas's models the forms of trust and compassion we want to cultivate.

Community listening not only foregrounds the process of creation but is productive in the way in engages audiences in new ways. This chapter helps to establish that community listening can take on visual forms, as a process seen, and therefore not limited to a verbal (e.g., heard, read) phenomenon. Being heard—a statement that implies a level of fulfillment and effectiveness—is a result not just of listening but of how one listens. Community listening as a visual engagement invites others to interpret those images in the context of their own lives, inviting many forms of listening that are situational, personal, and generative. I agree with García's observation that "how we listen no doubt tells us something about our ways of seeing, being, and doing. We are constituted differently, and yet, strung together by a universe of stories, stories-so-far, and the possibilities of new stories."[35] When we listen, as passersby viewing an art installation in an unexpected place, we bring ourselves to that process—our culture, history, identity—and positionality here matters. The public art of community listening provokes critical reflections about how we are constituted differently by colonial structures. The result is public engagement that invites stronger, more empathetic alliances across difference.

It is important to note that not all public art is inherently successful in the ways I describe in this chapter; it is my hope that through this analysis of Thomas's work, I have sketched out some of the ways that community listeners might gauge the effectiveness of public art in their own communities. As I look at public art elsewhere, Thomas's work has taught me to simultaneously listen as well. I listen for the voices that want to be heard, the competing histories that appear as stories. I listen for that which reveals something about the relationships between the artist, those depicted, and the landscapes in which the work is situated. I listen for the questions the work asks of me, and I try to answer them. And the moment I start doing that, by engaging in the public art of listening and the back-and-forth exchange it elicits, I recognize the work's productive power: its potential to alter perceptions, shake up realities, provoke responses, deepen commitments, and change minds.

---

35. García, "Creating Presence," 7.

Becoming Complicit

I begin this conclusion with a memory. On a trip to western North Carolina—a place I had never been before—on my bike, I remember climbing up an old logging doubletrack trail called Old Mitchell in the fall, when the red maples and yellowing oak trees meshed brilliantly with green pine needles. I was visiting from Florida, where we lived briefly between living in Arizona and Idaho, so needless to say, my legs were readjusting to the rocky terrain and I had to stop often. On one of these stops, while confirming my location on a map, I noticed I was just above an area called the Boggs Wilderness. I stopped dead in my tracks and looked out through the trees toward this area—wilderness areas are closed to mountain bikes, but for all intents and purposes, I was in the same forest. It was in this moment—when I looked out into lands I had never seen before, yet one that shared my family name, forever enshrining my belonging—that I thought deeply and differently about what it means to understand the landscape as a settler.

My ancestors, those distant relatives on my father's side who passed down my last name, Boggs, arrived on this continent from Ireland in the mid-seventeenth century. Before the United States won its independence, people with my last name had spread out all over the country. People with my last name have fought in every US war, including opposing sides of the Civil War; my father still has the sword carried by our ancestor who fought for the North. They have occupied positions in politics, from senators to governors, worked as lawyers, merchants, and tradesmen. People with my last name are bound up in so many ways to the stories of western expansion. One was a friend of Kit Carson, another married into Daniel Boone's family, another traveled with the infamous Donner Party (though apparently parted ways before they entered the Sierra Nevada). There is a Boggsville in Colorado and Boggs Mountain in Northern California. Boggs is a name that appears on tombstones, government documents, building names, and elsewhere all over the country, so I should not be surprised that one of these ancestors had a wilderness area named after him (assuming "him") somewhere. The Boggs Wilderness in North Carolina does not belong to me or anyone related to me—I have absolutely zero connection to it in my life at all—yet I sit with the knowledge that stolen Cherokee land bears my name.

All this is to say that the encounter was a reminder that the trails I run or ride, whether in Arizona, Idaho, or North Carolina, were made for me as a settler, narrated for me as a settler, written for me as a settler, and accommodate me as a settler. The trail is curated by the narratives that produced it, which are often dependent upon Indigenous erasure. The settler perspective as *the way* to understand humans' relationship to the natural world, is however, a partial perspective at best—a lie, if we're being honest—and therefore it limits the ways even I am meant to experience these lands. Neither the map nor any sign I saw told me the area is ancestral Cherokee land. I had to Google that when I came home. "Whose land is the Boggs Wilderness in?" The question parses out the known, the included—my name—from the unknown, the Cherokee, the people who knew and cared for that land since time immemorial. The life of one of my ancestors seemingly replaced thousands of years of Indigenous belonging.

•

I continue to return to the question: how can I leverage my skills and privileges against settler colonialism as a settler occupying stolen Indigenous lands?

My coverage of actions like those described in chapter 7 and elsewhere were nearly always preceded by a phone call the night before. My correspondents would mention nothing specific on the phone other than instructions about when and where actions would take place and that they needed me there. I would get up very early, and equipped with my camera and voice recorder, I would ride my bike as close as I could in the dark, hide my bike in the forest, and hike up to the approximate location on the road. When I got there, I quickly realized that my role as a community writer was much more complex than the article that would come from my time there. It wasn't just the coverage that was necessary but my presence as well. Before the police showed up, as I talked to those locked down, I instinctually asked if anyone needed anything, from food and water to sunscreen. When the police came, I obviously identified myself as press, but when they requested that I get off the road, I realized that—other than the police and Snowbowl personnel—I was the only witness to demonstrators' removal and arrest. My photos and video would turn out to be crucial evidence in court should someone need it. During the day of the actions, I received texts from demonstrators' friends and family, asking if their loved ones were okay. And it meant the world to them that I could provide reassurances and updates. I also remember feeling embarrassed by my lack of preparedness about these important responsibilities. During those actions, I spent all day with them under these conditions; at the end of the day, I felt guilty for going home to write an article as they went to jail. While I showed up and did as much as I could under my important—yet freely chosen—role as press, I was not complicit in their struggle in the same way. But there are many ways to be and become complicit, which is the focus I want to take in this concluding chapter as I map out answers to questions over how to resist recreational colonialism.

Actions in solidarity or in support of Indigenous struggles against settler colonialism take place during key moments and places, and whether big or small, individual actions or those in coordination with Indigenous peoples can all be useful, even as settlers understand that at the end of the day, they are still a part of a legacy of colonization. But solidarity, alliance, and support are all too often confused with what people mean when they refer to themselves as an "ally," a term that unfortunately has been fully absorbed into performative liberal politics, from universities and nonprofit organizations to corporations and state and local governments. It has become an identity that people claim at the end of a retreat, a certificate earned after a series of workshops on diversity or "sensitivity training." Proof of allyship is marked through self-identification, by a sticker on an office door, the terms of which are so watered down it has become fundamentally meaningless.

"Accomplice" has surfaced from Indigenous anarchist thinking as a more useful term. It's worth pointing out that this term emerged specifically out of the context of the controversy over development on the Peaks, reflecting frustrations with how settlers, scholars, environmental groups, and other entities fell short in their apparent commitments to support Indigenous resistance to development at Snowbowl and elsewhere. While "accomplice" has started to be absorbed into scholarly and political discourse across the country and around the world, those who deploy it often do so out of context, without crediting Indigenous Action Media for the discussion they started.

As described in a zine written by a collective of Indigenous anarchists who were involved in the direct actions on the San Francisco Peaks and elsewhere, "Accomplices, not Allies: Abolishing the Ally Industrial Complex" sought to change the terms by which we imagine meaningful alliance: "When we fight back, or forward, together, becoming complicit in a struggle towards liberation, we are accomplices."[1] Commitment to liberation and decolonization means settler accomplices, in a sense, are working against themselves, their lived and embodied identity as beneficiaries of colonialism. A key question therefore remains: can settlers, who benefit from the continuation of colonialism, who therefore maintain unacknowledged investments in settler colonialism, ever truly be accomplices?

Fortunately, meaningful discussions centering on questions like this are ongoing among feminist and Indigenous scholarship and within radical spaces. While much of these conversations attempt to locate alternative processes toward reconciliation, or "the act of restoring estranged or damaged social and political relationships"[2] and restorative justice, they are also useful toward articulating and understanding alliance across difference. In *Becoming Kin: An Indigenous Call for Unforgetting the Past and Reimagining Our Future*, Patty Krawec explains why reconciliation practices from settler governments that hinge on apologies for the horrors of colonialism can sometimes lead to further divisions as they are not on Indigenous terms. The acknowledgment and apology are a start, but without a process of accountability that leads to changes in behavior, changes to the way people think, the relationship remains unchanged. With respect to reconciliation, Leanne Betasamosake Simpson has noted it has become "institutionalized," and she worries that Indigenous "participation will benefit the state in an asymmetrical fashion." With no change in behavior, or process from which to change the relationship, an apology could easily be a conversation stopper instead of a starter, whereby "the historical 'wrong' has been 'righted' and further transformation is not needed."[3] Krawec, Simpson, and Robin Wall Kimmerer, like so many Indigenous scholars and writers before them, from Vine Deloria Jr. to Winona LaDuke, contrast settler and Indigenous ways of knowing and being in the world and use the structural limitations of language as a primary animating example. Krawec and others point to the English language as dualistic and objective, while most Indigenous languages—Anishinaabe for her—are more relational and open to the changing conditions of humans and the world around us. Kimmerer breaks this down further by contrasting the English language, which is dominated

---

1. Indigenous Action Media, "Accomplices."
2. Coulthard, *Red Skin, White Masks*, 107.
3. L. Simpson, *Dancing on Our Turtle's Back*, 22.

by nouns, with most Indigenous languages, which contain many more verbs.[4] While of course there are important distinctions to be made among the hundreds of Indigenous languages, the overarching commonalities that produce what Vine Deloria Jr. described generally as "a Native view," are worth lingering on. Consequently, a noun-world is one full of people, places, and things that *are*—static and unchanging—and possibility framed as a matter of this *or* that. In other words, a noun-world readies us to objectify the world, to view it as static, unchanging, and disconnected. A verb-world, however, recognizes *both, and, also,* the world and all of us as in process, becoming, and in relation. For settlers, especially those who might be defensive at even being called settlers, this simple yet consequential observation provides a framework for how to think about solidarity in terms that Indigenous peoples might more easily recognize:

> Being a settler or colonizer is not something you *are*; it is something you *do*. It describes your relationship to this land and the people in it. Remember that settlers come to impose a way of living on top of the existing people. Settler colonialism destroys in order to replace. If you are going to stop being a settler and start being kin, that's where we start. With what you do.[5]

The problem with "ally," and to a certain extent "accomplice," is that expressions of solidarity under this framework can too easily be absorbed into performative politics of *being*—as opposed to *doing*. With respect to "accomplice," Klee Benally wrote, "this provocation was disposed of its intent," and such an outcome "was predicted."[6] Solidarity is actions we take that put us on the side of the oppressed and not the oppressor, that put us in relationship with the original people of this land rather than those who impose other systems on them.[7] Unfortunately the term "accomplice" has followed the same path as "ally" as the preferred terminology in liberal activist speak. This is why I find myself drawn to the action verbs Indigenous Action Media originally used to define an accomplice, specifically the phrase "becoming complicit." "Becoming" denotes the as-yet-unfulfilled process that leads to being, and "complicit" works with its synonymic cousin "implicate" to generate forms of affect that

---

4. See Kimmerer's essay "Learning the Grammar of Animacy" in *Braiding Sweetgrass*. This essay is particularly good for further reading on the point I'm making here, and her writing is beautiful, but it has also been noted that her work risks universalizing "Indigenous wisdom." I am doing my best to be mindful of this important critique here.

5. Krawec and Estes, *Becoming Kin*, 178–79.

6. K. Benally, *No Spiritual Surrender*, 200.

7. Krawec and Estes, *Becoming Kin*, 179.

demand self-reflection as a prerequisite to a relationship that is always changing. Indeed, decolonization itself is "an act of becoming."[8] Instead of pro-
claiming oneself an ally or an accomplice, "becoming complicit" refers to the
process through which one recognizes how they are implicated. Reckoning
with the ways we are complicit is a productive place from which to break with
the past, come to understand our historical role in oppressive structures, and
ultimately to reimagine how we are in relation. Becoming complicit opens
space for individual journeys—knowing there will be mistakes, regrets, and
missed opportunities. Because it is a process, one that is situated and personal,
it doesn't really matter where one is on this path as long as they commit to
staying on it.

Becoming complicit is crucial to resisting recreational colonialism. As I
lean toward a conclusion for this book, I recognize this project as incomplete
and imperfect. What about hunting, fishing, foraging, canoeing and kayak-
ing, golfing, and so many other forms of outdoor recreation? I could realisti-
cally engage and analyze only so many sites of inquiry under the framework
of recreational colonialism in the span of one book. As an intervention into
the relationships between outdoor recreation and the systems that sustain settler colonialism, I hope this book will sustain future discussion and analysis
among a variety of audiences. Throughout, I have used outdoor recreation and
its discourses as a means of prodding the edges of important questions: What
does it mean to be a settler on stolen Indigenous land? How has my proximity
to settler colonialism curated my experiences in these lands, how I understand
myself, and my relationship and responsibility to Indigenous peoples? What
does meaningful alliance and repair actually look like—is it even possible? All
of these questions are for those committed to becoming complicit.

I understand that many folks and organizations want a checklist or
a universal process they can put on an infographic or structure a training
around, but becoming complicit is not about trying to establish a set of dos
and don'ts—it's about dignity, respect, and the messy and ongoing process of
making better relations with Indigenous communities and the landscapes we
love. In the process, becoming complicit requires us to recognize how one's
understanding of place and of being is directly tied to the discourses—histories, myths, stories, philosophies, and cultural depictions—of those places.
For folks in outdoor recreational spaces—from individual participants, race
directors, and coalitions to industry leaders, land managers, and directors of
outdoor recreation and environmental education programs—I'll list some
actionable ways folks can begin to challenge the structures and assumptions

---

8. Barker and Pickerill, "Radicalizing Relationships," 1721.

that allow recreational colonialism to persist. This list is not meant to be exhaustive, but taken together, these considerations work to articulate a set of values, ethics, and intentions from which repair can begin.

1. **Dignity.** Recognize that your passion for outdoor recreation can never be more important than the physical, cultural, and spiritual survival of Indigenous peoples. Indigenous peoples have cared for the lands in which you engage—for all intents and purposes—since the beginning of time. If Indigenous people articulate restrictions on outdoor recreation, respect the fact that they have done so for important reasons and that they are not obligated to explain those reasons in a way that you'll fully understand. It is "not Indigenous peoples' responsibilities to teach Settler people, it remains the responsibility of the Settler to learn."[9]

2. **Respect.** Respect the fact that when it comes to controversies involving tribal opposition to the recreational activity you enjoy on stolen land, there might not be a compromise that exists. If Indigenous people oppose skiing on a particular mountain or rock climbing on specific formations, don't do it.

3. **Whose law?** Just because access or a form of recreation is technically legal on Indigenous people's ancestral land (a.k.a. on "public land" or "Crown land") does not mean Indigenous people are okay with it. Do your research. On land controlled by tribes, respect for tribal law and Indigenous sovereignty is the minimum.

4. **Research and listen.** Indigenous people and beliefs are not a monolith. Like all groups of people, individuals have different opinions, and while there are commonalities, there are hundreds of tribes informed by different belief systems. Retire the phrase, "the Native Americans believed . . ." from all articles, promotional material, and branding. The outdoor recreational landscape should not have Indigenous cultural and spiritual information filtered through the lens of settlers. Talk and listen to Indigenous people. Quote and cite Indigenous writers and historians. Furthermore, understand that as with all governments, the decisions made or positions held by tribal councils or tribal governments do not always reflect the will of the people.

5. **Stop appropriating.** There needs to be a full stop on Indigenous art, cultural representation, iconography, and language used in branding and promotion of settler-owned products, events, and media. Taking something that belongs to Indigenous people and deploying it out of context,

---

9. Barker and Pickerill, 1721.

giving it new meaning, and making money off it are all deeply unethical practices rooted in colonialism.

6. **Landback.** Support Indigenous efforts to reclaim stolen land, even if you enjoy outdoor recreation on those lands. It's a complicated and ongoing Indigenous-led conversation with a lot of nuances. It's important to listen. The frontier, the West, the wilderness, the outdoors, public lands, Crown lands—each of these terms are based on different narrations, perspectives designed to move us away from one singular reality: they are all stolen Indigenous land, lands in which settlers have been unwanted guests for more than four hundred years. So actions taken in solidarity "must seek to simultaneously address the dominating power being exercised over Indigenous individuals and communities, and also the power historically and currently directed to structure territory in such a way that Indigenous peoples are not able to tap into traditional relational networks."[10]

7. **Come to know yourself.** Specifically, for those descended from European settlers, those racialized as white in what is now the United States, Canada, Australia, New Zealand, and elsewhere, consider how you understand the world as a settler. Ask yourself, what does it mean to be a settler on stolen Indigenous land? How has your proximity to settler colonialism curated your experiences in these lands, how you view and understand yourself, and your relationship to Indigenous peoples? Beyond words and branding, what does meaningful alliance and repair actually look like? How can you live in a way that makes your commitments to Indigenous sovereignty actionable? This involves humble, everyday ruminations, reflections, and epiphanies, and it requires settlers to think about their relationship to Indigenous peoples, lands, and the violent legacies they inherit and from which they benefit.

8. **Be critical of stories.** The landscape is physical, material, but also discursive. The land is a multitude of stories that are always unfolding—they have been told long before settlers got here and will be told long after we're gone. The land has multiple histories, often competing and contradictory to the ones we've been told. Through research, observation, and reflection, inquire into the ways the landscape has been narrated through histories, mythologies, folklore, and literature but also law and land-use policy. Take note of who tells those stories, who is centered in those stories, which identities are accommodated through those stories, and how those stories affect the way you engage with those landscapes.

10. Barker and Pickerill, 1717.

9. **Whose land?** Learn about the Indigenous names for the places and land-scapes in which you engage—some places will have Indigenous names reflecting multiple tribes and forms of cultural significance. Who inhabited that land before settlement? What are the processes that led to the theft of that land? What efforts are in motion to reclaim that land? How can you move beyond simple "acknowledgment" and toward justice? This can be anything: including Indigenous people more directly in decision-making processes, getting involved in mutual aid efforts of all kinds that directly benefit Indigenous communities, or making monetary donations to Indigenous-led organizations and community leaders to aid in their work.

10. **Build inclusive practices.** If you're an event organizer (for a trail run or mountain bike race, for example), work with local tribes to ensure that (1) the event is compatible with Indigenous protocols for that land, particularly around the presence of sacred sites. (2) Be mindful of how you tell the story of that land to participants (see #8 in this list). Hint: the beginning of the story is not when settlers arrived and began to mine it for gold; this is only part of the story. (3) Beyond simple permissions, think about how your event can be enriched through direct tribal involvement and proceed in terms Indigenous people help to define. How can you strategize alongside Indigenous peoples to challenge settler colonialism, bust myths, and provoke new understandings about history and positionality?

•

The outdoor recreation community—its industries, advocacy organizations, lobbying groups, and everyday participants—have reached an inflection point, marking 2025 as a pivotal moment for critical intervention. With record-breaking participation and spending across the board, the outdoor recreation economy is now valued at over $1.1 trillion. As I type this, there are several key pieces of legislation on the table that will expand access, reach, and influence of outdoor recreation across the country, and half of US states have established offices of outdoor recreation. These indicate a rather sudden shift in attention to outdoor recreation and an understanding of the political power it represents. There are also a variety of emerging academic programs at the undergraduate and graduate level designed to prepare future leaders in the outdoor recreation industry. With a few exceptions, these programs are largely dominated by faculty from business, management, economics, and parks and recreation and therefore lack curriculum from the humanities and social sciences that would prepare students to facilitate meaningful collaborations with Indigenous communities and important discussions about colonialism and white supremacy on stolen land.

Thankfully, there is an ever-growing list of local and national organizations that take a justice-centered approach to inclusion and belonging needs within and among marginalized communities. These organizations look like anything from local queer hiking groups to a growing list of national organizations like Outdoor Afro, Latino Outdoors, the National Brotherhood of Skiers, and Natives Outdoors. These organizations typically have leadership with solid backgrounds in environmental justice and solidarity politics and have been successful in enabling queer and BIPOC outdoor enthusiasts to safely enjoy the outdoors while creating a needed sense of community in those spaces.

Due in large part to organizations like this, the most recent participation report from the outdoor recreation industry marks a significant jump in ethnic diversity among first-time participants in outdoor recreation. However, among "core" outdoor participants—those who participate regularly, quantified by nine or more outings per year—ethnic diversity in the outdoors plummets. Indeed, despite the gains in diversity celebrated by the outdoor industry, these core participants are actually increasingly white.

My analysis on recreational colonialism suggests there are cultural, historical, and material reasons why core participation in the outdoors is increasingly white despite largely successful campaigns aimed at increasing representation. While the outdoor industry promotes "DEI in the outdoors!" across websites, social media, marketing, and events, BIPOC folks may find themselves without support when they enter those spaces alone. Representation will only get folks so far. If settlers are not asked to confront the variety of ways "the outdoors"—both as a physical space and a cultural idea—has been curated in ways that sustain the structures from which settler colonialism depends, BIPOC folks are simply on their own in a space that is exclusive at best and downright dangerous at worst. As long as white settlers who dominate those spaces do not engage in the hard, reflective work of becoming complicit, the reach of inclusion and diversity initiatives in the outdoors will remain limited.

At a time when it seems so many converging interests are clamoring to get a slice of this pie, actionable inclusion, accessibility, and justice-oriented movements lack a meaningful sense of cohesion and are therefore vulnerable to co-optation by corporate and governmental entities. We must lift up those making good relations with the land, and with local cultures and Indigenous communities, those concerned about impact and effect, those who speak *with* and not *for*, those willing to do the self-reflective work that begins from the assumption that the land is not a cash machine or a "playground," as we so often hear, but the material space from which complex stories are written and accumulate. Those stories reflect competing histories and meaning-making systems and ultimately reveal how we are constituted differently in the landscapes we love. The so-called outdoors requires prophetic and humble people and organizations who understand their wider responsibility in this story-making process. Cultural and environmental sustainability is the next generation of so-called public lands policy, and we can only move forward by listening to Indigenous peoples and infusing dignity and respect into every level of the process.

BIBLIOGRAPHY

Abbey, Edward. *Desert Solitaire: A Season in the Wilderness.* New York: Ballantine, 1971.

Abel, Elizabeth. *Signs of the Times: The Visual Politics of Jim Crow.* Berkeley: University of California Press, 2010.

Adorno, Theodor W. *Minima Moralia: Reflections on a Damaged Life.* New York: Verso, 2005.

Adorno, Theodor W. "Veblen's Attack on Culture." In *Prisms,* 73–94. Cambridge, MA: MIT Press, 1983.

Aitchison, Cara. "Theorizing Other Discourses of Tourism, Gender and Culture: Can the Subaltern Speak (in Tourism)?" *Tourist Studies* 1, no. 2 (2001): 133–47.

Aitchison, Cara, Nicola MacLeod, and Stephen Shaw. *Leisure and Tourism Landscapes: Social and Cultural Geographies.* London: Routledge, 2001.

Alaimo, Stacy, and Susan Hekman. Introduction to *Material Feminisms,* edited by Stacy Alaimo and Susan J. Hekman, 1–19. Bloomington: Indiana University Press, 2008.

Alcoff, Linda. "The Problem of Speaking for Others." *Cultural Critique,* no. 20 (Winter 1991–92): 5–32.

Alene Gone Bad. "Paatuwaqatsi Run." *Journey to Badwater* (blog). Last modified December 19, 2018. https://alenegonebad.blogspot.com/2009/09/paatuwaqatsi-run.html.

American Alpine Club. *Desert Pioneers.* 2014. https://exhibits.americanalpineclub.org/clubhouse/desert-pioneers/.

Anderson, Joyce Rain. "Walking with Relatives." In *Unruly Rhetorics: Protest, Persuasion, and Publics,* edited by Jonathan Alexander, Susan C. Jarratt, and Nancy Welch, 45–59. University of Pittsburgh Press, 2018.

Anderson, Kim, Maria Campbell, and Christi Belcourt. *Keetsahnak / Our Missing and Murdered Indigenous Sisters.* Edmonton: University of Alberta, 2018.

Aristotle. *Politics: Books VII and VIII.* Translated by Richard Kraut. Oxford: Clarendon, 1997.

Arizona Daily Sun. "City of Flagstaff Approves Snowbowl Snowmaking Contract for 20 More Years." August 9, 2014. https://azdailysun.com/news/local/city-of-flagstaff-approves-snowbowl-snowmaking-contract-for-more-years/article_9a89939e-1f90-11e4-84e2-001a4bcf887a.html.

Arizona Daily Sun. "Court Greenlights Hopi Challenge against Flagstaff's Sale of Reclaimed Wastewater to Snowbowl." January 8, 2014. https://azdailysun.com/news/local/court-greenlights-hopi-challenge-against-flagstaff-s-sale-of-reclaimed/article_3198671c-782d-11e3-98c9-0019bb2963f4.html.

Arizona Daily Sun. "Snowmaking Opponents File for Time." July 7, 2010. https://azdailysun.com/news/local/snowmaking-opponents-file-for-time/article_7c83bc26-a770-5d35-b759-3cd87a6d448e.html.

Arizona Snowbowl. "The Next Chapter: Sharing Snowbowl's Future." June 13, 2019. https://www.snowbowl.ski/the-next-chapter-sharing-snowbowls-future/.

Ashcroft, Bill, Gareth Griffiths, and Helen Tiffin. *The Empire Writes Back: Theory and Practice in Post-Colonial Literatures.* 2nd ed. New York: Routledge, 2002.

Associated Press. "Name of Ski Mountain Will No Longer Include Derogatory Term." November 29, 2021. https://apnews.com/article/business-mountains-maine-native-americans-c471ea145159ca8a41c9a75c3cecfaa4.

Associated Press. "What's Merriam-Webster's Word of the Year for 2023? Hint: Be True to Yourself." November 27, 2023. https://apnews.com/article/merriam-webster-word-of-year-2023-a9fea610cb32ed913bc15533acab71cc.

Augé, Marc. *Non-Places: Introduction to an Anthropology of Supermodernity.* New York: Verso, 1995.

Baker, Nena. *The Body Toxic: How the Hazardous Chemistry of Everyday Things Threatens Our Health and Well-Being.* New York: North Point, 2008.

Baldy, Cutcha Risling. *We Are Dancing for You: Native Feminisms and the Revitalization of Women's Coming-of-Age Ceremonies.* Seattle: University of Washington Press, 2018.

Barad, Karen. "Posthumanist Performativity: Toward an Understanding of How Matter Comes to Matter." In *Material Feminisms,* edited by Stacy Alaimo and Susan J. Hekman, 120–56. Bloomington: Indiana University Press, 2008.

Barker, Adam J. *Making and Breaking Settler Space: Five Centuries of Colonization in North America.* Vancouver: University of British Columbia Press, 2021.

Barker, Adam J., and Jenny Pickerill. "Radicalizing Relationships to and through Shared Geographies: Why Anarchists Need to Understand Indigenous Connections to Land and Place." *Antipode* 44, no. 5 (2012): 1705–25.

Barker, Adam, and Russell Myers Ross. "Reoccupation and Resurgence: Indigenous Protest Camps in Canada." In *Protest Camps in International Context: Spaces, Infrastructures, and Media of Resistance,* edited by Gavin Brown, Anna Feigenbaum, Fabian Frenzel, and Patrick McCurdy. Bristol, UK: Bristol University Press, 2017.

Barker, Joanne. *Critically Sovereign: Indigenous Gender, Sexuality, and Feminist Studies.* Durham, NC: Duke University Press, 2017.

Bartlett, Steve. "Huntley Ingalls, 1928–2018." American Alpine Club. Accessed September 26, 2022. http://publications.americanalpineclub.org/articles/13201215133/Huntley-Ingalls-1928-2018.

Barton, Ben F., and Marthalee S. Barton. "Ideology and the Map: Toward a Postmodern Visual Design Practice." In *Professional Communication: The Social Perspective,* edited by Nancy R. Blyler and Charlotte Thralls, 232–52. Newbury Park, CA: SAGE, 1993.

Bauer, Kira. "Protecting Indigenous Spiritual Values." *Peace Review* 19, no. 3 (2007): 343–69.

Bell, Brooklyn. "Outside Magazine: Chip Thomas, Telling Navajo Stories with Street Art." You-Tube, February 28, 2020. https://www.youtube.com/watch?v=vD_3p4UIcE8.

Benally, Jeneda. "The Holy San Francisco Peaks, Arizona: Cultural and Spiritual Survival of South-Western Indigenous Nations." In *Sacred Species and Sites: Advances in Biocultural Conservation*, edited by Gloria Pungetti, Gonzavo Oviedo, and Della Hooke, 409–12. Cambridge, UK: Cambridge University Press, 2012.

Benally, Klee [@eelk]. "The Gesture of DOI Changing Anti-Indigenous Names on Stolen Lands . . ." Twitter, September 21, 2022. https://twitter.com/eelk/status/1572662258173616128.

Benally, Klee. "Klee Benally Sentenced to 'Community Service,' Affirms Commitment to Defending Sacred Peaks." Indigenous Action Media, 2012.

Benally, Klee. *No Spiritual Surrender: Indigenous Anarchy in Defense of the Sacred.* N.p: Detritus Books, 2023.

Benally, Klee. "The San Francisco Peaks and the Politics of Cultural Genocide." In *Edge of Morning: Native Voices Speak for the Bears Ears*, edited by Jacquelin Keeler, 86–103. Salt Lake City: Torrey House, 2017.

Benally, Klee, and R. T. Cody, dir. *The Snowbowl Effect.* Flagstaff: Indigenous Action Media, 2005.

Berkhofer, Robert F. *The White Man's Indian: Images of the American Indian from Columbus to the Present.* New York: Knopf, 1978.

Betz, Eric. "Mud Mayhem Draws Charges." *Arizona Daily Sun,* September 21, 2011. https://azdailysun.com/news/local/crime-and-courts/mud-mayhem-draws-charges/article_fd2fb486-1308-57a9-bd92-87f0b0a5bd13.html.

Bhabha, Homi K. "DissemiNation: Time, Narrative and the Margins of the Modern Nation." In *The Location of Culture,* 219–322. New York: Routledge, 2004.

Bioeconomics. "Economic Significance of Arizona Snowbowl to the Flagstaff and Coconino County, Arizona Regional Economy." Indigenous action Media, March 2, 2012.

Bird, Elizabeth. "Savage Desires: The Gendered Construction of the American Indian in Popular Media." In *Selling the Indian: Commercializing and Appropriating American Indian Culture,* edited by Carter Jones Meyer and Diana Royer, 62–98. University of Arizona Press, 2001.

Bjørnstad, Eric. *Rock Climbing Desert Rock IV: The Colorado Plateau Backcountry: Utah.* Regional Rock Climbing Series. Guilford, CT: Falcon Guides, 2003.

Blanco, María Del Pilar, and Esther Peeren. "Possessions: Spectral Places/Introduction." In *The Spectralities Reader: Ghosts and Haunting in Contemporary Cultural Theory,* 395–99. New York: Bloomsbury, 2013.

Boggs, Kyle. "Anti-Snowbowl Direct Actions Intensify alongside Construction." *The Noise: Arts & News,* September 2011, 10–11.

Boggs, Kyle. "Arizona Testbowl: Denying Human Rights and Experimenting with the Ecological Integrity of the San Francisco Peaks." *Sustainability Review,* February 28, 2010. https://www.thesustainabilityreview.org/articles/arizona-testbowl-denying-human-rights.

Boggs, Kyle. "Borowsky Says He's Selling Snowbowl to Ski Franchise, yet Forest Service and City Say No New Leases Are on the Table." *The Noise: Arts & News,* February 2015, 11.

Boggs, Kyle. "Direct Action Halts Ski Resort Construction on Sacred Site." *Earth First! Journal,* March 5, 2012. http://earthfirstjournal.org/article.php?id=533.

Boggs, Kyle. "The Hopi Man Who Runs to Protect His Tribe's Water." *High Country News,* November 5, 2015. https://www.hcn.org/articles/the-hopi-man-who-runs-to-protect-his-tribes-water.

Boggs, Kyle. "The Material-Discursive Spaces of Outdoor Recreation: Rhetorical Exclusion and Settler Colonialism at the Arizona Snowbowl Ski Resort." *Journal for the Study of Religion, Nature and Culture* 11, no. 2 (June 8, 2017): 175–96. https://doi.org/10.1558/jsrnc.18841.

Boggs, Kyle. "No Really, What's in the Wastewater?" *The Noise: Arts & News,* September 2009, 12–13.

Boggs, Kyle. "Our Water Systems, Our Future: Inconvenient Truths Revealed in Snowbowl Talks." *The Noise: Arts & News,* December 2010, 10–11.

Boggs, Kyle. "The Peaks in Context Snowbowl Village Revisited." *The Noise: Arts & News,* August 2009, 12–13.

Boggs, Kyle. "Replacing Columbus Day with Indigenous Peoples Day Isn't Enough." *High Country News,* October 4, 2016. https://www.hcn.org/articles/replacing-columbus-day-with-indigenous-peoples-day-isnt-enough.

Boggs, Kyle. "Resistance Continues for Snowbowl Opposition." *The Noise: Arts & News,* March 2011, 10, 17.

Boggs, Kyle. "The Rhetoric of Exclusion on the San Francisco Peaks." *The Noise: Arts & News,* July 2012, 10–11.

Boggs, Kyle. "Storm Clouds Darken over the San Francisco Peaks as the City Debates Water for Snowbowl." *The Noise: Arts & News,* September 2010, 10–11, 37.

Boggs, Kyle. "Storm Clouds Darken over the San Francisco Peaks as the City Debates Water for Snowbowl, Part 2." *The Noise: Arts & News,* October 2010, 10–11.

Boggs, Kyle. "That's Not Why I Ride a Bike." *The Noise: Arts & News,* November 2010: 16.

Boggs, Kyle. "A Thousand Different Mountains on the San Francisco Peaks." *The Noise: Arts & News,* September 2009, 12–13.

Boggs, Kyle. "Tree Sit Halts Construction of Reclaimed Wastewater Pipeline." *The Noise: Arts & News,* September 2012, 10–11.

Bonds, Anne, and Joshua Inwood. "Beyond White Privilege: Geographies of White Supremacy and Settler Colonialism." *Progress in Human Geography* 40, no. 6 (December 2016): 715–33. https://doi.org/10.1177/0309132515613166.

Borowsky, Eric, and J. R. Murray. Letter to Deputy Secretary of Agriculture Kathleen Merrigan. June 29, 2009.

Bourdieu, Pierre. "Social Space and Symbolic Space." In *Practical Reason: On the Theory of Action,* 1–18. Oxford: Polity, 1998.

Brown, Gavin, and Anna Feigenbaum. *Protest Camps in International Context: Spaces, Infrastructures and Media of Resistance.* Bristol: Policy Press, 2017.

Brune, Michael. "Pulling Down Our Monuments." Sierra Club, July 22, 2020. https://www.sierraclub.org/michael-brune/2020/07/john-muir-early-history-sierra-club.

Bruyneel, Kevin. *Settler Memory: The Disavowal of Indigeneity and the Politics of Race in the United States.* Chapel Hill: University of North Carolina Press, 2021.

Burns, Cameron. "Shiprock's East Face." *American Alpine Journal* 69, no. 37 (1995): 66–72.

Busbridge, Rachel. "On Haunted Geography." *Interventions: International Journal of Postcolonial Studies* 17, no 4 (2014): 469–87.

Butler, Judith. *Bodies That Matter: On the Discursive Limits of "Sex."* New York: Routledge, 1993.

Butler, Richard. "Geographical Research on Tourism, Recreation and Leisure: Origins, Eras and Directions." *Tourism Geographies* 6, no. 2 (2004): 143–62.

Byrd, Jodi. *Transit of Empire: Indigenous Critiques of Colonialism.* Minneapolis: University of Minnesota Press, 2011.

Cajete, Gregory. *Look to the Mountain: An Ecology of Indigenous Education.* Durango, CO: Kivakí Press, 1994.

Campbell, Neil. *The Rhizomatic West: Representing the American West in a Transnational, Global, Media Age.* Lincoln: University of Nebraska Press, 2008.

CBC News. "CBC Closing Comments on Indigenous Stories 'Commendable,' says N.W.T. Man." December 1, 2015. https://www.cbc.ca/news/canada/north/cbc-closing-comments-on-aboriginal-stories-reaction-1.3345137.

CBC News. "Jogger Decries Offensive Mountain Biking Trail Names in Kelowna." November 4, 2016. https://www.cbc.ca/news/canada/british-columbia/jogger-decries-offensive-mountain-biking-trail-names-in-kelowna-1.3835409.

Chavez, Tazbah Rose. "Nüümü Poyo: A Story of Reclamation." *Uncommon Path—An REI Co-Op Publication* (blog), January 10, 2020. https://www.rei.com/blog/news/nuumu-poyo-a-

Clark, Gregory. *Rhetorical Landscapes in America: Variations on a Theme from Kenneth Burke.* Columbia: University of South Carolina Press, 2004.

Clemens, Chris. "Running with the Hopi." christarzanclemens.com, September 20, 2014. https://www.christarzanclemens.com/2014/09/running-with-the-hopi/.

Climbing House. "Dirtbag Explained." March 24, 2012. http://climbinghouse.com.

Coconino County Planning and Zoning Commission. "In the Matter of Public Hearing Reference Development of Hart Prairie." Transcript, January 29, 1974. "Richard and Jean Wilson Collection, 1995." Subgroup one, "Save the Peaks" 1964–1977, box 1.1. Northern Arizona University, Special Collections and Archives, Flagstaff, Arizona.

Coconino National Forest. "Environmental Impact Statement for Snowbowl Facilities Improvement." US Forest Service, 2005. http://www.fs.usda.gov/detailfull/coconino/landmanagement/projects/?cid=stelprdb5347260.

Colborn, Theo, Dianna Dumanoski, and John Peterson Myers. *Our Stolen Future: Are We Threatening Our Fertility, Intelligence, and Survival?—A Scientific Detective Story.* New York: Penguin, 1997.

Cole, Cyndy. "ADEQ: City Hid Wildcat Violations." *Arizona Daily Sun,* May 10, 2013. https://azdailysun.com/news/local/adeq-city-hid-wildcat-violations/article_4af8c1de-3b34-5896-8678-9787136fe518.html.

Cole, Cyndy. "Secret Snowbowl Talks Break Open." *Arizona Daily Sun,* March 9, 2010. https://azdailysun.com/news/local/govt-and-politics/secret-snowbowl-talks-break-open/article_777a27d5-d46f-56e1-9255-b07cebdfa07e.html.

Cole, Cyndy. "Snowbowl Beats Second Lawsuit." *Arizona Daily Sun.* Last modified July 30, 2019. https://azdailysun.com/news/local/snowbowl-beats-second-lawsuit/article_7a58a09b-560f-5aca-ac22-7600fb848fce.html.

Cole, Cyndy. "Tribes: New Snowmaking Plan No Better." *Arizona Daily Sun,* March 19, 2010. https://azdailysun.com/news/local/govt-and-politics/tribes-new-snowmaking-plan-no-better/article_60b56145-867e-5a58-8204-e0af765856ec.html.

Coleman, Annie G. "The Unbearable Whiteness of Skiing." *Pacific Historical Review* 65, no. 4 (1996): 583–614.

Coleman, Annie G. "The White West: Ski Town Image, Tourism, and Community." In *Ski Style: Sport and Culture in the Rockies,* 147–81. Lawrence: University Press of Kansas, 2004.

Connell, R. W., and James W. Messerschmidt. "Hegemonic Masculinity: Rethinking the Concept." *Gender and Society* 19, no. 6 (2005): 829–59.

Conrad, David. "Community Murals as Democratic Art and Education." *Journal of Aesthetic Education* 29, no. 1 (1995): 98. https://doi.org/10.2307/3333522.

Coulthard, Glen Sean. *Red Skin, White Masks: Rejecting the Colonial Politics of Recognition*. Minneapolis: University of Minnesota Press, 2014.

Cram, E. *Violent Inheritance: Sexuality, Land, and Energy in Making the North American West*. Oakland: University of California Press, 2022.

Cronon, William. "The Trouble with Wilderness: Or, Getting Back to the Wrong Nature." *Environmental History* 1, no. 1 (1996): 7–28.

Culler, Jonathan. *Framing the Sign: Criticism and Its Institutions*. New York: Blackwell, 1988.

De Certeau, Michel. *The Practice of Everyday Life*. Berkeley: University of California Press, 1984.

Deer, Sarah. *The Beginning and End of Rape: Confronting Sexual Violence in Native America*. Minneapolis: University of Minnesota Press, 2015.

Deleuze, Gilles, and Félix Guattari. *A Thousand Plateaus: Capitalism and Schizophrenia*. Translated by Brian Massumi. 13th ed. Minneapolis: University of Minnesota Press, 2009.

Deloria, Philip Joseph. *Playing Indian*. New Haven: Yale University Press, 1998.

Deloria, Vine, Jr. *God Is Red: A Native View of Religion*. Golden, CO: Fulcrum, 1994.

DeLuca, K. "A Wilderness Environmentalism Manifesto: Contesting the Infinite Self-Absorption of Humans." In *Environmental Justice and Environmentalism: The Social Justice Challenge to the Environmental Movement*, edited Ronald D. Sandler and Phaedra C. Pezzullo, 27–55. Cambridge, MA: MIT Press, 2007.

DeLuca, Kevin, and Anne Demo. "Imagining Nature and Erasing Class and Race: Carleton Watkins, John Muir, and the Construction of Wilderness." *Environmental History* 6, no. 4 (2001): 541–60.

DeLuca, Kevin Michael. *Image Politics: The New Rhetoric of Environmental Activism*. London: Routledge, 2012.

Depoe, Stephen P., John W. Delicath, and Marie-France Aepli Elsenbeer. *Communication and Public Participation in Environmental Decision Making*. Albany: State University of New York Press, 2004.

Dikovitskaya, Margarita. *Visual Culture: The Study of the Visual after the Cultural Turn*. Cambridge, MA: MIT Press, 2005.

Dilworth, Leah. *Imagining Indians in the Southwest*. Washington, DC: Smithsonian, 1996.

Dobrin, Sidney. "Writing Takes Place." In *Natural Discourse: Toward Ecocomposition*, edited by Sidney Dobrin and Christian R. Weisser, 11–26. Albany: State University of New York Press, 2002.

Dobrin, Sidney I., and Sean Morey. *Ecosee: Image, Rhetoric, Nature*. Albany: State University of New York Press, 2009.

Downey, Allan. *The Creator's Game: Lacrosse, Identity, and Indigenous Nationhood*. Vancouver: University of British Columbia Press, 2018.

Doyle, Kathryn. "Switch to Minimalist Running Shoes Tied to Injuries, Pain." *Reuters*, January 9, 2014. https://www.reuters.com/article/us-running-shoes-injury-idUSBREA081CS20140109.

Dussias, Allison. "Cultural Conflicts Regarding Land Use: The Conflict between Recreational Users at Devils Tower and Native American Ceremonial Users." *Vermont Journal of Environmental Law* 2, no. 13 (2001): 40.

Edensor, Tim, and Sophia Richards. "Snowboarders vs Skiers: Contested Choreographies of the Slopes." *Leisure Studies* 26, no. 1 (2007): 97–114.

Emerson, Ralph Waldo. *Ralph Waldo Emerson*. Edited by Richard Poirier. Oxford, UK: Oxford University Press, 1990.

Endres, Danielle. "The Rhetoric of Nuclear Colonialism: Rhetorical Exclusion of American Indian Arguments in the Yucca Mountain Nuclear Waste Siting Decision." *Communication and Critical/Cultural Studies* 6, no. 1 (2009): 39–60.

Epstein, Andrew. "Mark Rifkin, *Settler Common Sense: Queerness and Everyday Colonialism in the American Renaissance* (University of Minnesota Press, 2014)." *New Books in Native American Studies,* August 21, 2014. https://podcasts.apple.com/us/podcast/ mark-rifkin-settler-common-sense-queerness-and/id427425949?i=1000364276553.

Escudero, Nicki. "Students Climb to New Heights." *The Lumberjack,* September 3–9, 2003.

Estes, Nick. *Our History Is the Future: Standing Rock versus the Dakota Access Pipeline, and the Long Tradition of Indigenous Resistance.* New York: Verso, 2019.

Finney, Carolyn. *Black Faces, White Spaces: Reimagining the Relationship of African Americans to the Great Outdoors.* Chapel Hill: University of North Carolina Press, 2014.

Fishman, Jenn, and Lauren Rosenberg. "Guest Editors' Introduction: Community Writing, Community Listening." *Community Literacy Journal* 13, no. 1 (2018): 1–6. https://doi.org/10.1353/ clj.2018.0016.

Flagstaff Police Department. "2021 Flagstaff Police Department Annual Report." Accessed October 2, 2022. https://issuu.com/flagstaffpolicedepartment/docs/annual_report_2021-_final.

Flint. "Paatuwaqatsi—Water Is Life Ultra Race Report." *Flintland* (blog), September 15, 2013. https://flintland.blogspot.com/2013/09/paatuwaqatsi-water-is-life-ultra-race.html.

Fontana, Bernard L. *Tarahumara: Where Night Is the Day of the Moon.* Tucson: University of Arizona Press, 2016.

Fonseca, Felicia. "Hopi Lawmakers Drop Top Attorney, Suspend Others." *Native Times,* May 16, 2010. https://nativetimes.com/index.php/news/tribal/3607-hopi-lawmakers-drop-top-attorney-suspend-others.

Foss, Sonya K. "A Rhetorical Schema for the Evaluation of Visual Imagery." *Communication Studies* 45, no. 3–4 (1994): 213–24.

Foucault, Michel. *The Archaeology of Knowledge.* New York: Pantheon, 1972.

Foucault, Michel. *The History of Sexuality.* New York: Pantheon, 1978.

Foucault, Michel. *The Order of Things: An Archaeology of the Human Sciences.* New York: Vintage, 1973.

Franks, Trent. Letter to Secretary of Agriculture Tom Vilsack. July 26, 2009.

García, Romeo. "Creating Presence from Absence and Sound from Silence." *Community Literacy Journal* 13, no. 1 (2018): 7–15. https://doi.org/10.1353/clj.2018.0017.

Gedicks, Al. *Resource Rebels: Native Challenges to Mining and Oil Corporations.* Cambridge, MA: South End, 2001.

Gilbert, Matthew. *Hopi Runners: Crossing the Terrain between Indian and American.* Lawrence: University Press of Kansas, 2018.

Gilio-Whitaker, Dina. "Appropriating Surfing and the Politics of Indigenous Authenticity." In *The Critical Surf Studies Reader,* edited by Dexter Zavalza Hough-Snee and Alexander Sotelo Eastman, 214–32. Durham, NC: Duke University Press, 2017.

Gilio-Whitaker, Dina. *As Long As Grass Grows: The Indigenous Fight for Environmental Justice from Colonization to Standing Rock.* Boston: Beacon, 2019.

Glowacka, Maria, Dorothy Washburn, and Justin Richland. "Nuvatukya'Ovi, San Francisco Peaks: Balancing Western Economies with Native American Spiritualities." *Current Anthropology* 50, no. 4 (2009): 547–61.

Goins, Cole. "Embodying Key Principles and Ethics of Deep Listening." American Press Institute, September 4, 2018. https://americanpressinstitute.org/embodying-key-principles-and-ethics-of-deep-listening/.

Goldberg, Ryan. "The Drug Runners." *Texas Monthly,* July 25, 2017. https://features.texasmonthly.com/editorial/the-drug-runners/.

Golightly, Sean. "'My Integrity or My Job': This Northern Arizona National Forest Supervisor Felt She Had to Choose." *Arizona Daily Sun,* August 7, 2022. https://azdailysun.com/news/local/my-integrity-or-my-job-this-northern-arizona-national-forest-supervisor-felt-she-had-to/article_3c41f8ae-13a1-11ed-940a-e325a4056b8b.html.

Gómez-Barris, Macarena. *The Extractive Zone: Social Ecologies and Decolonial Perspectives.* Durham, NC: Duke University Press, 2017.

Gordon, Avery. *Ghostly Matters: Haunting and the Sociological Imagination.* Minneapolis: University of Minnesota Press, 1997.

Grabham, Emily. "'Flagging' the Skin: Corporeal Nationalism and the Properties of Belonging." *Body & Society* 15, no. 1 (2009): 63–82.

Grand Circle Trails. "Ultra Adventures." Last modified December 19, 2018. http://grandcircletrails.com.

Gregory, Derek, and Credo Reference (Firm). *The Dictionary of Human Geography.* 5th ed. Malden, MA: Blackwell, 2009.

Griffin, Susan. *Woman and Nature: The Roaring Inside Her.* San Francisco: Sierra Club Books, 2000.

Haas, Jason. "Sacred or Profane: A Future for Navajolands Climbing?" *Rock and Ice,* February 2014.

Hall, Colin Michael, and Stephen Page. *The Geography of Tourism and Recreation: Environment, Place, and Space.* New York: Routledge, 1999.

Haraway, Donna. *Simians, Cyborgs, and Women: The Reinvention of Nation.* New York: Routledge, 1991.

Harding, Sandra. *Sciences from Below: Feminisms, Postcolonialities, and Modernities.* Durham, NC: Duke University Press, 2008.

Harvey, David. "Space as a Keyword." In *David Harvey: A Critical Reader,* edited by Noel Castree and Derek Gregory, 270–94. Malden, MA: Blackwell, 2006.

Hayles, N. Katherine. *How We Became Posthuman: Virtual Bodies in Cybernetics, Literature, and Informatics.* Chicago: University of Chicago Press, 1999.

Hein, Hilde. *Public Art: Thinking Museums Differently.* Rowman Altamira, 2006.

Hekman, Susan. "Constructing the Ballast: An Ontology for Feminism." In *Material Feminisms,* edited by Stacy Alaimo and Susan J. Hekman, 85–119. Bloomington: Indiana University Press, 2008.

Hersher, Rebecca. "Key Moments in the Dakota Access Pipeline Fight." NPR, February 22, 2017. https://www.npr.org/sections/thetwo-way/2017/02/22/514988040/key-moments-in-the-dakota-access-pipeline-fight.

Heywood, Ian. "Climbing Monsters: Excess and Restraint in Contemporary Rock Climbing." *Leisure Studies* 25, no. 4 (2006): 455–67.

Hill, Charles A., and Marguerite Helmers. *Defining Visual Rhetorics.* Mahwah: Routledge, 2004.

Hinshaw, Wendy Wolters. "Writing to Listen: Why I Write across Prison Walls." *Community Literacy Journal* 13, no. 1 (2018): 55–70. https://doi.org/10.1353/clj.2018.0021.

Hirst, Stephen. *I Am the Grand Canyon: The Story of the Havasupai People.* 3rd ed. Grand Canyon, AZ: Grand Canyon Association, 2006.

Hopi Tribe. "Hopi File Lawsuit over Sewage Effluent Contract." August 22, 2011. http://www.hopi-nsn.gov/wp-content/uploads/2016/05/Hopi-Tribe-returns-to-Court-to-protect-San-Francisco-Peaks-from-reclaimed-wastewater-after-Flagstaff-City-Council-delays-decision-on-settlement.pdf.

Hopi Tribe v. City of Flagstaff, Ariz. No. 1 CA-CV 12-0370. 2013.

Hopi Tribe v. US Forest Service. Civil Case No. 1:12-cv-01846 (RJL) 2012.

Horkheimer, Max, and Theodor W. Adorno. "The Culture Industry: Enlightenment as Mass Deception." In *Dialectic of Enlightenment,* 94–136. New York: Continuum, 1994.

Howard, Kathleen, and Diana F. Pardue. *Inventing the Southwest: The Fred Harvey Company and Native American Art.* Flagstaff: Northland, 1996.

Huhndorf, Shari. *Going Native: Indians in the American Cultural Imagination.* Ithaca, NY: Cornell University Press, 2001.

Indigenous Action Media. "Accomplices, Not Allies: Abolishing the Ally Industrial Complex." May 4, 2014. http://www.indigenousaction.org/accomplices-not-allies-abolishing-the-ally-industrial-complex/.

Indigenous Action Media. "Direct Action to Protect Holy Peaks Continues." August 14, 2011. https://www.indigenousaction.org/direct-action-to-protect-holy-peaks-continues/.

Indigenous Environmental Network. "Court Rules in Favor of Native Youth Attacked at Flagstaff Dew Downtown Event." January 23, 2014. https://www.ienearth.org/court-rules-in-favor-of-native-youth-attacked-at-flagstaff-dew-downtown-event/.

Ingersoll, Karin Amimoto. *Waves of Knowing: A Seascape Epistemology.* Durham, NC: Duke University Press, 2016.

Inter Tribal Council of Arizona. Letter from 20 tribes of the Inter Tribal Council of Arizona to Mayor of Flagstaff Sara Presler. August 27, 2010.

International Indian Treaty Council. Letter to the Committee on the Elimination of Racial Discrimination. August 17, 2011.

Irigoyen-Rascón, Fructuoso, and Alfonso Paredes. *Tarahumara Medicine: Ethnobotany and Healing Among the Rarámuri of Mexico.* Norman: University of Oklahoma Press, 2015.

Jackson, Rachel C., and Dorothy Whitehorse DeLaune. "Decolonizing Community Writing with Community Listening: Story, Transrhetorical Resistance, and Indigenous Cultural Literacy Activism." *Community Literacy Journal* 13, no. 1 (2018): 37–54. https://doi.org/10.1353/clj.2018.0020.

Jacoby, Karl. *Crimes against Nature: Squatters, Poachers, Thieves, and the Hidden History of American Conservation.* Berkeley: University of California Press, 2003.

Jameson, Fredric. *Postmodernism, Or, the Cultural Logic of Late Capitalism.* Durham, NC: Duke University Press, 1991.

Jensen, Robert. "The High Cost of Manliness" *Smirking Chimp,* September 14, 2006. http://www.smirkingchimp.com/node/543.

Jocks, Chris. "Guest Column: Changing Times for Snowbowl and a History of the Ski Resort." *Navajo-Hopi Observer News,* December 14, 2021. https://www.nhonews.com/news/2021/dec/14/guest-column-changing-times-snowbowl-and-history-s/.

Johnson, Gavin. "Considering the Possibilities of a Cultural Rhetorics Assessment Framework." *Constellations,* August 26, 2020. https://constell8cr.com/pedagogy-blog/considering-the-possibilities-of-a-cultural-rhetorics-assessment-framework/.

Karakey, Bryanna, and Stacie Leach. "Bouldering: A Risk at Every Turn, a Pleasure with Every Step." *The Lumberjack* 6, no. 98 (February 24–March 3, 2011).

Katz, Jackson. *Tough Guise: Violence, Media, and the Crisis in Masculinity.* Media Education Foundation. 1999.

Keene, Adrienne. "Engaging Indigeneity and Avoiding Appropriation: An Interview with Adrienne Keene." *English Journal* 106, no. 1 (2016): 55–57.

Kiewa, Jackie. "Rewriting the Heroic Script: Relationship in Rockclimbing." *World Leisure Journal* 43, no. 4 (2001): 30–43.

Killingsworth, Jimmie, and Jacqueline S. Palmer. *Ecospeak: Rhetoric and Environmental Politics in America.* Carbondale: Southern Illinois University Press, 1992.

Kimmel, Michael S. *Guyland: The Perilous World Where Boys Become Men.* New York: Harper, 2008.

Kimmerer, Robin Wall. *Braiding Sweetgrass: Indigenous Wisdom, Scientific Knowledge and the Teachings of Plants.* Minneapolis: Milkweed, 2013.

Kniazkov, Maxim. "Treading on a Shrine: Sacred Site Now an ATV Playground." *The Colorodoan,* August 14, 2005. Available at https://thumpertalk.com/forums/topic/233081-treading-on-a-shrine-sand-mtn-closure/.

Krawec, Patty, and Nick Estes. *Becoming Kin: An Indigenous Call to Unforgetting the Past and Reimagining Our Future.* Minneapolis: Broadleaf, 2022.

Kozak, David. "The Unclimbable Summits?" *American Alpine Journal* 26, no. 58 (1984): 122–25.

KQED Arts. "Street Artist Portrays Navajo Life with Large Scale Murals." *PBS News Hour,* June 3, 2018. https://video.kqed.org/video/street-artist-portrays-navajo-life-with-large-scale-murals-1528048405/.

Kusz, Kyle. "Extreme America: The Cultural Politics of Extreme Sports in 1990s America." In *Understanding Lifestyle Sport: Consumption, Identity, and Difference,* edited by Belinda Wheaton, 197–214. London: Routledge, 2004.

LaChapelle, Dolores. *Deep Powder Snow: 40 Years of Ecstatic Skiing, Avalanches, and Earth Wisdom.* Durango, CO: Kivakí Press, 1993.

LaDuke, Winona. "Environmental Justice." Northern Arizona University, public talk, 2/1/2011.

LaDuke, Winona. *Recovering the Sacred: The Power of Naming and Claiming.* Cambridge, MA: South End, 2005.

Langlois, Krista. "These Places Are Sacred Native American Sites—Not Playgrounds." *Outside Online,* July 5, 2018. https://www.outsideonline.com/2322921/new-rules-respectful-recreation.

Lefebvre, Henri. *The Production of Space.* Cambridge, MA: Blackwell, 1991.

Leroux, Darryl. *Distorted Descent: White Claims to Indigenous Identity.* Winnipeg: University of Manitoba Press, 2019.

Lesh, Charles. "Writing Boston: Graffiti Bombing as Community Publishing." *Community Literacy Journal* 12, no. 1 (2017): 62–86. https://doi.org/10.1353/clj.2017.0022.

Limerick, Patricia Nelson. *The Legacy of Conquest: The Unbroken Past of the American West.* New York: W. W. Norton, 2006.

Lonetree, Amy. *Decolonizing Museums: Representing Native America in National and Tribal Museums.* Chapel Hill: University of North Carolina Press, 2012.

Long, Jonathan, and Kevin Hylton. "Shades of White: An Examination of Whiteness in Sport." *Leisure Studies* 21, no. 2 (2002): 87–103.

Loudin, Amanda. "Climbing Routes Are Riddled with Racist and Misogynistic Names. Meet the People Trying to Change It All." *Washington Post,* November 30, 2020. https://www.washingtonpost.com/gender-identity/climbing-routes-are-riddled-with-racist-and-misogynistic-names-meet-the-people-trying-to-change-it-all/.

Lowman, Emma Battell, and Adam J. Barker. *Settler: Identity and Colonialism in 21st Century Canada.* Winnipeg: Fernwood, 2015.

MacCannell, Dean. *The Tourist: A New Theory of the Leisure Class.* Los Angeles: University of California Press, 2013.

MacDonald, Dougald. "Desert Pioneer Eric Has Died." *Climbing,* October 15, 2015.

MacInnes, John. "The Crisis of Masculinity." In *The Masculinities Reader,* edited by Stephen Whitehead, 311–29. London: Polity, 2001.

"Majestic Monument Valley 50K and More." *For Love of Trails* (blog), March 17, 2015. http://happyplacetrails.blogspot.com/2015/03/majestic-monument-valley-50-k-and-more.html.

Makley, Matthew S., and Michael J. Makley. *Cave Rock: Climbers, Courts, and a Washoe Indian Sacred Place.* Reno: University of Nevada Press, 2010.

Malwhinney, Janet. "'Giving Up the Ghost:' Disrupting the (Re)production of White Privilege in Anti-Racist Pedagogy and Organizational Change." Master's thesis, Ontario Institute for Studies in Education of the University of Toronto, 1998.

Mar, Tracey Banivanua, and Penelope Edmonds. *Making Settler Colonial Space: Perspectives on Race, Place and Identity.* New York: Springer, 2010.

Marsiglio, William. *Men on a Mission: Valuing Youth Work in Our Communities.* Baltimore: Johns Hopkins University Press, 2008.

Martin, Derek Christopher. "Apartheid in the Great Outdoors: American Advertising and the Reproduction of a Racialized Outdoor Leisure Identity." *Journal of Leisure Research* 36, no. 4 (December 2004): 513–35. https://doi.org/10.1080/00222216.2004.11950034.

Martine, Dwayne. "Monument Valley Tribal Park 'Mitten' Intact." Navajo Parks and Recreation, May 5, 2006. http://navajonationparks.org.

Massey, Doreen B. *For Space.* Thousand Oaks, CA: SAGE, 2005.

May, Jon. "'A Little Taste of Something More Exotic': The Imaginative Geographies of Everyday Life." *Geography* 81, no. 1 (1996): 57–64.

McCain, John, Jon Kyl, and Ann Kirkpatrick. Letter to Secretary of Agriculture Tom Vilsack. July 6, 2009.

McCain, John, Jon Kyl, and Ann Kirkpatrick. Letter to Secretary of Agriculture Tom Vilsack. November 20, 2009.

McCain, John, Jon Kyl, and Ann Kirkpatrick. Letter to Secretary of Agriculture Tom Vilsack. March 8, 2010.

McClintock, Anne. "The Angel of Progress: Pitfalls of the Term 'Postcolonialism.'" *Social Text* 31–32 (1992): 84.

McClung, John. "My First Ultra: Paatuwaqatsi 50k Report." *Barefoot in Arizona* (blog), October 11, 2012. https://bfinaz.blogspot.com/2012/10/my-first-ultra-paatuwaqatsi-50k-report.html.

McDonald, Laughlin. *American Indians and the Fight for Equal Voting Rights.* Norman: University of Oklahoma Press, 2010.

McDougall, Christopher. "Born to Run." Talks at Google, October 27, 2009. https://gtalks-gs.appspot.com/talk/born-to-run-mountain-view.

McDougall, Christopher. *Born to Run: A Hidden Tribe, Superathletes, and the Greatest Race the World Has Never Seen.* New York: Alfred A. Knopf, 2009.

McDougall, Christopher. "The 'Born to Run' Author's Discovery of the Tarahumara Running Tribe." *Runner's World,* June 20, 2018. https://www.runnersworld.com/runners-stories/a20954821/secrets-of-the-tarahumara/.

Mehall, Luke. *The Great American Dirtbags: More Tales of Freedom and Climbing from the Author of "Climbing Out of Bed."* N.p.: Benighted, 2014.

Meinig, Donald William. *The Interpretation of Ordinary Landscapes: Geographical Essays*. Oxford, UK: Oxford University Press, 1979.

Merchant, Carolyn. *Ecological Revolutions: Nature, Gender, and Science in New England*. 2nd ed. Chapel Hill: University of North Carolina Press, 2010.

Mike, Aaron. "Navajo Rising." *Common Climber*. Accessed February 7, 2024. https://www.commonclimber.com/navajo-rising.html.

Mills, Sara. *Discourse*. 2nd ed. London: Routledge, 2004.

Moor, Robert. *On Trails: An Exploration*. New York: Simon and Schuster, 2016.

Morgan, Onyx [Venessa] Sloan. "Empty Words on Occupied Lands? Positionality, Settler Colonialism, and the Politics of Recognition." Antipode, January 4, 2015. https://antipodefoundation.org/2014/07/02/empty-words-on-occupied-lands/.

Morgensen, Scott Lauria. "The Biopolitics of Settler Colonialism: Right Here, Right Now." *Settler Colonial Studies* 1 (2011): 52–76.

Morgensen, Scott Lauria. *Spaces between Us: Queer Settler Colonialism and Indigenous Decolonization*. Minneapolis: University of Minnesota Press, 2011.

Morgensen, Scott Lauria. "Theorizing Gender, Sexuality and Settler Colonialism: An Introduction." *Settler Colonial Studies* 2 (2012): 2–22.

Morgensen, Scott Lauria. "White Settlers and Indigenous Solidarity: Confronting White Supremacy, Answering Decolonial Alliances." *Decolonization* (blog), May 4, 2015. https://decolonization.wordpress.com/2014/05/26/white-settlers-and-indigenous-solidarity-confronting-white-supremacy-answering-decolonial-alliances/.

Morris, Christopher W. *The Social Contract Theorists: Critical Essays on Hobbes, Locke, and Rousseau*. Lanham, MD: Rowman & Littlefield, 1999.

Mullen, Maggie. "Climbers Ignore Native Americans Request at Devils Tower." Wyoming Public Radio, June 30, 2017. https://www.wyomingpublicmedia.org/post/climbers-ignore-native-americans-request-devils-tower.

Mullin, Molly. *Culture in the Marketplace: Gender, Art, and Value in the American Southwest*. Durham, NC: Duke University Press, 2001.

Murphy, Rod, dir. *El Chivo*. 2016.

Murphyao, Amanda, and Kelly Black. "Unsettling Settler Belonging: (Re)Naming and Territory Making in the Pacific Northwest." *American Review of Canadian Studies* 45, no. 3 (2015): 315–31.

Nabokov, Peter. *Indian Running: Native American History and Tradition*. Santa Fe: Ancient City Press, 1987.

Nash, Roderick. *Wilderness and the American Mind*. 4th ed. New Haven: Yale University Press, 2001.

National Environmental Policy Act of 1969 § 102, 42 U.S.C. § 4332, 1994.

Navajo-Hopi Observer News. "Hopi Tribe Rallies Against the City of Flagstaff." September 7, 2011. https://www.nhonews.com/news/2011/sep/07/hopi-tribe-rallies-against-the-city-of-flagstaff/.

Navajo Nation et al. v. U.S. Forest Service. 408 F. Supp. 2d 866 (D. Ariz. 2006).

Navajo Nation et al. v. U.S. Forest Service. 479 F.3d 1024 (9th Cir. 2007).

Navajo Nation v. U.S. 535 F.3d 1058, 1068 (9th Cir. 2008) (*en banc*).

New Mexico PBS. "NMPBS ¡COLORES! Golden Migration at Valle de Oro with Chip Thomas." YouTube, November 15, 2016. https://www.youtube.com/watch?v=6899P_APxqM.

Oelschlaeger, Max. *The Idea of Wilderness: From Prehistory to the Age of Ecology*. New Haven: Yale University Press, 1991.

Office of the Assistant Secretary for Planning and Evaluation. "2020 Poverty Guide-lines." US Department of Health and Human Services. Accessed October 4, 2021. https://aspe.hhs.gov/topics/poverty-economic-mobility/poverty-guidelines/prior-hhs-poverty-guidelines-federal-register-references/2020-poverty-guidelines.

Oravitz, Jeff. "Less Than One Percent of the Peaks Developed." *Arizona Daily Sun,* August 27, 2010. http://azdailysun.com/news/opinion/mailbag/less-than-percent-of-peaks-developed/article_dca25ac4-4d6a-58b8-9a22-0fcc3863143a.html.

O'Riley, Michael F. "Postcolonial Haunting: Anxiety, Affect, and the Situated Encounter." *Postcolonial Text* 3, no. 4 (2007): 1–15.

Ormes, Robert. "A Bent Piece of Iron." *Saturday Evening Post,* July 22, 1939.

Ortiz, Michelle Angela. "Amplifying Community Voices through Public Art." *Community Literacy Journal,* 2020, 14.

Outdoor Industry Association. "Outdoor Recreation Participation Report, 2017." https://outdoorindustry.org/wp-content/uploads/2017/05/2017-Outdoor-Recreation-Participation-Report_FINAL.pdf.

Outdoor Industry Association. "2022 Outdoor Participation Trends Report." https://outdoorindustry.org/resource/2023-outdoor-participation-trends-report/.

Outdoor Industry Association. "U.S. Outdoor Recreation Industry Soars to $1.1 Trillion." https://outdoorindustry.org/press-release/u-s-outdoor-recreation-industry-soars-to-1-1-trillion/.

Parker, Chris. "Climbing's Greatest Route Names." *Rock and Ice,* October 15, 2015.

Pearson, Andy. "Race Report: The Magnificent Monument Valley 50." *Ievenranthisfar* (blog), March 18, 2015. https://ievenranthisfar.tumblr.com/post/113990988946/race-report-the-magnificent-monument-valley-50.

Peters, Jason. "Public Art as Social Infrastructure: Methods and Materials for Social Action at Environmentally Contaminated Sites." *Reflections: A Journal of Public Rhetoric, Civic Writing & Service Learning* 19, no. 2 (Fall/Winter 2019–20): 106–29.

Pietsch, Bryan. "How Veterans of #Vanlife Feel about All the Newbies." *New York Times,* April 2, 2021. https://www.nytimes.com/2021/04/02/us/living-in-a-van-coronavirus-pandemic.html.

Powell, M., D. Levy, A. Riley-Mukavetz, M. Brooks-Gillies, M. Novotny, and J. Fisch-Ferguson. "Our Story Begins Here: Constellating Cultural Rhetorics." Enculturation, October 25, 2014. http://www.enculturation.net/our-story-beginshere.

Propper, Catherine. "The Study of Endocrine-Disrupting Compounds: Past Approaches and New Directions." *Integrative and Comparative Biology* 4, no. 1 (2005): 194–200.

Randazzo, Ryan. "Arizona Snowbowl Plans $60M Expansion to Ease Congestion, Upgrade Facilities at Flagstaff Resort." *Arizona Republic,* June 12, 2019. https://www.azcentral.com/story/news/local/arizona/2019/06/12/snowbowl-ski-resort-near-flagstaff-announces-plans-major-upgrades-arizona/1432492001/.

Ratcliffe, Krista. *Rhetorical Listening: Identification, Gender, Whiteness.* Carbondale: Southern Illinois University Press, 2005.

Razack, Sherene, ed. *Race, Space, and the Law: Unmapping a White Settler Society.* Toronto: Between the Lines, 2002.

Reese, Cory. "Monument Valley 50 Race Report—2015." *Fast Cory* (blog), March 18, 2015. http://www.fastcory.com/2015/03/monument-valley-50-race-report-2015.html.

Restivo, Michael. "Fred Beckey: The Original Climber Dirtbag." *The Clymb.* Last modified December 19, 2018. http://theclymb.com. Site discontinued.

Rifkin, Mark. "The Frontier as (Movable) Space of Exception." *Settler Colonial Studies* 4, no. 2 (April 3, 2014): 176–80. https://doi.org/10.1080/2201473X.2013.846393.

Rifkin, Mark. *Settler Common Sense: Queerness and Everyday Colonialism in the American Renaissance*. Minneapolis: Minnesota University Press, 2014.

Riley-Mukavetz, A. "Towards a Cultural Rhetorics Methodology: Making Research Matter with Multi-Generational Women from the Little Traverse Bay Band." *Rhetoric, Professional Communication and Globalization* 5, no. 1 (2014): 108–25.

Robins, Kevin. *Into the Image: Culture and Politics in the Field of Vision*. New York: Routledge, 1996.

Robinson, Victoria. *Everyday Masculinities and Extreme Sport: Male Identity and Rock Climbing*. New York: Berg, 2008.

Rodriguez, Olga R. "California Ski Resort Changes Name to Remove Offensive Word." Associated Press, September 21, 2021. https://apnews.com/article/sports-california-business-native-americans-2020-tokyo-olympics-4d974f061651ce3ce2d740c14bd9221e.

Rogers, Richard A. "Deciphering Kokopelli: Masculinity in Commodified Appropriations of Native American Imagery." *Communication and Critical/Cultural Studies* 4, no. 3 (September 2007): 233–55. https://doi.org/10.1080/14791420701459715.

Roggeman, Pete. "Bike Companies Killed the Fat Bike." NSMB, January 21, 2015. https://nsmb.com/articles/bike-companies-killed-fat-bike/.

Rojek, Chris. *Decentring Leisure: Rethinking Leisure Theory*. Thousand Oaks, CA: SAGE, 1995.

Rojo, Jaime, and Steven Harrington. "Jetsonorama's New Piece in Telluride and 'Wastewater Snow.'" *HuffPost*. https://www.huffpost.com/entry/jetsonorama-wastewater-snow_b_10227064.

Rom, Zoë. "The Case for Re-Naming Public Lands." *Trail Runner Magazine* (blog), April 28, 2021. https://www.trailrunnermag.com/people/culture-people/the-case-for-re-naming-public-lands/.

Ronto, Paul. "The State of Ultra Running 2020." RunRepeat.com. Accessed December 31, 2022. https://runrepeat.com/state-of-ultra-running.

Rose-Redwood, Reuben. "Rethinking the Agenda of Political Toponymy." *ACME: An International E-Journal for Critical Geographies* 10, no. 1 (2011): 34–41.

Rose-Redwood, Reuben, and Derek Alderman. "Critical Interventions in Political Toponymy." *ACME: An International E-Journal for Critical Geographies* 10, no. 1 (2011): 1–6.

Rose-Redwood, Reuben, Natchee Blu Barnd, Lucchesi Annita Hetoevéhotohke'e, Sharon Dias, and Wil Patrick. "Introduction: Decolonizing the Map: Recentering Indigenous Mappings." *Cartographica* 55, no. 3 (2020): 151–62.

Rosiek, Jerry Lee, Jimmy Snyder, and Scott L. Pratt. "The New Materialisms and Indigenous Theories of Non-Human Agency: Making the Case for Respectful Anti-Colonial Engagement." *Qualitative Inquiry* 26, no. 3–4 (March 1, 2020): 331–46. https://doi.org/10.1177/1077800419830135.

Rothman, Hal. *Devil's Bargains: Tourism in the Twentieth-Century American West*. Lawrence: University Press of Kansas, 1998.

Rowe, Aimee Carrillo. *Power Lines: On the Subject of Feminist Alliances*. Durham, NC: Duke University Press, 2008.

Royster, Jacqueline Jones. "When the First Voice You Hear Is Not Your Own." *College Composition and Communication* 47, no. 1 (Feb. 1996): 29. https://doi.org/10.2307/358272.

Ruiz, Bernardo. *The Infinite Race*. "30 for 30" ESPN series. Season 3, episode 45, 2020.

Rychter, Tacey. "Climbers Flock to Uluru before a Ban, Straining a Sacred Site." *New York Times*, July 11, 2019. https://www.nytimes.com/2019/07/11/world/australia/uluru-climbing-ban.html.

Said, Edward. *Orientalism*. New York: Vintage, 1994.

Samet, Matt. *Death Grip: A Climber's Escape from Benzo Madness*. New York: St. Martin's, 2013.

Sanchez, John, Mary E. Stuckey, and Richard Morris. "Rhetorical Exclusion: The Government's Case against American Indian Activists, AIM and Leonard Peltier." *American Indian Culture and Research Journal* 23, no. 2 (1999).

Save the Peaks Coalition. "U.S. Government Ignores Public Health Dangers of Sewer Water Snowmaking Concerned Citizens File New Lawsuit to Force Government to Study and Disclose Effects of Ingesting Snow Made from Treated Sewage Effluent." 2009.

Save the Peaks Coalition v. U.S. Forest Service. No. CV 09-8163-PCT-MHM (D. Ariz. Feb. 18, 2011).

Schimel, Kate, and Brooke Warren. "Recreation Is Redefining the Value of Western Public Lands." *High Country News*, May 14, 2018. https://www.hcn.org/issues/50.8/recreation-recreation-is-redefining-the-value-of-western-public-lands.

Segal, Lynne. "Being a Man Just Ain't What It Used to Be." *Times Higher Education Supplement*, 2006.

Senda-Cook, Samantha. "Long Memories: Material Rhetoric as Evidence of Memory and a Potential Future." *Western Journal of Communication* 84, no. 4 (2020): 419–38. https://doi.org/10.1080/10570314.2020.1714073.

Senda-Cook, Samantha. "Materializing Tensions: How Maps and Trail Mediate Nature." *Environmental Communication* 7, no. 3 (2013): 355–71.

Senda-Cook, Samantha. "Rugged Practices: Embodying Authenticity in Outdoor Recreation." *Quarterly Journal of Speech* 98, no. 2 (2012): 129–52.

Shackell, James. "This Porter Has Hiked the Inca Trail Hundreds of Times, but Never Seen Machu Picchu." The Intrepid Foundation. https://www.theintrepidfoundation.org/theintrepidfoundation/post/this-porter-has-hiked-the-inca-trail-hundreds-of-times-but-never-seen-machu-picchu.

Shirley, Joe, Jr. "On the Sanctity of the San Francisco Peaks." Letter from Navajo Nation president Dr. Joe Shirley Jr. to Secretary of Agriculture Tom Vilsack. April 5, 2010.

Simpson, Audra. "Indigenous Identity Theft Must Stop." BostonGlobe.com, November 17, 2022. https://www.bostonglobe.com/2022/11/17/opinion/indigenous-identity-theft-must-stop/.

Simpson, Leanne Betasamosake. *Dancing on Our Turtle's Back: Stories of Nishnaabeg Re-Creation, Resurgence and a New Emergence*. Winnipeg: Arbeiter Ring, 2011.

Slotkin, Richard. *The Fatal Environment: The Myth of the Frontier in the Age of Industrialization, 1800–1890*. Norman: University of Oklahoma Press, 1998.

Slotkin, Richard. *Regeneration through Violence: The Mythology of the American Frontier, 1600–1860*. Middletown, CT: Wesleyan University Press, 1973.

Smith, Linda Tuhiwai. *Decolonizing Methodologies: Research and Indigenous Peoples*. 2nd ed. New York: Zed, 1999.

Snowbowl Vertical Files. Special Collections and Archives. Northern Arizona University, Flagstaff.

Soja, Edward. *Thirdspace: Journeys to Los Angeles and Other Real-and-Imagined Places*. Malden, MA: Blackwell, 1996.

Spivak, Gayatri Chakravorty. "Can the Subaltern Speak?" In *The Post-Colonial Studies Reader*, edited by Bill Ashcroft, Gareth Griffiths, and Helen Tiffin. London: Routledge, 1995.

Spracklen, Karl. *Whiteness and Leisure*. Palgrave Macmillan, 2013.

Stewart, Jon. "Christopher McDougall." *The Daily Show*. Accessed December 23, 2022. https://www.cc.com/video/re7vx8/the-daily-show-with-jon-stewart-christopher-mcdougall.

Straub, Julia. *Paradoxes of Authenticity: Studies on a Critical Concept*. Piscataway, NJ: Transcript, 2012.

Styres, Sandra. "Literacies of Land: Decolonizing Narratives, Storying, and Literature." In *Indigenizing and Decolonizing Studies in Education: Mapping the Long View*, edited by Linda Tuhiwai Smith, Eve Tuck, and K. Wayne Yang. New York: Routledge, 2019.

TallBear, Kim. *Native American DNA: Tribal Belonging and the False Promise of Genetic Science*. Minneapolis: University of Minnesota Press, 2013.

Taylor, Bron. *Dark Green Religion: Nature Spirituality and the Planetary Future*. Berkeley: University of California Press, 2010.

Taylor, Diana. *The Archive and the Repertoire: Performing Cultural Memory in the Americas*. Durham, NC: Duke University Press, 2007.

Taylor, Dorceta E. *The Environment and the People in American Cities, 1600s–1900s: Disorder, Inequality, and Social Change*. Durham, NC: Duke University Press, 2009.

Thompson, Audrey. "Summary of Whiteness Theory." http://www.kooriweb.org/foley/resources/whiteness/summary_of_whiteness_theory.pdf.

Thoreau, Henry David. *Walden*. 1st Shambhala, 150th anniversary ed. Boston: Shambhala, 2004.

Tiedje, Kristina. "The Promise of the Discourse of the Sacred for Conservation (and Its Limits)." *Journal for the Study of Religion, Nature and Culture* 1, no. 3 (2007): 326–39.

Todd, Zoe. "An Indigenous Feminist's Take on the Ontological Turn: 'Ontology' Is Just Another Word for Colonialism." *Journal of Historical Sociology* 29, no. 1 (March 2016): 4–22. https://doi.org/10.1111/johs.12124.

Todrys, Katherine Wiltenburg. *Black Snake: Standing Rock, the Dakota Access Pipeline, and Environmental Justice*. Lincoln: University of Nebraska Press, 2021.

Triece, Mary E. *Urban Renewal and Resistance: Race, Space and the City in the Late Twentieth to the Early Twenty-First Century*. Lanham: Lexington Books, 2016.

Trilling, Lionel. *Sincerity and Authenticity*. New York: Harcourt Brace Jovanovich, 1971.

Truglio, Brian. *Racing the Rez*. Wolf Hill Films for Native American Public Telecommunications, 2012.

Tuck, Eve. "Suspending Damage: A Letter to Communities." *Harvard Educational Review* 79, no. 3 (September 1, 2009): 409–28. https://doi.org/10.17763/haer.79.3.n0016675661t3n15.

Tuck, Eve, and K. Wayne Yang. "Decolonization Is Not a Metaphor." *Decolonization: Indigeneity, Education & Society* 1, no. 1 (2012): 1–40.

Turner, Frederick Jackson. *The Significance of the Frontier in American History*. Mansfield Centre: Martino Publishing, 2014.

United Nations Human Rights Council. "Report of the Special Rapporteur on the Rights of Indigenous Peoples." August 30, 2010, 21st session, agenda item 3. https://www.ohchr.org/Documents/HRBodies/HRCouncil/RegularSession/Session21/A-HRC-21-47-Add1_en.pdf.

Urry, John. *The Tourist Gaze: Leisure and Travel in Contemporary Societies*. London: SAGE, 1990.

US Department of Agriculture. "Final Environmental Impact Statement for Arizona Snowbowl Facilities Improvement, Vol. 1." National Forest Service, Coconino National Forest, 2005.

US Department of Agriculture. "Policy and Procedures Review and Recommendations: Indian Sacred Sites Report to the Secretary of Agriculture." Office of Tribal Relations, Washington, DC, 2012.

US Department of the Interior. "Secretary Haaland Takes Action to Remove Derogatory Names from Federal Lands." Press Release, November 19, 2021. https://www.doi.gov/pressreleases/secretary-haaland-takes-action-remove-derogatory-names-federal-lands.

Varga, Somogy. *Authenticity as an Ethical Ideal*. New York: Routledge, 2012.

Veblen, Thorstein. *The Theory of the Leisure Class.* Oxford, UK: Oxford University Press, 2009.

Veracini, Lorenzo. "Settler Collective, Founding Violence and Disavowal: The Settler Colonial Situation." *Journal of Intercultural Studies* 29, no. 4 (2008): 363–79.

Veracini, Lorenzo. *Settler Colonialism: A Theoretical Overview.* New York: Palgrave Macmillan, 2010.

Veracini, Lorenzo. *The Settler Colonial Present.* New York: Palgrave Macmillan, 2015.

Vilsack, Tom. Letter to Eric Borowsky and J. R. Murray. January 29, 2010.

Washington Trails Association. "8 Trails That Tell a Native American Story." Last modified July 28, 2019. https://www.wta.org/go-outside/seasonal-hikes/fall-destinations/trails-to-native-american-indigenous-story.

Western States Endurance Run. "Lottery." Accessed December 31, 2022. https://www.wser.org/lottery/.

Williams, Jacqueline. "Australia to Ban Climbing on Uluru, a Site Sacred to Indigenous People." *New York Times,* November 1, 2017. https://www.nytimes.com/2017/11/01/world/australia/uluru-ayers-rock-climbing-ban.html.

Wilson, Alexander. "The View from the Road: Recreation and Tourism." In *The Culture of Nature,* 19–51. Cambridge, MA: Blackwell, 1992.

Wilson, Shawn. *Research Is Ceremony: Indigenous Research Methods.* Halifax: Fernwood, 2008.

Wise, Tim, and Kevin Myers. *White Like Me: Reflections on Race from a Privileged Son.* Read-HowYouWant.com, 2010.

Wokler, Robert, Bryan Garsten. *Rousseau, The Age of Enlightenment, and Their Legacies.* Princeton: Princeton University Press, 2012.

Wolfe, Patrick. "Settler Colonialism and the Elimination of the Native." *Journal of Genocide Research* 8, no. 4 (December 2006): 387–409.

Woods, Alden. "Hopi Lose Arguments on Snowbowl Snowmaking in State Supreme Court Ruling." *AZCentral,* November 29, 2018. https://www.azcentral.com/story/news/local/arizona/2018/11/29/hopi-lose-arguments-snowbowl-snowmaking-state-supreme-court-ruling/1997219002/.

Yang, Billy. "Christopher McDougall." *Billy Yang Podcast,* May 25, 2018. https://billyyangpodcast.libsyn.com/christopher-mcdougall-byp-014.

Yellowstone National Park Lodges. "Stagecoach Adventure." Accessed September 6, 2022. https://www.yellowstonenationalparklodges.com/adventure/wild-west-adventures/stagecoach-adventure/.

Yeutter, Clayton. Letter to Secretary of Agriculture Tom Vilsack. Prepared by Hogan and Hartson. July 6, 2009.

Young, Alex Trimble. "Settler Sovereignty and The Rhizomatic West, or, The Significance of the Frontier in Postwestern Studies." *Western American Literature* 48, no. 1/2 (2013): 115–40.

Zak, Dan. "Book Review: *Born to Run* by Christopher McDougall." *Washington Post,* June 21, 2009. http://www.washingtonpost.com/wpdyn/content/article/2009/06/19/AR2009061901078.html.

Zappen, James P. "Digital Rhetoric: Toward an Integrated Theory." *Technical Communication Quarterly* 48, no 3 (2005): 319–25.

INDEX

www.ingramcontent.com/pod-product-compliance
Lightning Source LLC
Chambersburg PA
CBHW020346270326
41926CB00007B/336